Red Sea
and
Indian Ocean
Cruising
Guide

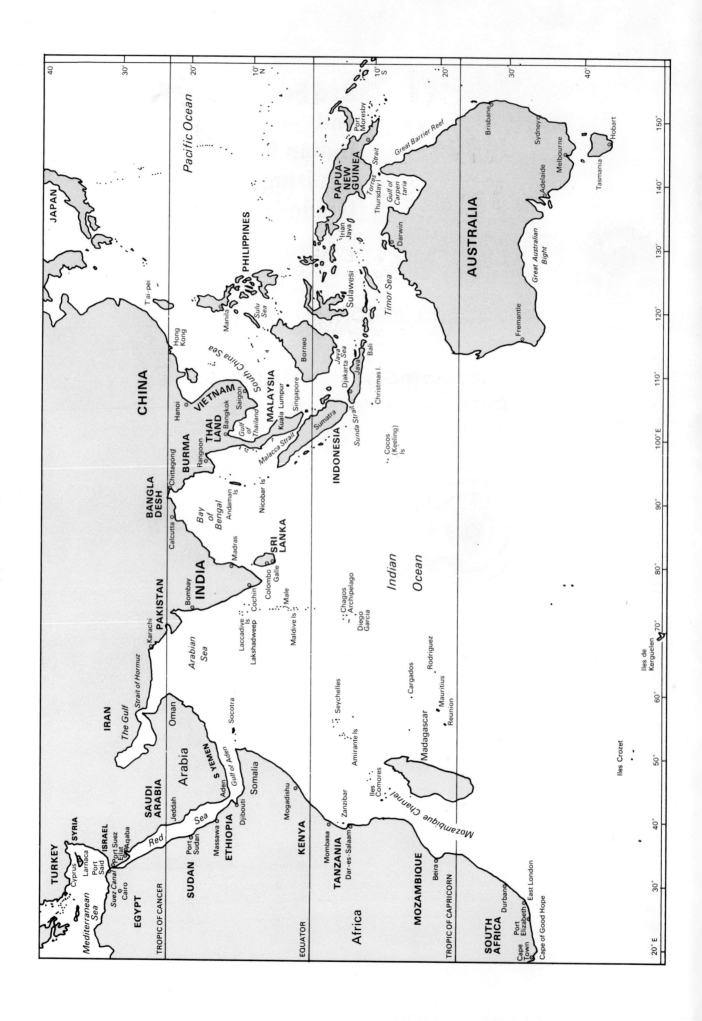

Red Sea and Indian Ocean Cruising Guide

A yachtsman's guide from the Suez Canal to Southern India, Sri Lanka, Singapore, Indonesia and Northern Australia.

ALAN LUCAS

Imray Laurie Norie & Wilson Ltd
St Ives Huntingdon England

Published by
Imray, Laurie, Norie & Wilson Ltd
Wych House, St. Ives, Huntingdon,
Cambridgeshire PE17 4BT. England

CAUTION

Whilst every care has been taken to ensure accuracy, neither the Publishers nor the Author will hold themselves responsible for errors, omissions or alterations in this publication. They will at all times be grateful to receive information which tends to the improvement of the work.

British Library Cataloguing in Publication Data

Lucas, Alan
  Red Sea and Indian Ocean cruising guide.
  1. Yachts and yachting — Indian Ocean
  I. Title
  797.1′24″09165   GV817.I/

ISBN 0-85288-096-0

Typeset by Cromwell Graphics, St. Ives, Cambridgeshire
Printed by Tabro Litho Ltd, St. Ives, Cambridgeshire

CONTENTS

Preface

Preface

To my wife, Patricia, and son, Ben, who lived every
minute of this book as they have others in the past and
who by their presence can only encourage more.

This cruising guide presumes the reader intends to sail his small ship from the Mediterranean Sea to Australia via
the Red Sea, India, Malaysia, Singapore and Indonesia. In other words, eastabouts. It does not deal with the
equally popular passage westabouts across the Atlantic and Pacific Oceans. However, a third alternative is briefly
looked at; this is the route down the Atlantic Ocean then under Africa and Australia running with the westerlies
and is the classic clipper route and should not be looked upon as a cruise in any sense of the word.

The routes and countries described in this book have enjoyed increasing popularity as British and European
yachtsmen realise how close this wonderworld of different sights and sounds really is. A mere 1500 easily sailed
miles from the Mediterranean Sea lies the Indian Ocean, the world's second largest expanse of water and one surrounded by a bewildering array of people, cultures and pursuits. And scattered across its surface are coral reefs,
cays and atolls as well as towering continental islands such as the Seychelles, Mauritius and Réunion.

As if the Indian Ocean and all it has to offer were not enough, the Red Sea rewards one with some of the world's
most beautiful coral gardens whilst guaranteeing a rapid transit for any southbound sailing boat, so reliable are
its northerly winds. And when the passage draws to a close and Australia rises above the horizon, the European
yachtsman can anticipate with some enthusiasm a return to his or her own way of life for Australia is an oasis of
western living standards, attitudes and economy. And whilst the latter has suffered a similar recessional hammer-
ing as other developed economies, it still manages to offer employment to the occasional transient. As a result
there is every reason to presume that employment will be found and the ship's coffers will be refilled ready for
the passage home to Europe.

Considering the number of ports and anchorages between Europe and Australia, it scarcely needs saying that
this book cannot include them all in precise and illustrative detail. It does, however, describe and illustrate all sensible routes as well as potential cruising diversions along the way.

All in all, the author believes this guide will give the navigator a valuable insight into the problems and pleasures of the trip to come. Absolute accuracy of detail is too subject to change to be guaranteed so it must be
emphasised here that this book is intended as a companion to, not a replacement for, official pilots and charts.

Alan Lucas
Rome 1985

CHARTS

The hydrographic charts used in the navigation and research for this book were a mixture of old and new measure-
ment, whilst the echo sounder used by the author was in fathoms. Because most users of this book are in the midst
of conversion and to avoid potentially dangerous incorrect conversion, soundings throughout the anchorage and
port section of this book are in metres. It should be stressed that the charts and maps in this guide are based on
the author's own sketches and are not in any way to be used as a substitute for the official charts.

INTRODUCTION

Culture Shock

POVERTY

Westerners love using the term 'culture shock' when describing conditions in another country, especially countries as different as those in Asia. And whilst the term is not necessarily derogatory in any way its insinuation is enough to discourage travellers as they imagine a situation intolerable to their sensitivities.

It is interesting that a cruising yachtsman can be surrounded by natives in their dugout canoes at a Pacific Island anchorage and think of it only as romantic experience; neither pity nor envy is felt, one just enjoys this classic involvement. Yet the same people surrounded by natives in their dugouts in a place like Sri Lanka, for example, can feel intimidation and discomfort. Why?

The main reason can be summed up in one short word — food. The Pacific Islander may have a very low income — if any at all — but he is mostly well fed and content. His island and the surrounding waters provide all he needs and to date his country has not been pressured into becoming yet another vibrant, industrial economy. He may ask a traveller for various odds and ends, but nearly always in exchange for something else. He never begs.

The same person in an overpopulated, rapidly developing, but still heavily dependent country knows hunger, for progress has passed him by. His country is still ancient enough to demand that he remain in his dugout canoe, from which he must eke a living, but not quite modern enough to pay him welfare that his impossible situation demands. As a result, this man needs your help and suddenly a 'romantic' situation turns sour. Nobody likes having their dream shattered and we all try to avoid another person's misery.

To the sensitive, the culture shock of certain parts of Asia is to feel impotent in terms of being able to offer any worthwhile assistance. To the insensitive, it is to be annoyed by the constant approach of beggars. To either person the easiest way out of the situation is to avoid it.

Considering that poverty in the world is far more common than anyone cares to admit, beggars are suprisingly few and far between when taking the broad view of Asia. But when confronted by such a person, whether in the

A shiny new yacht in harbour is a promise of gifts to desperately poor fishermen. In most cases they want only simple items such as useful containers, fishing lines and hooks.

street or alongside in a canoe, the visitor can meet his dilemma halfway by giving a little. That hoary saying, 'if you give to a beggar he will never go away' is absolutely wrong and I suspect it was invented by the very worst European miser as the truth is, if you don't give to a beggar he will, in all probability, pester you.

Under the circumstances, the easiest way around this problem is to always carry a few coins in your pocket and have a hand ready to excavate its contents. It is my experience that a beggar will expect only a little and not ask for more and certainly he will not haunt you as so often happens when refusal is practised.

The 'middle course' of being ready to give small coins can extend into other facets of life in Third World countries. For example, many fishermen appreciate containers of any description. Thus, that empty detergent bottle becomes a worthy gift that costs you nothing and proves very useful to the recipient. And a little psychology can work wonders at times. It did for us off the Indian coast as I will relate.

To set the scene it should be appreciated that the Indian coast literally swarms with fishermen in boats that range from ancient two-man sailing dugouts to reasonably efficient looking diesel launches. Most spectacular are the enormous twenty-man stitch-planked canoes measuring over fifty feet long and often powered by a twenty horse outboard, being narrow beamed the craft move swiftly and can overtake any displacement sailing or motor boat with ease.

Aboard our yacht *Tientos*, my wife, son and I steamed over a ruffled calm sea not ten miles off the coast. We steered through fleets of fishing boats each consisting of dozens of craft of all types. Quite suddenly, a number of twenty-man canoes broke from their fleet and sped after us. Candidly, I felt a touch of 'pirate-paranoia' for there was almost an aggressive air in the way they gave chase.

It rapidly became obvious that they were simply pleading for food; those not involved in the running of their canoes standing up and rubbing their stomachs. The broad smiles convinced me that underlying it all was a sense of humour. But humour or not, we could scarcely spend the remainder of the day passing out ship's supplies nor did we want to appear totally insensitive to their needs. That's when psychology entered into it.

Beckoning the closest canoe alongside we handed over a full bunch of bananas. There was enough for all and then some. This did the trick; the canoe with the bananas became the prime target, all other canoes veering off towards it. We continued unmolested feeling rather pleased with ourselves.

Just as giving nothing will only prolong the nuisance factor, so too will giving in excess upset the balance. The big-tipper leaves a tough legacy behind him for all parties so moderation is important.

Hygiene is another potential shock to the westerner visiting a Third World country. Frankly, the standards are low, but this is not to say the people are dirty. To the contrary, most folk are fastidious about personal cleanliness and the village water outlet is the busiest facility around. But poverty or near poverty levels deny the standard of hygiene the westerner likes to see. You cannot expect a shop assistant on five dollars a week to afford paper tissues. The back of the hand is eminently suitable — and cheap — when sniffles prevail and the fact that that same hand might then dive into a sack of flour, raisins or whatever as it serves a customer is par for the course. There is simply nothing the visitor can do about this.

These canoes chased the author off the west Indian coast in pursuit of food. A poor but happy band of fishermen, they were rewarded with a huge bunch of bananas.

Whilst learning to live with standards somewhat below our own it is heartening to note that sickness is minimal. A short stomachache for a day or two is about the norm whilst some folk escape totally unscathed. Unfortunately, however, the yachtsman tends to be the first sufferer because of the super sterile environment from which he comes. It is one thing to come from a developed society, quite another from the isolation of a vessel that has been out of touch with society of any description for many weeks.

Balanced against this is the fact that having one's own home (the vessel) along when sickness strikes makes for faster recovery for one is not concerned by hotel food, board cost and other shorebound obligations.

Having made sickness sound like a promise rather than a threat to anyone sailing to distant lands, it must be emphasised here that the yachtsman is wide open to ills and chills regardless of where he or she ventures because of the already noted isolated existence. In my twenty-five years of cruising and continuous living aboard I find sickness strikes just as readily when I enter a western port as it does in an eastern port. It is reasonable to assume, therefore, that the real enemy is isolation, not the prevailing hygiene standards.

Theft is probably the most popular fear amongst the cruising fraternity in a Third World country. Yet it is mostly baseless for it does not take into consideration the many factors that can also prevent theft. For example, some ports are securely fenced off denying access to the berth by the general public. In many Arab ports private boats are restricted to just one part of the harbour where shore access is guarded twenty-four hours a day by an armed sentry and in a few countries, so strict is the religion that theft simply does not occur.

In all my years of cruising, including time in such countries as Indonesia, Sri Lanka, India and many Arab countries, I have never locked my vessel. I have, in fact, suffered loss to a thief in my own country, Australia!

These are important tips for behaviour especially in Islamic countries:

Offer nothing with your left hand. This is reserved for menial functions.
Standing with hands on the hips during conversation is a traditional pose of defiance. Avoid this stance.
Do not point with the finger. Use the thumb only.
Do not beckon with the finger. Cup the hand and beckon with the palm down.
Ask before aiming the camera. A few Moslems see a camera as a thief of their spirit.
Do not kiss and cuddle in public. This is considered gross.
Wear nothing less than long socks and shoes with a dress or shorts and decent shirt when visiting bureaucracy. Westerners sloppily dressed are seen as rank peasants who do not deserve to be served. Most stories of officiousness are related by visitors who tried to clear their ship dressed in work-shorts and scuffs.

Safe and Unsafe Countries

Most Europeans come from a country that has colonised another country in the not so distant past. The English were in India, Sri Lanka and Malaysia, to name just a few, whilst the Dutch had Indonesia and the Italians dabbled in Ethiopia and whether they admit it or not, the North Americans effectively colonised many a country by imposing their own economy and values overseas. Surely there can be no better example of that than the Philippines.

Be that as it may, the purpose here is not to distribute guilt amongst the ruling nations but to make the yachtsman consider his image in previously colonised areas. He is a reminder of subservience or cultural destruction and, in some cases, brutality and at best, his forefathers were never wanted, or so it is thought now.

How does this affect the visitor nowadays?

Surprisingly, there is very little apparent vindictiveness, I have had an Arab tell me of the bloody, but hugely successful, overthrow of the British, yet the fact that I was obviously of British stock did not seem to occur to him at all. We were the best of friends. I have watched Arab television talk of 'the American threat off our shores' then give the latest dollar exchange rate so that Russian visitors may change their currency into the only foreign currency acceptable in that country, the American dollar!

The fact is, nearly all countries dealt with in this book have been under the yoke of foreign domination at some time or another. Yet none seem to hold any malice at either governmental level or on the street. But malice can be found by digging deep enough and the purpose of this chapter is, first, to warn against digging deep and, second, to advise on each country's attitude towards the visitor, in a condensed and instantly accessible form. But first let us see how not to 'dig deep'.

Europeans are accustomed to domination. We accept as normal fairly smooth-running businesses and government departments as well as the right to complain loud and clear when necessary. The more aggressive amongst us are not especially liked, even in our own countries, but we are tolerated.

It is a serious mistake to take this attitude into Third World and non-European countries where everything is different, from the idea of efficiency to belief in what is important and what is unimportant. The sight of an American, his face bright red with veins about to burst as a wait in a customs office becomes unbearably extended has little effect on the clerk causing the extension and a Swedish girl shouting obscenities at an Indian waiter because he brought her tea instead of coffee merely guarantees even poorer service late whilst the waiter gives

Poverty and crowded conditions do not necessarily make a country unsafe to cruise.

thanks that independence gave him the freedom not to have to live with such bumptiousness. The fact is, complaints about service or facilities fall on deaf ears. Such things are a western fetish, not in the local style. It is best to grin and bear it and in this way services and facilities might, in fact, improve. I recall being in a mad rush to clear my vessel with a certain harbour master, lest I miss the immigration office which was soon to close for the weekend, and was alarmed to find him prostrating himself before Allah. He saw me, indicated a reluctant willingness to desist from prayer to serve me and was obviously delighted when I insisted that he finish his prayers. This he then did in double quick time because, I suspect, the courtesy demanded reciprocation. There was no doubt that my feigning a no-rush attitude allowed me to get back to immigration before their office closed because reciprocation included being served before a number of other, less relaxed customers.

In a nutshell, the secret to enjoying a cruise is to relax when formalities and the time they take become unbearable. Keep a low profile, don't complain and recognise that even two long hours in an immigration office is but a minuscule percentage of your total time in the country. It is absurd to undermine your potential for enjoyment by taking along your own standards, leave them at home.

The following is a list of all countries in the area covered by this book with a short look at their attitudes towards the cruising person.

EGYPT   Although rotten with corruption and often bureaucratically unbearable, the fact is, Egypt welcomes the cruising boat. There are no restrictions, subject to correct formalities outlined in the ports and anchorage section of this book.

SAUDI ARABIA   One of the wealthiest countries in the world, with a fair population of indentured labour and brains, Saudi Arabia is closed to the tourist. This is intended as a means of maintaining religious purity, their Islamic beliefs being benign but strict.

The private boat may, however, enter Saudi Arabia at either Yenbo or Jeddah where most facilities can be enjoyed. Cruising the coast, whether cleared in legally or not, is *definitely not allowed* and can be practised only at the risk of having the boat impounded.

SUDAN   Despite political upheavals of late, Sudan must rate as the Arab world's most relaxed country. There does not appear to be any restriction imposed on boats and their crew visiting and a blind eye is mostly turned to those folk anchor-hopping the coast before clearing legally at Port Sudan.

ETHIOPIA   This is a country constantly at war with no tolerance whatsoever of outsiders. Very definitely its coast cannot be cruised nor may any of its ports be entered by private vessels.

NORTH YEMEN   This country has changed its attitudes several times, being very receptive to visitors in the mid-seventies only to virtually close its doors in the early eighties. Contemporary visitors have found themselves restricted to their vessels after entering Hudaydah and then being obliged to pay an outlandish port fee. Subject to contrary reports en route, this country should be avoided.

DJIBOUTI   No problems here. Expensive, sometimes unfriendly, but nevertheless happy about visits from private boats.

SOUTH YEMEN   The capital, Aden, presents no problems and might even rank as the world's least formal harbour in terms of minimal paperwork. However, cameras are not allowed ashore and certain restrictions might be imposed. Despite this, it is often possible to get a cruising permit for the coast.

OMAN   Rather like a small Saudi Arabia in religious attitude, tourists are not admitted. However, the law of the sea prevails and private vessels may enter at Salalah but must not cruise the coast before or after clearing.

PAKISTAN   No troubles. People and officials are generally welcoming but watch the news for any events which might reverse this situation temporarily for Pakistan is adjacent to Afghanistan which is at present involved in near civil war.

INDIA   This amazing country of contrasts offers no obstacles to the visiting yachtsman beyond presenting him or her with a mountain of paperwork which must be climbed every time a port is entered. Visas may be necessary for some visitors and a preliminary check with the nearest Indian embassy is suggested.

SRI LANKA   Is very receptive to nautical tourists and even has laws especially related to them. Unfortunately, these laws oblige one to pay an unreasonable port and agent's fee, but the cost is worthwhile to anyone anxious to see what must be the world's most beautiful mountain scenery.

BANGLADESH   This very poor country, still suffering the backlash of unrest, is not recommended, although cruising its limited coast is probably possible.

BURMA   With her port of entry in Rangoon, a private vessel may visit and cruise Burma on a seven day visa and special permission gained through any Burmese embassy. Port facility information can be gained directly from: Burma Ports Corporation, 10 Pansodan Street, Rangoon, BURMA. No further information will be found in this book.

THAILAND   The bulk of Thailand projects beyond the scope of this book and that part is accessible both physically and politically. But the part included here, between Burma and Malaysia, on the western side of the Malaysian peninsula, should be given a wide berth owing to the presence of pirates. This is dealt with in greater detail in the chapter, Pirates.

HONG KONG   This British satellite in the Far East is included in this book for those who prefer it to Australia as a destination. It is discussed in greater detail later. Here it need only be stated that it is perfectly safe politically although economically confused as the time draws closer for return to mainland China ownership.

PHILIPPINES   Stay away from the southern areas. The Sulu Sea is one of the worst areas in the world for pirates, whilst the southern island, Mindanao, is the home of the majority of Philippino religious and political dissidents. The only safe area is north of Mindanao with Manila or Cebu City the two best places for formal entry.

INDONESIA   The last country before reaching Australia (unless New Guinea is visited), Indonesia is very much a tourist area where the visiting yachtsman is welcome, if somewhat bureaucratically intimidated by their annoying Sailing Permit which must be obtained before entry, details of which will be found in the relevant anchorage and port section of this book.

PAPUA NEW GUINEA   Recently independent from Australia, this is one of the most remarkable countries to be found anywhere presenting to the tourist a fantastic mixture of cultures and standards and is perfectly safe politically; cruising folk are welcome.

AUSTRALIA   Australia will have been settled for only 200 years in 1988 and started as an English convict penal colony growing into one of the world's richest and most advanced nations. Politically stable and offering everything the average traveller expects at home, there is no problem in cruising its 11,546 miles of coastline as long as proper entry is made in the first place. The formality that truly sets Australia apart from most of the countries so far visited is its paranoia about quarantine; animals, foodstuffs, foodscraps and so on *must not be landed under any circumstances*. It is definitely not a place to take the family pet.

INDIAN OCEAN ISLANDS   All islands in the south Indian Ocean may be visited, though Madagascar and the Seychelles, being Marxist ruled, might prove cool and restrictive politically. There are no grounds for fear, however.

Islands in the north Indian Ocean are more restricted for reasons difficult to discover. The Amindivi, Laccadive, Andaman and Nicobar Islands are all Indian territory and are all off limits to cruising people, the Maldive Islands are very tourist-orientated but parts are restricted to maintain cultural and religious purity. The visiting boat may only arrive and depart from the capital, Male.

See the sections 'The Arabian Sea' and 'South Indian Ocean' for a fuller description of the islands.

EAST COAST OF AFRICA   Somalia, occupying the northeast tip and extending westward into the Gulf of Aden, is out of bounds to all private vessels. The island of Socotra, although politically part of South Yemen, must also be avoided.

Kenya and South Africa are safe enough enjoying, as they do, buoyant economies and political stability, whilst Mozambique and Tanzania may or may not be safe depending on the situation at the time. The cruising grapevine is best referred to for these two countries.

Pirates

I am constantly surprised by the Mediterranean yachtsman who thinks of the Middle and Far East as being hellholes of piracy, nothing could be further from the truth. In fact, one of the most dangerous areas regarding piracy is not the Far East but the area off the southern coast of Florida where you stand an excellent chance of losing your life to a drug peddler. Yet hundreds of Mediterranean based boats cross the Atlantic bent on cruising that area.

There is also a lot of misinformation, I recall one yachting author who wrote that, 'there have been only three cases of piracy in the Red Sea since the Suez Canal reopened in 1975.' Now that might be heartening to those who

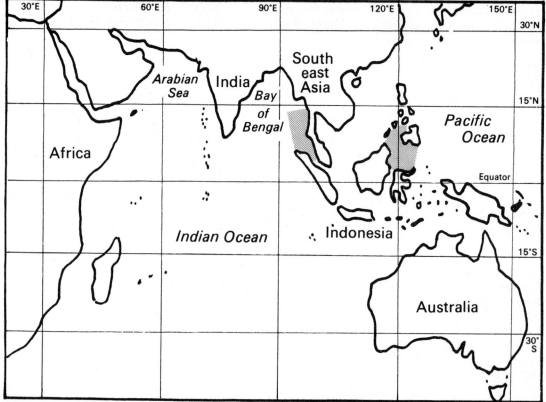

PIRATES
The two areas of potential piracy are indicated here. To the left is the northern part of the Malacca Strait whilst to the right is the Sulu Sea.

think every Arab in the Red Sea is a pirate, but it is totally wrong. In fact, each act of piracy occurred *outside* the Red Sea, *not* within and the name 'Red Sea' was for reference only. The incidents occurred at Socotra and Somalia and anyone venturing to those countries is either misinformed or not informed at all.

Somalia and Socotra need not be included in this chapter because they are not suggested as places of rest and recreation anywhere in this book. Other places are mentioned however, that do, in fact, have a piracy problem and these areas are the Malacca Strait and the Sulu Sea. They will be looked at separately here.

MALACCA STRAIT

This busy approach channel to Singapore separates the Indonesian island of Sumatra from the Malaysian peninsula. Sharing this peninsula, not far to the north, is the country of Thailand.

Partly caused by poverty, but mostly caused by the fact that the first to try got away with it, a flourishing business grew out of the stealing of small items from the decks of ships. This was accomplished by drawing alongside a ship under way up or down the strait then climbing aboard. Resistance proved minimal because there is not an officer or able seaman alive who does not prefer his life to the loss of a fire extinguisher, shackle or whatever else might be taken and, anyway, the company are the real losers. So willing were most commercial ships' officers and crews to allow their vessel to be raped rather than offer what might prove to be a bloody resistance, this form of piracy blossomed until something like 2000 ships a year were being attacked. Eventually the loss became obvious in company ledgers. Ship owners banded together and hired an Australian private detective firm to come up with an answer.

The exact nature of that answer and the effect it had is unknown to the author, but it is believed that one recommendation was to floodlight the aft deck where most pirates prefer to board and to carry one guard per ship. A sort of modern day version of 'riding shotgun'.

There is considerable debate as to who these pirates are: Indonesian, Malaysian or Thai? No one is sure and everyone says it is the other but it would seem from my limited research that the Thai fishermen represent the major proportion of pirates, a fact that tends to be substantiated by the area of greatest attack. This just happens to be towards the Thai side and end of the Malacca Strait.

Identifying the culprits is not important to the average yachtsman who really only wants to pass through the Strait in peace and security. It is good, therefore, to be able to report that yacht attacks are so rare as to be non-existent as long as the navigator steers a course favouring Sumatra as he enters or departs the strait. Once down into the narrower section there appears to be no danger of piracy at all.

SULU SEA

This small patch of water is surrounded on three sides by islands of the Philippines and on one side by the Malaysian section of Borneo. The Borneo end appears to be safe although the Sulu Sea is best avoided altogether because pirates tend to roam the entire area. Here is why.

The Philippines, under President Marcos is, for want of a kinder description, a dictated democracy. There are many pressures from within and without and these pressures were not eased by the slaying of Marcos' brother in 1983. There are many anti-government factions throughout the Philippines, but the oldest and most traditional enemy of the state is the population of Mindanao, the island nation's most southerly possession. Religious differences between north and south made the Mindanaons poor relatives and as poor relatives they periodically do their own thing to raise revenue. Piracy is one of them.

As in the Malacca Strait, large ships are favourite prey, but unlike the Malaccan Strait pirates, the Sulu Sea pirates will attack anything that looks worthwhile. As a result, a yacht might be considered profitable prey if only for the scrap value of her keel and if the victim must die in the effort then that is acceptable.

In truth, actual deaths are rare in this area, but they certainly have been recorded, one yachtsman losing his wife as she was shot through the head by a 'fisherman' coming up fast in an outboard-powered dugout canoe. And don't let the term 'dugout canoe' fool you; a vessel cut from a single tree can be up to 60 feet long and is necessarily narrow and as a result it is always very fast if given enough power.

The answer to the Sulu Sea pirate is simple: don't go there! There is absolutely no need to venture into this troubled area regardless of the destination or point of departure. It is also safe to presume that piracy does not extend beyond the boundaries of the Sulu Sea as it does not extend much beyond a specific part of the Malacca Strait.

Between the two extremes there may be encountered many acts which smack of potential piracy. There is nothing quite so worrying, for example, as a Malayan fishing boat rushing towards you only to turn broadside on at the last moment, to parallel your course for a few seconds, then roar away again. Whilst one can never quite discount it as a precursor to an aggressive act, it is nearly always aggressive only in the spiritual sense. A fisherman acting in this way is trying to pass all his bad luck across to you — or anyone else for that matter, including fellow fishermen.

The other area of concern occurs when surrounded by natives in their canoes or launches. Mostly these are simple folk who would love to see aboard your wonderful ship and to trade goods. Some beg for food and it is therefore good practise to carry plenty of items of appeal such as tinned fish (despite their diet of fresh fish in many areas), cotton T-shirts are welcome and so on. If begging becomes overwhelming and marginally aggressive then it pays to move on as soon as possible but this is rarely necessary.

In closing this subject it would be folly for the yachtsman to cruise any area naïve to the possibility of trouble as it can happen anywhere. But true acts of piracy will only be found in the two areas noted and both these areas can be avoided.

Destructive Winds

The Beaufort wind scale defines a hurricane as being of 64 knots and over. This is far more realistic than the absurdities one occasionally hears in yachting circles which seem to suggest that winds of this speed are merely exciting sailing breezes. Only a fool could be excited by such a wind for, in the areas of destructive winds, there is a good chance of the wind rising even higher. It is entirely possible that it will top 200 knots but, far more realistically, it might reach 100 knots. At this speed it is very definitely destructive; houses have their roofs peeled off and boats lose every stitch of software.

The diagram shows the areas covered by this book where destructive winds are likely to occur. In all areas they are a summer or wet-season phenomenon, the only absolute being that such winds do not occur in winter (the dry season). And then it is only an absolute of convenience because destructive winds have been recorded out of season but so rarely that the issue will not be considered here.

Any navigator using this book will have an Admiralty *Pilot* pertinent to the area being cruised or the Admiralty *Ocean Passages For The World*, or both. These excellent publications provide a wealth of technical information relating to destructive winds, leaving me free here to offer personal observations which may prove useful to the smallboat skipper.

Destructive tropical storms enjoy a number of names dependent on area. In Australia they are called 'cyclones'; in the China Sea 'typhoons'; in the Caribbean 'hurricanes'. In and around India they are referred to as cyclones or typhoons and in one part of Australia they are called 'willy-willies'. But call them what you will, their nature remains common and is potentially destructive.

I use the word 'potentially' above because a tropical storm is not always destructive. It depends on wind strength and the nature of the objects it is endeavouring to destroy. Logically, a suburb of weatherboard houses will be flattened before a suburb of brick houses. A vessel with excessive sail and minimal weight will roll before its opposite type; software will go before hardware.

With sensible planning there is absolutely no need to run into a tropical storm. The cyclone-free period can be used or the Equator, where no cyclone ventures, can be favoured. But presuming the obligation is to sail into a known area of destructive winds, then the following is pertinent.

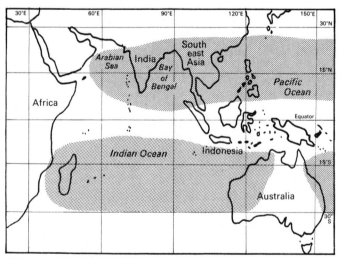

DESTRUCTIVE WIND ZONES
The two shaded areas indicate the limits of destructive winds in the northern and southern hemispheres. Each experiences its 'cyclone' or 'typhoon' season in summer only.

The author's son, Ben, stands beside a monument to one of Australia's great cyclones in which over 50 vessels and 300 men perished.

STORM LIMITS

Wherever destructive winds are known to occur, and regardless of their rate of occurrence, it is a fact that they never encroach upon the Equatorial belt. As a result, the area between latitudes 5° north and 5° south is completely free of such storms all year round.

Tropical storms breed in the vicinity of latitude 10° of their respective hemisphere and tend to track northwest in the northern hemisphere and southwest in the southern hemisphere. Their most destructive area tends to be between 15° and 20° although incursions to either side of those limits have been known. In the approximate area of 20° latitude the path often turns at right angles to continue north or south in the other quadrant and from this point on they usually die, or 'fill', as it is known. They will mostly fill regardless of their life span or track soon after encountering a large landmass but on very rare occasions, regeneration has been recorded after passing over a coast and venturing inland. This regeneration is always associated with a change of course which carries them back over the coast.

STORM SIGNALS

These are so many and varied that, frankly, one alone seldom proves anything whatsoever. However, as evidence stacks up the possibility of a serious storm in the vicinity cannot be ignored. If a corrected barometer falls more than 3 millibars below the mean, there is a depression somewhere which could intensify.

A long swell associated with the above is further proof and indicates the exact bearing from your position. If the depression is to the west it will, in all probability, move away and cause no distress whatsoever; if to the east then it will probably move towards you but veer to the north in the northern hemisphere and south in the southern hemisphere. This is tantamount to saying that if it follows a classic course it will move northwest in the northern hemisphere and southwest in the southern hemisphere.

If the above phenomenon occurs during relatively settled weather, the sky will fill from the storm centre with high cirrus, then altostratus and finally cumulus scud. In fact, storms of a serious nature rarely develop out of a clear blue sky. Mostly, the weather is unsettled for days and often weeks before and for this reason, the cloud test above is the least reliable.

Without meaning to sound flippant, the best sign is a verbal warning over the normal long or short-wave radio. All areas prone to destructive winds have excellent warning services based on modern radar and satellites. The Philippines, for example, experience more tropical storms per year than many other countries put together yet rarely do they suffer serious damage because of the excellence of its advance warning system.

Dislodged houses and domestic bric-a-brac are seen through the twisted remains of a ferro-cement hull under construction. This was the result of Townsville's (northeast Australia) cyclone *Althea* which topped 125 knots.

More of *Althea's* legacy is this trawler carried ashore by a 12 foot high storm surge. She wrecked a boat shed after slipping herself sideways.

AVOIDING THE BLOW

If the storm is truly inevitable then finding its exact position by wind direction offers a means of avoiding the worst area, not of avoiding the storm altogether. Be that as it may, the following is worthwhile for in moving out of the way of the centre, the strongest winds, followed by the most confused seas, are avoided.

The least destructive side of the storm until it alters course at around 20° is *towards* the Equator regardless of which hemisphere it is in and fortunately, it is also the direction in which the wind blows. Thus, when taking evasive action in the southern hemisphere you will sail north before a strong southeasterly wind. In the northern hemisphere you will sail south before a strong northeast wind.

To determine the probable direction of the storm centre is a matter of realising that the wind is blowing around and in towards the centre. In the southern hemisphere this is in a clockwise direction whilst in the northern hemisphere it is anticlockwise. Therefore, when facing the wind, the centre of its source will be somewhere around 90° to your left or right (southern and northern hemisphere respectively) depending on its proximity.

RIDING IT OUT

As long as the storm follows a normal path and does nothing untoward, like retreating along its previous path for a while before advancing again or turning suddenly to threaten you again, the wind will be behind you and will slowly decrease as you run away from its centre. Initially, however, the seas will be big and the wind around Force 8 or more. It is therefore a matter of sailing as fast as conditions permit with whatever sail area suggests itself.

If, on the other hand, the storm is not successfully avoided and winds of 70 knots and over are experienced, then bare poles and warps are indicated. But whatever tactics are employed, always presume the wind will increase and act accordingly; take in and stow all soft materials such as dodgers, sails and ropes. These items will flog themselves to death in the ultimate wind and may carry more substantial parts of the vessel with them in so doing.

STORM SURGE

A tropical revolving storm is like a huge vacuum cleaner. Its centre is of extremely low pressure and as a result, loose items within its proximity will fly skywards. But pertinent here is the effect this vacuum has on the sea; it endeavours to raise its surface level and it succeeds in varying degrees dependent on intensity.

The great cyclone of the 5th March 1899 which hit Australia's northeast coast and drowned over 300 men whilst sinking 50 of their pearling fleet, is said to have lifted the level of the sea 50 feet. This was established after finding lugger parts miles inland and stranded dolphins in cliff-face caves a similar height above mean sea level. Cyclone *Althea,* a storm that destroyed ten percent of the City of Townsville a few hundred miles away and 72 years later, lifted the sea nearly 12 feet. As a result, those vessels that survived, breaking free in the harbour, were scattered around the city's shoreline parks and roads.

It is this storm surge that can prove our greatest enemy; a benign phenomenon that insidiously lifts the sea level during the storm, but if not considered could easily break a vessel's warps even if wind were not present and once free the vessel becomes prone to enormous damage.

HIDING IN PORT

Having ridden out a number of tropical storms in crowded anchorages and ports, I have no illusions about the safety of such havens. They are only as safe as the other boat which, I fear, tends to break loose and start a domino action that is awesome to behold. The problem in port is that boats less well prepared than yours could be your undoing so it is wise, therefore, to check other boats around you after securing your own.

The one advantage of being in a commercial port is the access to heavy equipment after the storm should it be needed to lift your vessel back into the water. It is entirely possible for a number of vessels to find themselves on a surrounding road or park after being lifted there by surge. Quite obviously, a crane service is not available at an isolated anchorage; however, I recommend the latter over the former as long as it is not open to any point of the compass from which the wind might blow.

The best 'cyclone-hole' is a mangrove creek which is totally protected and narrow enough to allow warps to be taken to stout tree trunks. You should never underestimate the need for proper securing, once free to swing in any direction there is an excellent chance of stoving the bottom in on a mangrove tree which rapidly becomes a stump as the vessel drives aground.

PERSONAL SAFETY

Many lives are still lost in this age of advance warning systems simply because low-lying ground is inundated with the storm surge. That and the torrential rain always associated with a tropical storm create floods ahead of which many villagers cannot escape. This is especially true along certain parts of the coasts of India and the Philippines.

In developed countries where dwellings are more substantial and not as densely grouped, most lives are lost by injury. In Darwin's cyclone *Tracy,* for example, it is believed many folk perished when an apartment building collapsed, others died from wounds received from flying debris and some simply died of heart attack, so fearful can a fully developed cyclone be.

One of a number of small boats destroyed, this yacht is carried ashore by a moderately harmless cyclone in the New Guinea area.

Whilst one cannot prepare the aged against fear, it is possible to list a few do's and don'ts regarding the risk of injury. When it is realised that such items as coconuts, sheets of corrugated iron and other sundry missiles might fly around at speeds in excess of 100 miles per hour it can be appreciated that one should remain indoors. This applies to the yachtsman whether in port or in an isolated creek, for mangrove branches also become airborne. Do not be tempted to rush out on deck every time a worrying noise is heard. Unless the vessel is threatened, it is better to remain below. And if it is necessary to venture outside, keep a sharp watch for missiles and be ready to flatten yourself to the deck. This latter action is, in fact, often necessary just to prevent being blown overboard.

Under no circumstances leave the ship regardless of what may have blown away to beg retrieval; all too often something happens to deny safe return. Consider your life and the general welfare of the vessel as a whole far too important to jeopardise in the pursuit of petty items. Even a brand new sail flogging itself to death can prove to be petty under these circumstances.

GENERAL

After reading this chapter the yachtsman is apt to presume that destructive winds are the norm wherever they are prevalent. *Whenever* they are prevalent, yes, but not wherever because they are disciplined by natural factors, the most important being the right season. It has been admitted that unseasonal storms have occurred but they are too rare to deserve serious consideration. It can therefore be restated that destructive winds only occur in their allotted areas during their allotted times and this time is always summer.

AREAS OF TROPICAL STORMS

The following areas included in this book are subject to destructive winds, during the relevant season detailed later.

Arabian Sea   Most of the eastern half with risk in the western half as far as the island of Socotra.

Bay of Bengal   The whole area.

South China Sea.   The entire area but rare in the far south.

Indian Ocean south   Between 5° and 30° south across its full width.

India   The entire country except for extreme inland in the north.

Sri Lanka   Potentially the whole island but most common in the north.

Malaysia   Unlikely in the south, probable in the north.

Singapore   Extremely rare.

Indonesia   Unknown except for rare occurrences across the northern tip of Sumatra and southern coast of Java and the island chain across to Timor.

Philippines   Very common. Worst area in the world.

Papua New Guinea   Unknown except for rare occurrences along the south coast of the mainland and the Louisiade archipelago.

Australia   Northern Australia only as far south as 20° latitude with rare extensions down to 30°. Uncommon in the Torres Strait and between the Torres Strait and Darwin.

TROPICAL STORM SEASONS

Destructive winds are confined to the hottest time of the year wherever they occur. Because there is very little difference between summer and winter in these regions the two seasons are more generally referred to as the wet (summer) and dry (winter) season. In the northern hemisphere they are also called 'monsoons', the direction of wind indicating whether it is summer or winter. Thus, winter in the northern hemisphere is called the 'northeast monsoon' whilst the summer is called the 'southwest monsoon season'.

Whilst the above terms can be used in either hemisphere, 'wet' and 'dry' season mostly applies to the south whilst 'southwest monsoon' and 'northeast monsoon' apply to the north.

The following details the period of the year when destructive tropical storms can be expected in the areas described in this book. Further details regarding year-round weather will be found under the relevant heading in each area's or country's description in the 'Ports and Anchorages' section.

Arabian Sea The period of the southwest monsoon extends from May to September inclusive but tropical storm activity may extend beyond September. The cyclone season is from May to December inclusive with the most dangerous months being May, June, October and November. They are very rare during July, September and December and are unknown during August.

Bay of Bengal The circumstances here are exactly the same for the Arabian Sea except that there is no safe month. Cyclones may be expected between May and December with the month of greatest danger being November.

South China Sea Being in the northern hemisphere the South China Sea experiences its cyclones (called 'typhoons' here) during the southwest monsoon also, the greatest difference being in the possibility of typhoons extending into the northeast monsoon making any month of the year cyclone-prone. However, they are extremely rare between December and April inclusive but are very active during the southwest monsoon, the neighbouring Philippine Islands experiencing more tropical storms per year than any other part of the world. The most active months are July to October.

Indian Ocean south. December to April inclusive is the wet season here and therefore the cyclone season. January is the month of greatest frequency but often the most violent storms are either early or late in the season.

India The cyclone season here is identical to the Arabian Sea.

Sri Lanka Cyclones are unusual here but the danger period is similar to the Bay of Bengal.

Malaysia This country is the same as the Bay of Bengal.

Phillipines See South China Sea.

Australia Exactly as the southern Indian Ocean.

Coping with Coral

English and European yachting people who are either new to cruising or who have spent their time afloat exclusively in, or near, home waters will not have encountered coral reefs. As a result, the very idea of sailing in 'coral-infested waters' conjures up vivid pictures of shipwreck and hardship. They find it difficult to imagine conditions as they really are after consuming so much written and visual material that portrays living coral as a beautiful witch. This chapter, therefore, is intended to straighten out the facts and inject a little common sense into the subject.

Basically, a coral reef consists of millions upon millions of living organisms which thrive in tropical waters. As a rule of thumb, coral will be found only within the confines of the sun's movements. Thus, coral beyond 23⅓° north or south of the Equator is extremely unusual and generally only occurs where a warm current carries suitable water beyond this limit. Lord Howe Island, in the Tasman Sea off Sydney is a good example as is the coral in the northern extremes of the Red Sea.

Because living coral cannot survive at depths much greater than 100 feet it stands to reason that it cannot grow like an insidious cancer from the bottom of the ocean and suddenly appear where there was no coral before. It can only prosper upon geologically established foundations such as a coastal shoal or on the top of a submerged mountain. It can, and sometimes does, expand upon its charted territory by a matter of feet in a year and a reef not yet endangering surface navigation may indeed reach the surface one day, but these things are of more interest to the marine biologist than to the small boat navigator.

Not that insidious coral growth cannot eventually affect the small boat navigator, but so slow is the growth that any survey organisation easily keeps up with it. In fact, adjustments may be necessary only once or twice in a century or they may not be required at all because it is equally true that a reef can reduce in size. This is caused by any one of a number of phenomena from crown-of-thorns starfish attack to industrial pollutants. In twenty-five years of cruising amongst coral I have seen entire reef structures vibrantly alive one decade to be essentially drab and partly dead the next, only to see obvious evidence later of reblossoming. Never, in that time, have I seen absolute proof that a reef has grown up, or out, to any appreciable degree.

Along with the depth and temperature of water, another limiting factor in a coral organism's growth is air. It cannot survive for very long out of water, one tide being about the limit. For this reason coral will only grow as high as the *neap low tide level*. Thus, a coral plateau is exposed at spring lows and fully covered at spring highs. In fact, not all reefs fully cover at spring high tide. There are often boulders of dead coral conspicuous above the surface at even the highest tide. These are pushed up by storm activity and act as ideal reference points when sailing close to a reef.

Whilst the top of a large reef structure is naturally very rough on the feet of anyone collecting shells, and even rougher on a ship's bottom when she strikes the edge, the fact remains that much of the surface is uniformly even. I know of at least one wartime pilot who landed his bomber on a reef along the northeast coast of Australia; it goes without saying that he never got it off again although he and his crew *did* survive the landing.

The reason that a reef might present a tolerable landing strip to a stricken aircraft is because sand collects and fills the gaps between coral lumps. This is especially so towards the leeward edge, the windward edge being particuarly sawtoothed and thus the very worst part with which to collide and where most vessels unfortunately strike and it is for this reason that most such accidents result in the total loss of the vessel.

I digress. The point being made about sand accumulation on a reef plateau is the ready potential for a sand cay to appear. It can happen that sand piles up close to the leeward edge until it manages to remain above the high tide level in which position it can then become a collection point for birds who carry seeds out to it and thus start a struggling growth of coarse grass. If the growth gets beyond the grass stage it might even support small plants until a stunted forest results. This is a true cay, its forefather being a sand cay.

Typical reef types are illustrated leaving it only to be said here that nearly all headlands within tropical and semitropical waters boast a fringing reef which might extend to sea for two miles. More commonly it extends only half a mile or less. Similarly, continental islands nearly always have a fringing reef right around their perimeter which will vary in width from a few feet to one mile depending on environment and geographical shape. Sometimes whole bays will be literally filled with coral making a potentially great anchorage absolutely useless because nothing but a dinghy could possibly enter and then only at high tide.

Fringing reefs, it can be appreciated, can only 'fringe' if they have a land mass from which to extend. Isolated reefs, on the other hand, are truly that. They are *isolated* masses sitting atop a submerged mountain. They can be associated with continental islands but are mostly associated with sand and true cays.

When navigating in reef country there are a number of golden rules. These are listed here.

Always stand a watch as high as possible up the mast when eyeballing into reef country.

Never eyeball up to a reef against the sun. The reflection easily hides its otherwise conspicuous presence beneath the surface.

Get out of the habit of cutting close to headlands and continental islands. Always presume a fringing reef extends offshore whether the chart suggests this or not.

Nearly all coral infested areas in the world are well surveyed, allowing safe passage to those capable of elementary navigation. A constant watch is mandatory, however.

This vessel is careened on the hard-packed sand line between the beach and the fringing reef. The fringing reef can be seen still underwater between the hard sand and the deep water.

The green turtle is a most common reef dweller. It is protected in many areas of the world.

When making the final approach up to any type of reef prior to anchoring, keep a sharp lookout for isolated coral heads. Where the area is well charted these are nearly always shown, but presume their presence regardless. *Just as radar* seems to create as many accidents as it prevents, so too do beacons and lights upon isolated reefs, or so it seems. The reader would be astonished at the number of huge ships sitting hard aground and written off right next to a light beacon visible fully ten miles. I know of one incident where the ship actually bounced up onto the reef and bowled the light over! The lesson seems to be that we tend to take well-advertised reefs too close whilst we hold off unadvertised reefs for a considerable distance.

To return to generalities. Don't think of coral as if it is something waiting to rear up and grab you but conversely, never underestimate its potential for damage. Even the rudder, gently banging on a reef to an almost imperceptible swell can suffer untold damage and the most innocuous accident can slowly and insidiously develop into a total loss situation.

As an example of the above, I have a friend who was determined to sail his yacht into a lagoon. Having safely entered, he ghosted in very light airs across the emerald green surface heading for the windward corner, en route he gently grounded on an unseen coral head. Lulled by the peace of the scene he was slow to react and, to his horror, realised that the tide was falling fast and he could not get off. The result was total disaster as the vessel lay down with her topsides between two drying coral heads, the cabin side resting against one and the keel on the other. The vessel was eventually salvaged but the damage was appalling.

When anchoring in coral waters, two dominant bottoms will be found: mud and sand. A third, pure coral, is rare and should be avoided.

Mud will always be found under the lee of a reef that drops straight off with a minimum of isolated coral heads in the vicinity of the anchorage. This is true of both fringing and isolated reefs. The standard CQR or any favourite mud anchor is therefore suitable.

Sand with scattered coral patches will be found wherever the central plateau is well underwater whether it is the floor of a fully enclosed lagoon or a bay formed by a horseshoe-shaped reef. Where there is more sand than coral, any mud anchor will suit and where there are numerous coral patches with minimal clear sand, the Fisherman or Admiralty Pattern is recommended.

Regardless of what type of anchor is dropped over, or near coral, never trust pure rope. Many Mediterranean habits must be broken lest the vessel drift away from a frayed and parted warp. Use only chain or at least a long chain trace between anchor and rope.

The navigator using this book will first encounter coral at the other end of the Suez Canal in the Gulf of Suez. From there on, he will be in coral waters all the way to Australia unless he ventures into the Southern Ocean. But this is not tantamount to saying he must be on his toes every inch of the way. The popular vision of reefs scattered all over the ocean is patently absurd. The reef areas are well advertised and well indicated on the charts and in some places thousand of miles separate them.

Mail

It would be nice to think that efficient mail services are the exclusive property of developed countries. In that way the quality of services along the way might be accurately predicted. But the very worst mail service in the world, so it seems, is not in some desperate Third World nation whose inhabitants are just emerging from the Stone Age, it is in the model of developed countries today: Italy!

In Italy, letters commonly take up to two weeks just to get from the local post office to the nearest international airport. I base this on the fact that a flight between Rome and London takes about two hours yet mail has been known to take two hours *plus* two weeks — and that was whilst living within sight of Rome's international airport. The mind boggles at what happens when letters are posted from further away.

Before becoming too critical of just one country, I am reminded that in my own country — a super-efficient model of America — internal mail often takes five days over a journey that can be done in five hours. Everything considered, Third World nations are doing jolly well by comparison.

The fact is that none of the countries included in this book can be held responsible for the loss of any of the author's mail. A parcel to Sri Lanka took so long that it was given up for lost and a letter to Sudan was delivered to a totally irrelevant address and only by the sheerest chance did it find me. Further it must be said that The People's Democratic Republic of Yemen failed to despatch a package of my son's correspondence school tapes, but my wife accepts blame there; you do not send such potentially subversive material from a communist country! But all in all, the services functioned smoothly enough.

The cruising person is advised to keep his or her name and address brief and as simple as possible. Remember that Arabic script, for example, enjoys no similarity whatsoever to the Roman alphabet so a non-English-speaking Arab postal clerk will have to ask around as to where he puts your letter and the person who can interpret may be limited to simple visual impressions. As a result there is an excellent chance that a letter to Mr and Mrs Jones will be found in the 'M' (for Mr or Mrs) pigeonhole.

Fortunately, English is widely understood along the routes in this book but it definitely pays to limit your name to just the surname. Thus my name would be, *Lucas,* c/o Post Office, Wherever. I would then know to ask only for 'L' although in some places I would also check 'P' and 'O' and 'W'.

This precaution is only necessary where mail is sent to countries whose language bears no resemblance whatsoever to ours in the written form, in other words, all Arab and Eastern countries. However, it mainly applies to secondary centres where British colonialism spread but was not centred. For example a major town in India can cope with a complicated name and address whilst a mountain village may not.

The most secure address en route to Australia is care of the yacht agent in Galle, Sri Lanka as advertised in that section. Otherwise, one can only use *poste restante* for the post offices involved and this can cause some initial confusion. Take, for example, a letter sent to the post office in Aden. Strictly speaking, there is no such place as a town called Aden, it being an area. As a result, that letter will almost certainly be lodged in the post office at the city of Crater. As a result, a yachtsman searching for mail may be obliged to follow many a lead before locating it.

The grapevine is one of the best advisory services en route. Check with those folk sailing in the opposite direction and ask them how their mail fared in whatever country you hope to make a pick-up. But keep your pick-ups to a minimum and limit them to proven addresses.

Another way of simplifying mail delivery is to avoid sending and receiving parcels of any description. Many Third World and remote countries look on parcels as being highly suspicious. They are often held by customs where countless forms must be filled in and a king's ransom in duty must be paid before being released into your custody. You then find it is a plastic toy for the child's birthday which now owes four times its value!

Some countries are quite paranoid about the way an outgoing parcel must be wrapped. In India they insist upon each and every parcel being covered in cloth and then stitched! There are even businesses specialising in sewing the cover on parcels.

Considering the opportunity for madness, the sailor is advised to receive only simple letters en route and save the heavies for arrival in Australia. There, sanity returns regarding parcels although duty may still be applicable unless very definitely proven that you are a yacht in transit.

When sending mail from poorer or corrupt countries, beware of the clerk stealing the stamps. The system works thus; the clerk takes your money and personally places the stamps on your mail. Then, as soon as you leave, he removes the stamps and sells them again, dumping your mail with the rubbish. Where this practice is suspected, insist on seeing the letters franked or buy the stamps and drop them into a post box yourself.

This practice is not as rampant as one might expect considering the wages earned by many Third World postal clerks, but it has been known to happen, especially in Indonesia and for this reason I recommend that Indonesia be ignored as a reliable mailing area. Singapore is excellent, corruption being virtually wiped out, and Australia is not so far away that Indonesia cannot be passed through without the collection of important mail.

When having mail forwarded to any address, regardless of the country, allow for the possibility of it being returned to sender after one month. Try not to have it delivered ahead more than one month before your expected arrival.

In closing this chapter, it must be emphasised that while advising of the problems makes the whole system sound untenable, it is not and I have already said that I have lost nothing to speak of over the years. But one must learn a few tricks of the trade and these, in condensed form are:

Keep the address simple.
Listen to the grapevine for the best address.
Put your own stamps on once the standard rate is known.
Register all important letters.
Avoid receiving or sending parcels until Australia, although Sri Lanka proved secure enough, if cumbersome, in its system whilst Singapore and Hong Kong are very efficient.

The Tropical Market

A person from a northern country is very rarely aware of the different fruits and vegetables available in a tropical country, let alone what to do with them. The following, therefore, is a list of the common species found in markets from Sudan to New Guinea and how they might be cooked or prepared.

VEGETABLES

Taro   Very like a potato. Can be boiled, baked or fried.
Okra   Slightly slimey, can be used to thicken stews or fried.
Yam   Very starchy, can be washed to remove starch before eating.
Cassava   Some varieties can be toxic, needs repeated washing and thorough cooking. Best grated.
Choko   Skin better removed before cooking unless very young.
Coconut   A fruit or vegetable, there are two stages at which they can be picked or purchased, 'eating' and 'drinking'. 'Eating' is the fully ripe nut which can be made into coconut cream by grating the flesh then squeezing its liquid through cloth into a bowl. The natural water from the nut or plain water can be added to the gratings for a final squeeze which produces a thinner milk. The final cream can be used with a great variety of fleshes and vegetables. Chips of ripe coconut flesh make wonderful nibbles around a barbeque. Lightly fry and eat immediately. 'Drinking' is the green nut before it falls from the palm and before its flesh fully matures. Drink the liquid. Superb flavour.
Breadfruit   Can be baked or boiled whole or cut into chips. Always peel before cooking. The seeds can be boiled or roasted to eat as nuts.

Tropical markets mostly overflow with fresh local produce which is commonly unidentifiable by visitors from cold regions. Some of the best markets are in India.

TROPICAL FRUITS

Bananas   Some varieties are for cooking only, being small, green and quite hard. Otherwise eat as a fruit and the leaves can be used to wrap food in before cooking.

Pawpaw   Most versatile, the pawpaw can be used as a fruit eaten as it is when ripe, or cooked as a vegetable when green. Tastes a little like squash. The leaves can be boiled or steamed with a little coconut milk and eaten as a vegetable whilst the skin makes a fine compress for a tropical ulcer as well as easing insect bites when rubbed over the area. Pawpaw juice, apart from being very drinkable, can be used to tenderise meat.

Pummelo   Similar to a large, thick-skinned grapefruit, the flesh is often pink or red in colour. This seems especially so at the Port Sudan market. Is often quite dry. Delicious eaten as it is.

Jackfruit   Similar to breadfruit. Eat the flesh around the seeds. Seeds can be roasted and eaten as nuts.

Carambola (Five Corners)   Shaped like a star when cut and divided into five sections, this fruit has a tangy, thirst-quenching quality and its juice can be extracted as a drink only. The juice also helps remove stains from linen and helps clean brass (with salt added).

Soursop (Custard Apple)   Large, soft and green with black leaves, this magnificent fruit is best eaten when soft at which stage it is fully ripe but will not last long.

Mangosteen   Looking like a persimmon, this has a unique and delicious flavour.

Guava   Useful to make jam as they are high in pectin. Excellent to eat when ripe. Lemon coloured.

Mangoes   Surely the greatest taste treat of all fruits, the mango is eaten when yellowish and fully ripe although some native races eat them hard and green. Can be used as a vegetable in this state.

Pineapple   Often quite small in the tropics, they are mostly much sweeter than ones from colder climates. Absolutely superb when eaten fresh.

Citrus   Lemons, limes, tangerines and oranges are included here all of which will be found in the tropical market. Commonly oranges have green skins yet will prove sweet whilst others are close to the flavour of a lemon. Big juicy navel types are unknown.

Lychees   Oval, reddish with a hard scaly covering, eat the flesh around the seed.

Durian   Oval and prickly, tastes delicious but has a foul smell.

Grandadilla   Large green to yellow fruit which is yellow when ripe. Eat as it is or cook as a vegetable.

Victualling along the way

This subject is dealt with independently under the heading 'Facilities' in each and every port description throughout the 'Ports and Anchorages' section of this book. However, as a service to those wanting a quick reference for the entire route, the following is brief but pertinent.

DIESEL FUEL   In 1984, diesel cost around US$1.50 per gallon in Larnaca, Cyprus, where it is also easily loaded at the marina and being cheaper than in most European countries there is a natural temptation to fill every available space aboard with fuel. This is not necessary so carry just enough to guarantee passage to Suez (Port), at the southern end of the Suez Canal where it is not only much cheaper again but is easily loaded alongside.

Beyond Suez, all major ports have diesel fuel readily available at prices that tend to float slightly higher than Cyprus. In Aden it is cheaper and very easily loaded whilst in Galle in Sri Lanka, it is similar and also easily loaded.

Singapore boasts fuel barges whose masters actively sell their product and who take great care with visitors' topsides and decks. Indonesia is a fuel-producing country with outlets for the refined product in all ports and Australia can claim the same although its diesel price tends to match petrol making it the most expensive. At around US$1.80 per gallon in 1984 it was slightly higher than all countries involved except India where the price hit US$2.50 for the same quantity.

PETROL   tends to be around twice the price of diesel in all countries except Australia and India where it is similar. Nowhere will it be found bowsered on a jetty and must be carted from the nearest service station. In some towns this represents a walk or bus ride of up to one mile.

PARAFFIN   is very easy to buy in Cyprus, Sri Lanka, Singapore and Australia in which countries it is tied to the diesel price. It is available in all other countries but can be often annoying to locate. In India, for example, there is no problem buying it by the small bottle but bulk requires special clearance from a government department for some obscure reason.

METHYLATED SPIRITS is also available everywhere but often with peculiar conditions attached. In Port Sudan, for example, one can only buy through the black market making it devilishly expensive whilst in Sri Lanka it burns with all the purity of old sump oil. It is of good quality and easily available in India, Singapore and Australia suggesting that stocks be bought in Cyprus to carry out through to India at least and preferably Singapore.

OIL There is never any problem finding elementary types of oil for petrol or diesel engines although the high-detergent type demanded by the latter can take a little tracking down in some towns. Special purpose oils, on the other hand, can be difficult and sometimes impossible to locate and this is true of hydraulic gearbox oil. The yachtsman should carry an ample supply of this commodity or change his gearbox oil to engine lubricating oil where the manufacturer agrees with the practice (usually where an engine does not exceed 3000 rpm).

GAS The European yachtsman will never see gas as cheap again after leaving the Mediterranean. In other areas it is commonly twice and three times the price. It is, nevertheless, available in all main centres, albeit with the proviso that connecting up can prove difficult at times.

WATER Being such a fundamental staple of the human race, it hardly needs confirming that water will be found everywhere. Jetty outlets are not always easy to find or, when found, are sometimes surrounded by commercial users. However, in all ports mentioned in this book water will be found and put aboard even if it must be demijohned out by dinghy.

The classic fear of untreated water is well founded but in most areas it is treated. Local knowledge should be sought or, where this is absent and the water doubtful, boil all drinking water.

FOOD The tremendous range of processed foods we are accustomed to seeing in Europe will not be seen again until Singapore, then again in Hong Kong and Australia. However, India has a remarkably broad industrial base and does produce a great variety of tinned and dried food.

The cruising boat is best stocked to the hilt with processed foods in Cyprus after which basic replacements should be found in all other countries. Fresh food, of course, is available everywhere at often remarkably low prices. There are markets in all areas described herein.

WINE, SPIRITS AND BEER Italy has the cheapest imported spirits in the Mediterranean whilst Spain and Cyprus vie for the cheapest wine. Beer tends to be a similar price through the Mediterranean and France among the cheapest.

It is recommended that wine drinkers take all they can from Cyprus for not only will the quality be difficult to improve upon elsewhere but the price is amongst the cheapest in the world. And in some areas along the route wine is simply not available at all, or, if it is available, it is imported and sold at outlandish prices.

Beer and spirits can be purchased duty-free from Port Said or Aden at prices which compete with European retail prices. Beer is brewed in India at a slightly higher cost to the consumer and is excellent, whilst Sri Lankan beer is best used for paint remover.

Singapore has a wide range of alcoholic drinks as does Australia, but in both countries it is expensive, beer, for example, being as much as 250 per cent more.

PAINT Imported paint in Cyprus is expensive whilst the local product is very cheap and of excellent quality. It is thereforee suggested that an amount of local paint capable of lasting the duration of the voyage be put aboard in Cyprus. It will be found in all other areas if mixing brands is not objected to.

HARDWARE There are some surprisingly well-stocked hardware stores along the routes in some of the most unlikely places, but in terms of predictable availability, Cyprus is, once again, hard to better. Certain items, such as brassware, plastic buckets and demijohns, and stainless -steel buckets are cheap in India.

REPAIRS Marine plywood and a useful selection of boat timber is hard to find beyond Cyprus until Singapore is reached. However, basic repairs to hull and machinery can be carried out in all ports, although finding professional labour might prove difficult. Sail repairs cannot be effected until Singapore although certain awning and upholstery shops can often help out. Glues and resins are difficult if not impossible to locate in the Red Sea, India and Sri Lanka suggesting that these be carried aboard from the Mediterranean.

BOAT BITS Fundamental items such as galvanised shackles, engine oil filters, rope and so on will be found at hardware shops and service stations along the way. Specific engine or gearbox parts will not be found (easily) and yacht hardware is simply unknown until Singapore. There is a good selection of the latter in Larnaca and Limassol, Cyprus.

PASSAGES

Indian Ocean Routes

THE BEST ROUTE

The best route to anywhere by sailing boat is always downwind. That is why the famous trade-wind routes are so popular but also why there is room for speculation regarding the passage from Europe to Australia because it is a fact that trade winds, as we know them in the Pacific and Atlantic Oceans, as well as the south Indian Ocean, do not exist. However, there *is* a form of trade wind and a very well-developed monsoon across the north Indian Ocean, as we will see.

A RESUME OF WIND DIRECTION

Detailed maps and descriptions will be found later for each and every part of the routes under scrutiny. Here the broad spectrum of passage planning around anticipated winds will be reviewed.

Without labouring the point with specific details here, it can be said that the Red Sea provides a very useful and occasionally rumbustious north-northwesterly wind throughout the year. It can therefore be stated categorically that a southbound sailing vessel will have no trouble running down to the Indian Ocean from the Mediterranean Sea.

So much for the first 1500 miles. As we enter the north Indian Ocean at the Gulf of Aden, to cross the Arabian Sea, we have a choice of beating against a light to moderate northeasterly with no fear of typhoons, or of running fast and reliably before a spanking southwesterly but with risk of typhoons.

Which is preferred? Having been involved in a couple of destructive winds I cannot and will not make light of such a phenomenon. However, such is the nature of the north Indian Ocean typhoons (or cyclones) that their season can be sailed with fair safety as is detailed under the chapter 'Destructive winds'. I thus promote the idea of using the southwesterlies rather than fighting the northeasterlies.

A working elephant in Sri Lanka is but one of the many unusual sights awaiting the yachtsman along the routes described in this section.

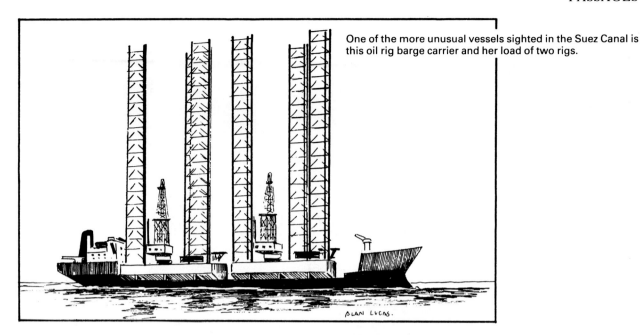

One of the more unusual vessels sighted in the Suez Canal is this oil rig barge carrier and her load of two rigs.

Because the southwest monsoon of the north Indian Ocean (The Arabian Sea and Bay of Bengal) prevails during the northern summer (May to October), it is obvious that one of these months should be used for the crossing, more if stops are to be made. However it makes sense to plan properly, since certain months are safer than others during this season. For example, for some obscure reason, August is entirely typhoon-free in the Arabian Sea despite the southwesterly season being fully developed. Thus it pays to enter the Arabian Sea at the beginning of August and be on the other side by the end of the month; the distance being around 2200 miles makes this possible for all but the slowest of craft.

Typhoons can occur during August in the Bay of Bengal but are most common during November, thus it is wise to reach Singapore before that month. Having made it safely to Singapore, enjoying a fair wind all the way from the Mediterranean, the wind should remain fair — albeit often totally windless — throughout the months of November to March, a period giving ample time to cruise down to Australia via the chain of Indonesian islands.

Between the months November and April there is a chance of a cyclone on the north Australian coast. However, they are rare in the Timor — Darwin area making that short 400 mile crossing an easy business of awaiting the right weather in Kupang, Timor.

Suggested alternative courses, as well as the one discussed above are shown graphically in the diagram on page 26. All will be looked at in detail here and cruising alternatives — as against making a passage — will also be explored.

Ancient practice and craft mingle with the 20th century in most Asian countries along the routes discussed here.

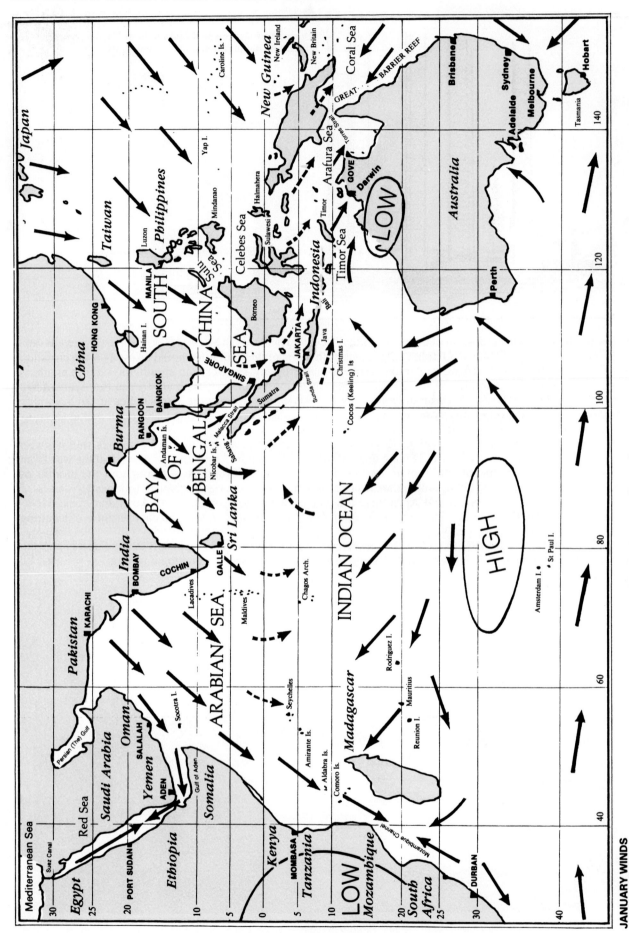

JANUARY WINDS

January, February and March are the best months for making westerly passage across the north Indian Ocean whilst they present the greatest likelihood of cyclonic activity in the southern hemisphere.

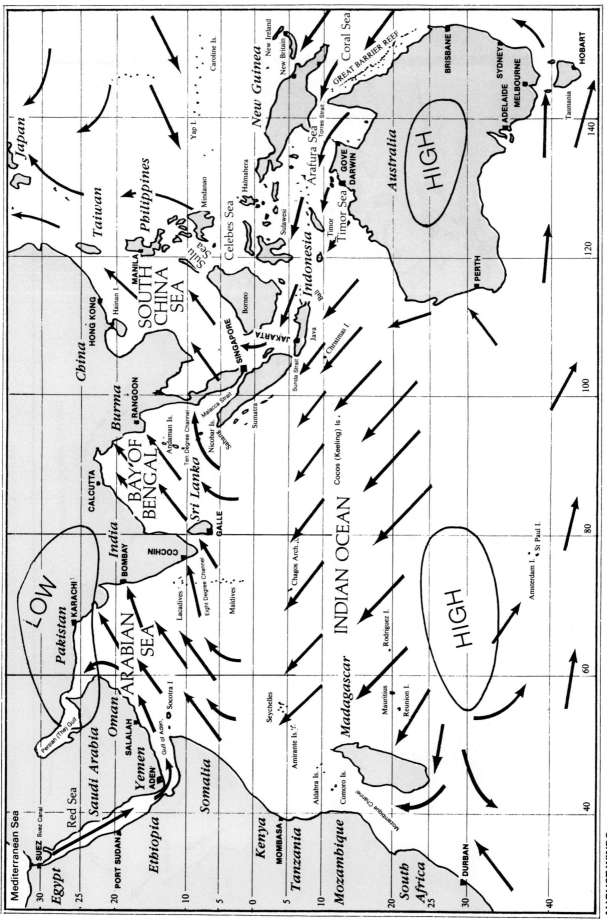

AUGUST WINDS
The months of May to November inclusive promise reliable, strong but safe southeasterly trade winds across the south Indian Ocean. In the northern hemisphere southwesterlies blow at a useful and reliable strength but this is the cyclone season with just a few months excepted as noted in this chapter.

23

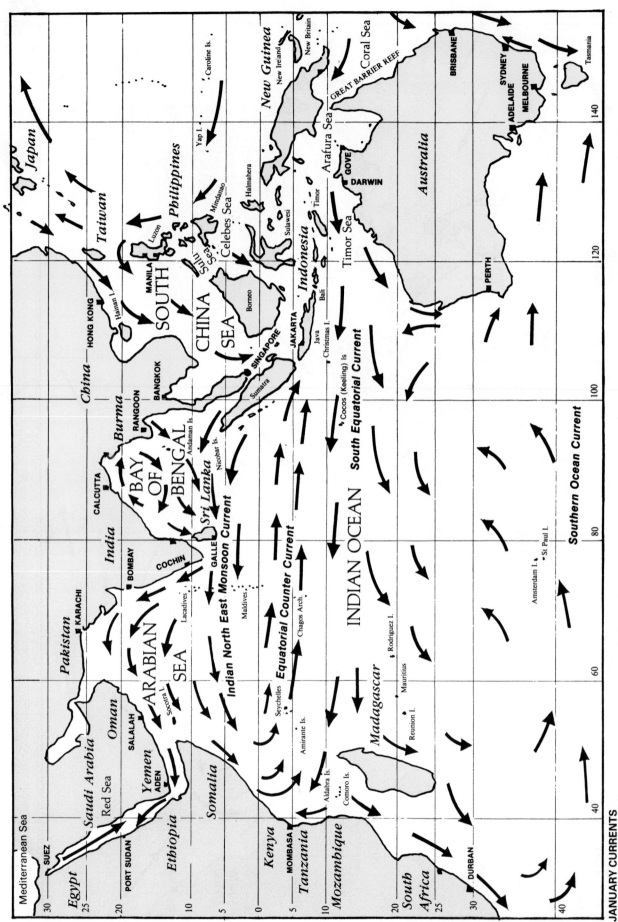

JANUARY CURRENTS
Currents are caused by the wind flow and thus conform to the same seasons as those for the trade winds and anti-trades. The two strongest currents will be found off the southeast coast of Africa and Australia whilst the Equatorial Counter Current is often absent.

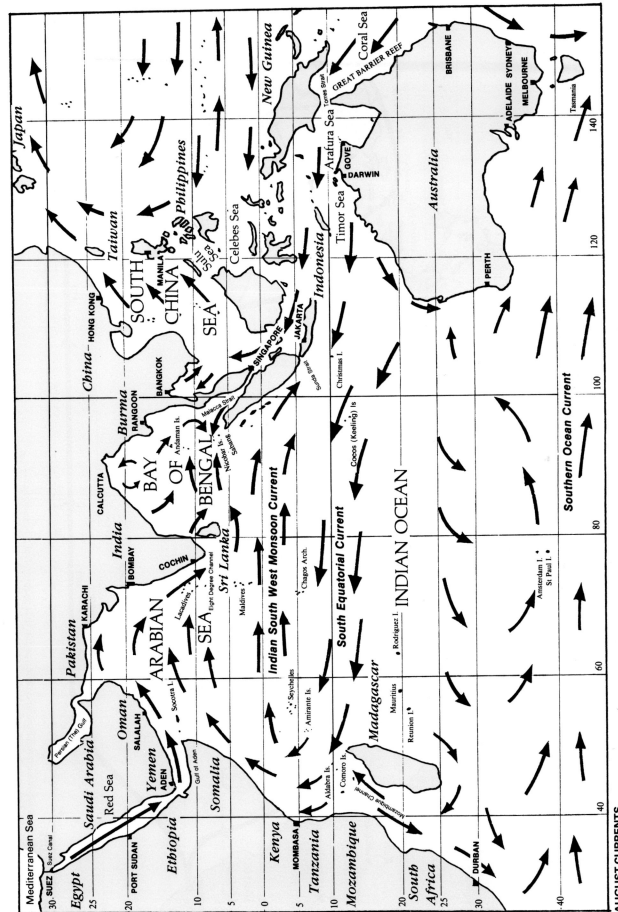

AUGUST CURRENTS

During the months May to November when the northern hemisphere's southwesterlies blow, the currents in that region reverse direction. The currents of the southern hemisphere remain constant.

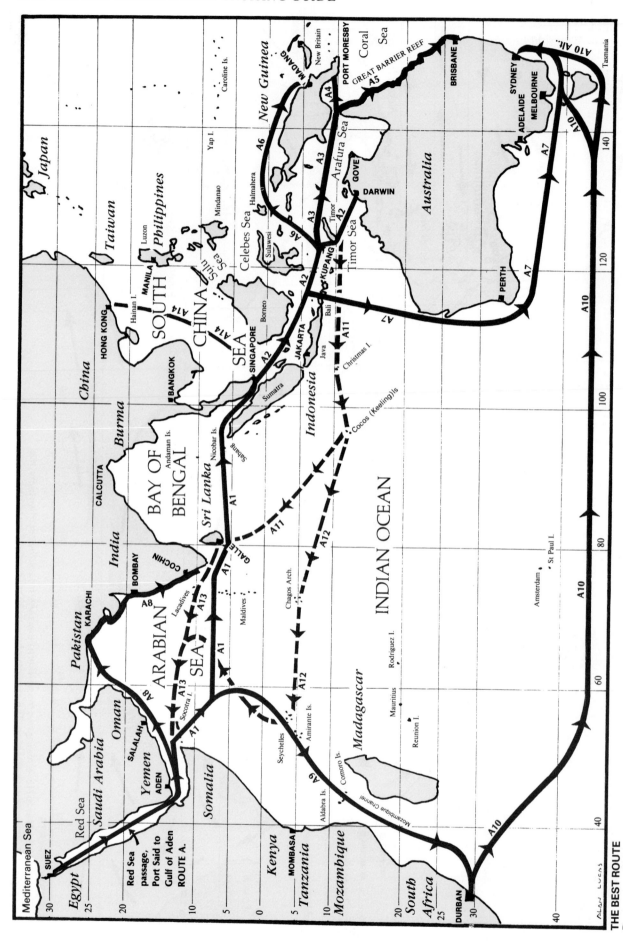

THE BEST ROUTE

Recommended routes are illustrated here and described in this chapter. Solid lines indicate easterly routes whilst dotted lines indicate westerly routes.

ROUTE A
Red Sea — Port Said to Aden

As emphasised under its own description, the Red Sea experiences a very dominant northerly wind which channels into the direction of the sea. Thus it is always NNW when blowing at any strength and for any duration. This occurs twelve months of the year with only rare short and sharp southerlies in the Gulf of Suez and fairly regular SSE winds from Aden up to the Ethiopian-Sudan border during the months December, January, February and March.

Gales can occur at any time of the year but the Red Sea never records a destructive wind, a fact that gives it a degree of security.

All considered, it can be appreciated that this route can be undertaken at any time of the year, but is best between the months April and November inclusive southbound, despite the inevitability of excessively hot weather and December to March northbound.

ROUTE A1
Aden to Singapore

The best time to leave the Red Sea and enter the Gulf of Aden is mid to late July depending on whether a victualling stopover in Aden or Djibouti is intended. In any case, it is best to enter the Arabian Sea in late July to early August by cutting between Somalia and Socotra, but under no circumstances being tempted to stop at either country. Reaching down to about 8° north, the southwesterly should be held yet its most violent area should be missed. At this time of year this area tends to extend east and northeast from Socotra.

The violence is relative, the month of August being free of destructive winds. However, during June, July and August the southwesterly can reach Force 7 and pile up considerable seas out from Socotra.

Vessels in need of victuals should stop at Galle; this small Sri Lankan port being well placed along the route and its services being quite outstanding for a small, struggling country, as outlined under its own heading.

Those intending to press on for Singapore should leave Sri Lanka no later than early October so that the Bay of Bengal can be crossed before its worst month for typhoons, November. But because the months May to November, and sometimes December, are typhoon-prone, the navigator should be prepared to lose his wind by steering towards the Equator should a destructive wind threaten. Such winds do not occur on the Equator or roughly 5° to each side.

The prevailing wind down the Strait of Malacca (between Malaysia and Sumatra) is northwesterly at this time of year; however, calms often dominate in this equatorial area at all times of the year. It is thus likely that the last few hundred miles will be covered by engine.

ROUTE A2
Singapore to Darwin

If Route A2 is to be covered in the one year, the vessel should be victualled and put to sea again to capture the northwesterlies which prevail throughout the Indonesian islands during December, January, February and March. Like the Singapore area, this time of year also experiences sweltering calms or contrary winds from thunderstorms, but at least the southern hemisphere's southeast trade wind is held at bay whilst a course to the southeast is shaped.

Kupang, the main town of Timor, is in a cyclone-free area but Darwin, a mere 400 miles away, is cyclone-prone. However, cyclones are rare in this area right across to Australia promising a good degree of safety to the navigator who will wait in Kupang for settled weather.

Upon arrival in Darwin, Route A2 is completed and the major destination is achieved. However, Australia is an enormous place offering a vast array of cruising alternatives and for this reason other destinations around its coast are studied and its cruising grounds are reviewed.

ROUTE A3
Timor to Thursday Island

The best time of year to cover this 1200 mile passage is around December, a fact that makes reaching Singapore well ahead of November doubly important. But it is not critical because the passage, during what is known in the southern hemisphere as the wet season, is mostly one of calms and variables with only about six weeks of truly useful northwesterly winds. Destructive winds are virtually unknown as long as the Australian coast is not favoured, and visibility is good enough most of the time to ensure accurate sights and landfall.

This route should not be attempted after March at which time the southeast trade wind is likely to return and then blow with a vengeance right through to November. It is a perfectly safe and dry time but would only be enjoyed by those folk enthusiastic about long and difficult beats to windward.

ROUTE A4
Thursday Island to Port Moresby

Vessels proceeding to the south coast of Papua New Guinea should sail directly across the northwest Coral Sea giving all due care and consideration to the many reefs and islets en route (see Torres Strait — Thursday Island description in 'Ports and Anchorages').

Despite the slight risk of cyclone activity, the passage is best made out of the southeast trade wind season for in this corner of the world they are the most constant and powerful trade winds to be found anywhere. The wet season between December and March inclusive, and January specifically, should be utilised.

ROUTE A5
Thursday Island down the Great Barrier Reef

Being in an area of very strong and persistent southeast trade winds, beating south along the Queensland coast is a trial by spray and discomfort. It *can* be done and an anchorage can be found every night but it cannot be seriously suggested as an easy way down the coast. It is risky but sensible to use, once again, the variable wet season from December to March and press south under engine.

The more sensible way to approach the Great Barrier Reef is to make for Sydney then cruise north along the east coast of Australia. A route to Sydney is noted later.

ROUTE A6
Timor to New Guinea's North Coast

The typical major destination at the end of this route is the glorious port and town of Madang from where the southwest Pacific can be cruised, albeit, often against headwinds.

Being along the Equator, no dominant wind pattern can be anticipated at any time of year however, variables favouring the eastern quadrant are common whilst northerlies emanating from the north Pacific's northeast trade wind are sometimes experienced during the months of January, February and March. Broadly speaking, the engine will be pressed into service more often than not and periods of maddening head swell with no wind must be expected occasionally.

ROUTE A7
Bali to Australia's West and South Coasts

During the wet season of December to April — not necessarily inclusive — a fair wind might be anticipated from Bali to Australia's northwest corner. More likely, however, calms will dominate and a southeasterly could prevail from 15° to 20° latitude. This is also the cyclone (called willy-willy here) season and care should be exercised towards Australia's northwestern region. Otherwise, the cyclone-free April to November southeast trade wind can be utilised.

In either season, headwinds can be expected down the west coast with a hope of fair slants at times, then westerlies should prevail across the south coast, although in summer (December to April) calms can prevail for days at a time.

ROUTE A8
Aden to India's West Coast

The fastest time of year for this passage is during the May to October southwest monsoon with August being the safest month in terms of typhoons. But because it is presumed the yachtsman will go to India to cruise its coast for a number of months, the southwest monsoon period becomes counterproductive placing a small boat on a constant lee shore.

Therefore, in a cruising context, it is recommended that Aden be departed around early December at which time the southwest monsoon will be over and the northeast trade winds will be establishing themselves. Mostly there is a distinct absence of wind or a presence of variables making it possible to sneak along the North Yemen coast with a minimum of headwinds. The further north one ventures, the less likely is one to encounter serious headwinds as long as the land near Pakistan is favoured.

En route, Salalah can be entered for supplies, rest and recreation, but this should be the only Omanian port entered. The coast should not be cruised owing to possible guerilla activity away from the control of the Sultan's army.

The coast can be cruised from Pakistan's capital, Karachi, all the way down to Cochin, and beyond if desired, but it should be all done before the return of the southwest monsoon in May.

At the prime cruising time — December to April inclusive — the west coast of India is predominantly calm being in a wind shadow. However, there are afternoon northerlies to help the southbound yacht along and at night it is not unusual to enjoy light offshore breezes. The mornings are mostly totally calm.

After a cruise of India's west coast it is possible to press on for Singapore during the early southwest monsoon which should be established by May but on the proviso that a cyclone could develop. In fact, if Singapore is the desired destination, early cyclones are unusual across the Bay of Bengal making May or June relatively ideal months for sailing east.

Otherwise, from the tip of India, the Maldives can be visited after which the Equator might be crossed around April, when the south Indian Ocean's southeast trade wind season should be well and truly established, offering good passage from the Chagos Archipelago to Durban. The European anxious to return home might consider this as an ideal route, for once around South Africa's Cape of Good Hope the South Atlantic southeast trade winds offer fast passage up to the Mediterranean.

ROUTE A9
Gulf of Aden to Durban, South Africa

Following along the lines of the above suggestion, this route presumes the yachtsman is keen to sail more or less directly from the Gulf of Aden to Durban as against cruising India first. Typically, this route would be taken by those intending to sail on to Australia via the Southern Ocean as discussed under Route A10. Whether the destination beyond Durban proves to be to Europe, via the South Atlantic, or across to Australia via the Southern Ocean, the summer season is the best time to be that far south if only on the basis of creature comforts. Happily, this fits into the best time to be leaving the Gulf of Aden relative to the northern hemisphere's cyclone season.

Leaving the Gulf of Aden in early August, the southwest monsoons are enjoyed during the cyclone-safe month during which time longitude 60° east should be reached before turning south. In fact, there is only advantage to be enjoyed by pressing further east before turning south and those wanting to visit the Maldives are encouraged to do so.

From 60° east, or further east if possible, turn south to cross the Equator and prepare ship for a strong but reliable southeasterly wind over the port beam. This should be found soon after the Equator and certainly by 8° south.

The Seychelles are a recommended stop after which the Comoros Islands might be visited although their anchorages will not prove especially comfortable or secure. In this area the wind should be east to northeast with periods of calm and variables as the Mozambique Channel is negotiated.

The Mozambique Current, running southwards at a good rate between the African mainland and Madagascar and later becoming the famous and often fast Agulhas Current, will assist southerly passage considerably. However, where the southeast trade wind is found again upon emerging from the Mozambique Channel, or worse, when a southwesterly gale blows against the current, the seas can be steep and at times dangerous. During such conditions it is sometimes better to be over the 100 fathom line (the continental shelf) where the current is at its weakest or possibly running in another direction.

ROUTE A10
Durban to Australia

After a stopover in Durban — possibly enjoying employment if the coffers are low, and certainly enjoying the hospitality of the Point Yacht Club — the crossing to Australia can be started in January. The exact month is not critical but is chosen here to provide the warmest weather and to gain the last of summer upon reaching Australia.

ROUTE A11
Darwin to Galle, Sri Lanka

This being the beginning of the return passage to Europe which, it is presumed for the sake of the exercise, will be via the Red Sea, it is best to reach Galle around late November, early December. This allows plenty of time for rest and recreation amongst the dozens of other westbound yachting people before the Arabian Sea's northeast trade wind becomes firmly established (in January).

Under these circumstances, Darwin is best departed around late August so that time can be spent in Bali, Christmas Island and Cocos (Keeling) Islands without fear of losing the wonderful southeast trade winds which prevail across the entire South Indian Ocean from April to November.

Bali, as noted under the section 'Indonesia' is one of the few Indonesian ports where a certain tolerance is shown to yachtsmen who enter without a Sailing Permit, three days usually being given. But rather than depend on prevailing attitudes, a Sailing Permit should be obtained well in advance, as detailed.

Christmas and Cocos Islands enjoy full descriptions near the end of this book as does the whole South Indian Ocean. Here it need only be emphasised that the southeast trade wind can be relied upon as a fair and honest wind as soon as Australia's wind shadow is cleared. It is also recommended that Cocos Islands be departed around late October for the two week passage to Galle. On the direct Great Circle route the trade wind should hold as far as the Equator after which calms, variables and a few thunderstorms will be encountered to Galle.

ROUTE A12
Cocos Island to Seychelles and beyond

The passage from Cocos (Keeling) Islands to the Seychelles, taking in the Chagos Archipelago en route, can be undertaken at any time during the southeast trade wind seas (April to November). Before the Seychelles became Marxist governed, and thus marginally restrictive to local cruising, this was the most popular route to the Red Sea from the southern hemisphere.

Leaving the Seychelles around late November to early December, steer north and east using the last of the south east trade winds. The purpose in making some easting here is to enjoy a fair slant on the Arabian Sea's northeasterlies when found. At this time of year this may not happen until about 10° north latitude.

ROUTE A13
Galle, Sri Lanka to Gulf of Aden

Beyond a shadow of doubt the best period of the year to make this westerly passage is during the months of January, February and March. These constitute the best of the northeast monsoon season and are entirely cyclone free. The same advice extends across the Bay of Bengal for those whose passage emanates from Singapore.

Upon entering the Red Sea during these months there is a fair chance of finding good southerlies as far north as the Ethiopian-Sudan border as detailed in the section 'The Red Sea'.

ROUTE A14
Singapore to Hong Kong

This passage is made entirely within the South China Sea, an area experiencing similar conditions to the Bay of Bengal and the Arabian Sea. Regrettably, it does not have a safe month during its typhoon-prone May to November southwest monsoon season although destructive winds are uncommon before July and are almost unknown in the extreme south of the region.

Considering the above, it makes sense to utilise the favourable southwest monsoon before July, May and June being usually safe. Otherwise, the safe January, February and March northeast monsoon can be sailed but at the cost of a hard beat to windward for much of the time.

The Fast Way Out

We are somewhat out of context here in describing a route that involves the Atlantic Ocean as well as the Indian Ocean. However, for those perhaps requiring such information, the fastest route from England to Australia will be discussed at here. This is known as The Clipper Route and is shown on the next page.

The Clipper Route was used commercially by the old sailing ships running from England to South Australia where gold, wool and grain were loaded for the return trip which passed under South America at the famous Cape Horn. It was a passage that could be undertaken at any time of year because of the reliability of most winds involved. The main concern, when in the Southern Ocean, was one of intense cold and the danger of icebergs across the path. It is for this reason that only the summer route will be looked at here.

The principle route utilised the North Atlantic northerlies down to the Equator after which the South Atlantic southeast trade winds were brought on the port beam. These carried the ships down to the 30th parallel in which region the course was altered to pass under South Africa, thence Australia, as the rumbustious westerlies of the Roaring Forties were found.

Children of a continuous procession of depressions around the Antarctic rim, the Southern Ocean westerlies actually vacillate between northwest and southwest, the former direction usually proving the strongest. But regardless of exact direction, these winds bring with them a formidable sea, unchecked, as it is, by any landmass across its path. It was for this reason that square-riggers carried a canvas screen behind the helm. This was not for such compassionate reasons as to protect the helmsmen, rather, it was to prevent their looking aft, taking fright and losing control of the ship.

Indicative of conditions in and below the Roaring Forties is the fact that Commander H. V. King was awarded an O.B.E. during the war just on the basis that he took his submarine *Olympus* to about 45° south in search of German raiders. The rigours of such a patrol did not go unnoticed at the top.

Having personally sailed in the Roaring Forties only in the region of South Australia, I can add little from experience. However, my impression during a gale was that although awesome, the waves are, at least, very well spaced. A small boat really does not suffer much until the tops start breaking. Then heavy-weather tactics may become necessary.

Depending on the exact course steered and the possible extra miles sailed in search of the best winds, the modern smallboat navigator should think in terms of 14,500 miles from England to Melbourne (Australia). Add 1000

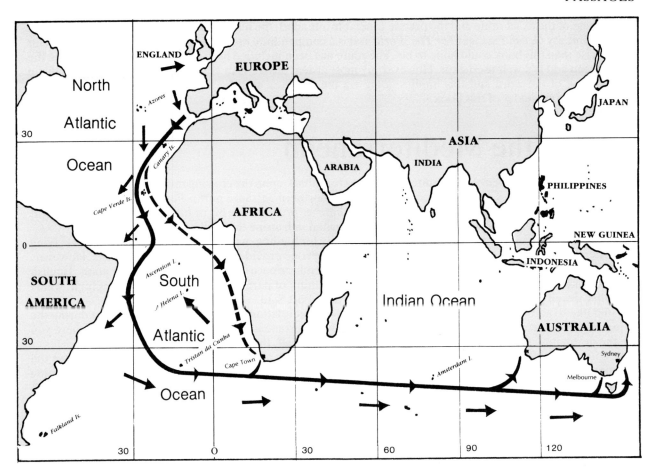

THE FAST WAY OUT
Those on the Atlantic seaboard anxious to make fast passage from Europe to Australia without the pleasures of cruising will find this route the fastest. The dotted line shows a possible alternative to carrying the South Atlantic trade winds across to Brazil but is plagued with calms or headwinds.

miles for Sydney and subtract the same for Perth. Depending on the size and potential of the vessel in question, the timetable may or may not include a victual stop at Cape Town. But it is my most heartfelt advice to make two or three stops en route to rest body and boat. The Cape Verde Islands are well placed for a casual visit en route whilst Cape Town is the logical victualling port.

The human timetable must now be balanced against wind and water. The Roaring Forties are best travelled in summer so as to reduce the ice hazard. Indeed, this can be eliminated altogether by seeking the westerlies at their northern limit. This might be around 35° south, a fact that will cost a little in speed but will improve comfort and peace of mind.

Considering the advantages of sailing in summer and the assumption that stops will be made along the way, the best time to leave England is June. This promises a domination of following winds from Portugal down to the Equator where doldrums must be expected. There could be as much as 600 miles of flukey winds and calms suggesting that the engine will be used.

The doldrums, and then later the southeast trade winds, will probably be found before the Equator because the South Atlantic trade winds reach north of the Equator during summer. Considering that once in the southeast trade wind belt the vessel will be working towards the southwest and being pressed onto the South American coast, the Equator should be crossed well to the east. Longitude 23° west is recommended.

The southeast trade wind will be carried over the port beam down to about Rio de Janeiro (Tropic of Capricorn) by which time the wind should slant into the east and possibly northeast. Soon after, another area of doldrums will be encountered before finding the westerly stream at about 30° south. This should be then run down towards Tristan da Cunha at which latitude the best weather should be found for the entire passage across to Australia.

Allowing three months for the passage to Tristan da Cunha (including three or four weeks rest at the Cape Verde Islands), the month is now late August or early September; still rather too cold. It is therefore suggested that a victualling stop be made at Cape Town taking at least one and preferably two months, longer if you like, for January and February are the warmest months for the passage across to Australia.

Regardless of the exact route and the precise timetable intended, the navigator should not plan, nor sail, without the Admiralty *Ocean Passages For The World* as it is a compendium of steamship and sailing routes and is far more precise than this book could hope to be. The route has been included here only because it does involve the Indian Ocean and is a well-used path. However my most ardent advice is to cruise from Europe to Australia in the true sense of the word and this implies going via the Red Sea and the north Indian Ocean as described throughout the remainder of this book.

Leaving the Mediterranean

Physically, the only way to leave the Mediterranean Sea to embark upon the cruising routes described in this book is to pass through the Suez Canal, and because the canal's northern entrance port is Port Said, it follows that the yachtsman is obliged to lay course for Port Said from whatever proves to be his or her last European country. It is the question of which country should be the last one visited in Europe that will be looked into here.

Because all European countries offer endless opportunity for fuelling, watering and victualling prior to leaving the Mediterranean, there is no real need to anguish over which one provides the best farewell facilities. However, for those seeking advice, I can do no better than to recommend Larnaca in Cyprus as a departure point. English is widely spoken here and the cost of living is low yet availability of parts, hardware and boatbits is high, whilst the country is well placed, being only 250 odd miles north of Port Said.

I would like to add that Cyprus is also conveniently placed in relation to the winds one can expect during the best period for departure. Alas, as anyone who sails the Mediterranean knows, it matters little from where you start, the destination is nearly always upwind. If there is wind at all, that is!

Facetiousness aside, a northerly is experienced between Cyprus and Port Said often enough to counter the claim that Larnaca is too far west to make it an ideal point of European departure. Candidly, the distance being only 250 miles, it really does not matter one way or the other. The advantages of being able to commission both the ship and her crew in a pleasant and affordable atmosphere are worth the slight disadvantage regarding the sailing of that infinitesimal distance.

In closing this section, the yachtsman is warned against having his passport stamped in Israel should Tel Aviv be visited en route to Port Said. Despite an accord between Egypt and Israel, the fact is things are tougher for those who carry any evidence of having visited Israel and this can be even more obvious in other Arab countries. Fortunately, a stamp is not obligatory in Israel and officials there will abstain, if requested, from marking a passport in any way.

PILOTAGE

NOTE The following descriptions of the Suez Canal and its major ports at each end, Port Said and Suez, are presented before the general description of the Red Sea in which will be found reference to Egypt as a whole.

The Suez Canal

This lockless, man-made canal connects the Mediterranean Sea with the Red Sea via three lake systems, is just under 90 miles long from its northern entrance at Port Said to its southern entrance at Suez and almost follows a perfect north-south course. The lakes, from north to south, are: Lake Timsah, on whose banks the major town of Ismailia is situated, Great Bitter Lake and Little Bitter Lake. Ismailia is the headquarters for the Suez Canal Authority and is where all small boats incapable of making the transit in one day are held overnight.

Opened 17th November 1869, the canal has twice been closed as a result of war. In 1956 the Suez Canal crisis, which resulted from Egypt nationalising the canal, caused its closure until the following year. Again, in 1967, the Israeli-Arab War blocked it for seven long years, then it was not reopened until June 1975. This latter period of closure led to the development of the supertanker whose role it was to keep the oil flowing from the (then) Persian Gulf to Europe via the Cape of Good Hope, South Africa. Since the canal reopened coinciding with a world shipping recession, the supertanker has become something of a huge white elephant, dozens being laid up in remote anchorages around the world. Their redundancy was relieved somewhat, however, by recent upgrading of the canal which now admits vessels of up to 200,000 tons unladen. In this way the supertanker can short-cut Africa when returning to the Gulf.

According to the *Red Sea and Gulf of Aden Pilot* the canal was used by 21,989 vessels in 1978 representing about 60 vessels per day. One of the pilots who stood a watch on *Tientos* in 1983 pointed out that the canal now handles over 100 ships per day, also claiming that the charge per ton stood at US$2.50 with vessels under 300 tons being admitted free of charge.

Before rejoicing at the thought of a free passage through the Suez Canal it should be emphasised that all vessels regardless of size are subject to administration charges. These amount to about US$60 per vessel.

FORMALITIES

Anywhere in Egypt formalities should be called 'formidabilities' for they are indeed formidable, especially where a transit of the Suez Canal is concerned. Look at the offices involved:

Immigration; Quarantine; Immigration again; Suez Canal manager; Suez Canal engineer; Bank; Insurance; Stamps; Post Office; Harbour master; Suez Canal manager again.

At any and all of the above offices a bribe (backsheesh) is not requested, but is expected, and if you do not know your way around, or attempt to clear the paperwork without paying bribes left right and centre, the formalities of getting through the canal could easily occupy three whole days. Although it will still cost the legitimate US$60.

Because doing one's own thing with any department in Egypt is an awesome prospect, a Suez Canal agent is best employed. There are a number of shipping firms engaged in this business and a couple who tend to specialise in private boats. In 1984, an agent's base fee floated around US$100 per boat regardless of size plus US$10 per person aboard. This tended to be a bottom rate below which they would not bargain. The reason is obvious: by the time they have finished paying bribes there is precious little left. Whether entering the canal from Port Said (the north) or Suez (the south) there will be no problem finding an agent. They are always looking out for business and will appear soon after arrival, if not during your arrival.

Having rounded up all the necessary paperwork, the boat itself will be subject to a number of inspections. These range from searches for bombs and other tools of the terrorist to a mechanical check to make sure the engine operates and the gearbox engages. And whilst such inspections can at times be casual, the way in which the launch master comes alongside can rarely be thus described. Bent stanchions and scuffed topsides are, I regret to report, par for the course in either Port Said or Suez. I recommend that all fenders be in place and that thoughts of a lengthy stay in Egypt be reconsidered as bureaucracy gets to you very quickly here.

When all is squared away, the agent will present a sheaf of papers and advise when to expect the pilot aboard.

This is nearly always before dawn, allowing even the slowest yacht to reach the halfway mark at Ismailia before dusk.

It should be pointed out here that a vessel may be cleared into the Suez Canal in such a way that she is free to drop her pilot at the other end and continue unmolested by further paperwork. Otherwise, where rest and recreation are required before launching off into the Red Sea, formalities are again obligatory at the other end; albeit, without any involvement with, or backsheesh to, the Suez Canal Authority.

PILOTS

There are 1500 Suez Canal pilots whose standard of boat handling is undisputedly high. However, some treat a private boat with contempt by doing no work at all, whilst others insist on actually doing the steering themselves all the way. Between the two extremes is the fellow who will keep an eye on things but allow the skipper to run his own boat. The one thing all pilots seem to have in common, however, is an expectation of a 'gift' after services have been rendered.

This 'gift' has more or less standardised at US$5 per pilot making the whole transit a ten dollar experience above and beyond money already paid out. Many people refuse to pay this bribe but nearly all find that certain advantages are lost. For example, the pilot might decide to hold them at one of the pilot stations for no apparent reason obliging them to take three days instead of two for the transit. As galling as it all is, I recommend that the going rate be paid and pride be swallowed in the interest of easing the visitor's lot.

To further relieve tension and to avoid unpleasant confrontation, carry US dollars in small denominations. One dollar bills are perfect but certainly do not expect change. The sight of a bigger bill than is expected is mere confirmation that you are offering more than the basic rate. Also, carry a few packets of cigarettes and hand them out to those officers recommended by the pilot. Usually such officers as customs and police rate at least one packet each. But don't hand them round willy-nilly, follow the pilot's advice.

SUEZ CANAL TRANSIT

In Port Said, many of the pilots object to having to find their own way across to the yacht centre at Port Fouad. As a result of this you might be asked to pick him up at the customs wharf close to the canal entrance proper on the starboard bank.

In Suez the pilot always comes to the so-called 'yacht club' jetty from where he is easily collected. Either way, and at either end, the pilot nearly always boards before dawn and his time is advised by the agent well in advance.

With the pilot aboard you will hold whichever side of the canal he indicates (usually the starboard bank as far as Ismailia then the port bank from there on, going either way). You will also be asked to go as fast as possible and when the engine is blowing black smoke he will still ask if you can go any faster!

Rarely does a small private vessel transit the entire length of the canal in one day even when it is physically possible. All boats are held overnight off the Authority's depot in the northwest corner of Lake Timsah at the rather pleasant town of Timsah. Incidentally, it is usually impossible to venture ashore here, without prior arrangement, as visitors are confined to their vessels.

Before dawn the next morning another pilot will board to continue the transit; if towards Suez, he will indicate the yacht club as the only place to berth or will be taken off by launch under way if you cleared at the other end for sea.

Passing in the Suez Canal. Vessels of up to 200,000 tons unburdened now use this vital link between the Mediterranean Sea and the Red Sea.

PORT SAID

POSITION 31°15′N 32°19′E   At the northern end of the Suez Canal in the southeast corner of the Mediterranean.

GENERAL DESCRIPTION   Port Said is a major seaport for Egypt generally and is the receiving port for southbound traffic into the Suez Canal. Divided by the harbour is the city of Port Said and the commercial area of Port Fouad.

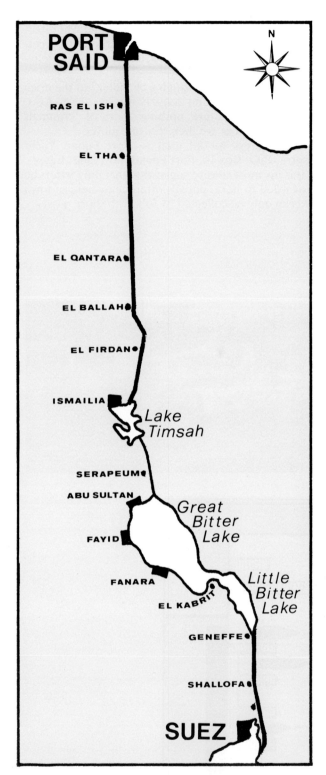

SUEZ CANAL
The Suez Canal is a man-made gutter joining the Mediterranean Sea with the Red Sea via three lake systems. It is now capable of back loading light supertankers of up to 200,000 tons.

The enthusiast shopper will enjoy Port Said proper but is obliged to secure a shore pass before being allowed ashore beyond the yacht basin. This involves the compulsory changing of US$150 per person into Egyptian pounds at the disadvantaged official rate; there is a black market rate considerably higher which is only available once ashore.

Those anxious to leave their vessel somewhere in Egypt in order to trek inland to see the sights of Cairo and Luxor are advised to consider the advantages of Suez (city and port) treating Port Said as a preliminary to entering the Suez Canal only.

The harbour of Port Said is a bustling, grimy place whose entrance is substantiated by two breakwaters extending offshore. The approach channel extends beyond and is marked by port and starboard lighted buoys.

APPROACH Being the delta of a large swamp area, the land around Port Said city is low and featureless. The city itself, however, boasts buildings high enough to form good landmarks when close aboard the coast. Soon after sighting the buildings the harbour mouth can be identified by the breakwaters and obvious traffic. Preliminary entrance should be made down the dredged, buoyed channel.

Within the harbour, the Port Fouad Yacht Centre will be found to port immediately beyond a shipbuilding yard. This is the only area permissible for private vessels. Do not anchor or berth anywhere other than here.

Those emerging from the Suez Canal heading to the Mediterranean will have a pilot aboard who will direct.

ANCHORAGE The visitor has no option as he or she is obliged to berth stern-to the Port Fouad Yacht Centre. The anchor will be dropped in foul mud towards the mouth of the basin and the stern will be warped to wherever indicated by Ali, the centre's general hand. Beware of too short a cable here as the mud is not good holding without ample scope.

Where the stern will not fit between the short timber finger piers, or the berths are fully occupied, anchor towards the shipyard and go stern-to the wall. Strictly speaking this is outside the centre's limits but a fence can be negotiated when going ashore. Under no circumstances be tempted to bypass the centre with or without a shore pass.

FORMALITIES Judging by a notice in red on an immigration form threatening serious consequences to anyone offering a bribe to an official, it would seem that unlike the Suez Canal transit, backsheesh is being controlled in Port Said. As a result, entry formalities are free of handouts and worry of whom to give what.

Whilst bureaucratic attitude towards private yachtsmen is far more restricting than to ordinary tourists, the fact is there is no animosity and paperwork is confined to the Yacht Centre. Upon arriving, remain on board until beckoned by an immigration officer then follow his lead until formalities are completed. Those requiring a shore pass must change US dollars as noted earlier and those intending to transit the canal will be approached by an agent who will handle all formalities.

Once having cleared immigration and customs it is necessary to report to the Yacht Centre's office to formalise berthing details and payment. Berths cost upwards of US$5 per day depending on the size of the craft.

FACILITIES The Port Fouad Yacht Centre is an obligatory facility offering the only berths in the harbour which are often animated by passing commercial traffic. There is also a lot of oil on the surface. Compensating marginally for these inconveniences are hot showers, toilets, 240 V AC power and plenty of running water to the berths.

Within the Centre's compound is a bar-café which never seems to open, shaded tables and chairs, an area of lawn and a shed in which repairs might be effected to awnings and sails, Ali having a sewing machine there.

Ali holds all mail for passing boats and will direct you to a box overflowing with letters and parcels reaching back to the seventies; a legacy of slow delivery, not the fault of Ali.

Fuel is purchased through a chandler but the price is higher than Suez and delivery messy at best. Also, certain chandlers are nothing short of 'criminals unhung', so gross are their 'try-on' quotes.

The address for all mail is: Port Fouad Yacht Centre, P.O. Box 16, Port Fouad, Port Said, Egypt.

It is my most sincere suggestion that only letters be forwarded to here, parcels often being held in town and can only be collected by folk with shore passes.

With anchor out and stern in, visiting vessels lie to timber finger piers at the Port Said Yacht Centre. When crowded, vessels may lie between the piers and the ship building yard, background.

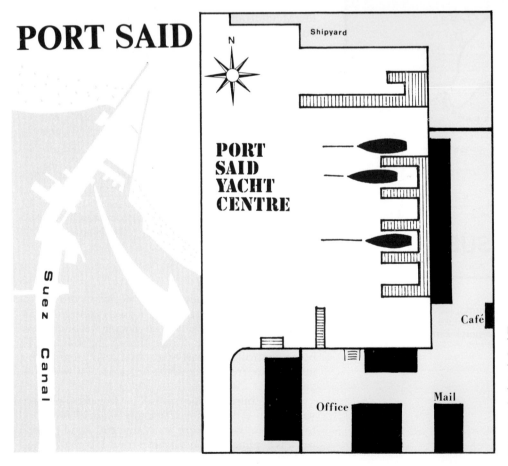

PORT SAID

PORT SAID YACHT CENTRE

N

Shipyard

Suez Canal

Café

Mail

Office

PORT SAID ANCHORAGE
The Port Said Yacht Centre is an obligatory facility for visiting boats awaiting the Suez Canal transit. A sliding scale is charged which tends to be a minimum of US$5 per day per vessel. Facilities alongside are basic.

SUEZ (PORT)

POSITION 29°58′N 32°34′E   At the head of the Gulf of Suez. The northernmost point of the Red Sea and the southern port for the Suez Canal.

GENERAL DESCRIPTION The area in and around both the port and city of Suez is of little physical interest. However, thanks to a more secure berth and a better deal on shore passes, it represents the best place in Egypt from which to sightsee.

Of great interest to the enthusiast ship-watcher is the traffic entering and emerging from the Suez Canal within easy view from the yacht basin. Everything from American battle wagons to submersible oil rig carriers will be seen as the visitor is reminded that the Egyptians run their canal very well indeed despite the prophets of doom in the 1950s.

APPROACH The southbound vessel approaches from the canal itself under instructions from the pilot. He will direct the visitor into the yacht basin off the so-called Suez Yacht Club. As we will see, this is a club in name only.

Vessels approaching from the Red Sea and Gulf of Suez will come upon hundreds of anchored ships awaiting Suez Canal transit after which the dredged channel up to the main port will be encountered. This channel is critical only to deep-draught vessels.

During this approach it is likely that launches of local chandlers and canal pilot agents will heave alongside endeavouring to capture your business. Dismiss all chandlers for their prices are always excessive whilst pilot agents are very competitive.

ANCHORAGE Approaching from the Red Sea, a visiting vessel is obliged to temporarily anchor in Port Ibrahim where shown on the map. After preliminary formalities it is necessary to move around to the basin off the Suez Yacht Club. This is in Suez Creek and enjoys excellent security both from weather and theft.

The price here is standard at US$6 per day for all vessels, the money being collected by the Club yardman. There are fore-and-aft drum moorings which are often fully occupied in which case a similar disposition can be organised with anchors. It is permissible to lay alongside the Club jetty but this inconveniences those wishing to load fuel and water.

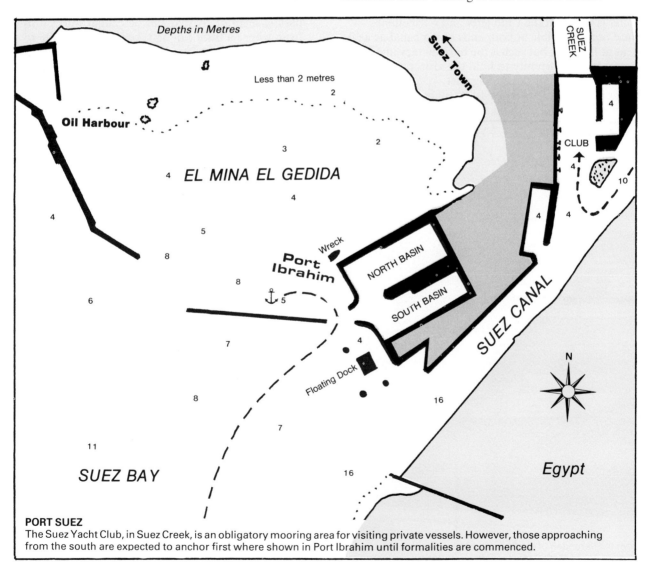

PORT SUEZ
The Suez Yacht Club, in Suez Creek, is an obligatory mooring area for visiting private vessels. However, those approaching from the south are expected to anchor first where shown in Port Ibrahim until formalities are commenced.

FORMALITIES These will be effected by the Suez Canal Pilot Agent for those entering from the south whilst those emerging from the canal will be obliged to clear with customs and immigration again. Officers come to the Club.

Shore passes are available through immigration here for US$50 per person changed into local currency. The pass is of shorter duration than the other (ten days instead of one month) but is ample for those wishing to quickly sightsee the interior.

FACILITIES The Suez Yacht Club is not a club in any accepted sense of the word being more a building in which empty rooms prevail over an area devoted to the storage of rowing skiffs. This appears to be a popular sport here as is evidenced by the pontoon dock especially for the launching of shells. Functioning showers and toilets are in this part of the building and soft drinks may be available from time to time. The Club yard is an ideal safe place for children to run around.

Diesel fuel is remarkably cheap here even after allowing for a three hundred per cent mark-up for visitors. It costs around US$25 per 44 gallon drum delivered to the club jetty from where it must be siphoned into the ship's tank.

Water is on tap at the Club jetty and is excellent.

Haul-out is possible at both ends of the canal as well as at Ismailia, but such is the bureaucracy involved and the opportunity to hold the visitor at ransom that it is strongly advised against.

Shopping in Suez city is good with all basics available including good fresh meat and vegetables at very low prices.

PORT SUEZ
From the moorings, the Suez Yacht Centre is very handy although its facilities are minimal. Mooring here is obligatory.

Eating out is no trouble with a choice across the board from dives to good hotels.

Souvenirs are available in a number of Indian-owned shops where beautifully engraved plates, brass sphinxes and so forth are available.

Sightseeing is no trouble from Suez presuming a shore pass is secured. A taxi can be caught into Cairo from where a train can be taken down the Nile to see such famous sights as the Valley of the Kings at Luxor.

Transport is in the form of local buses, trains and planes throughout the Suez, Cairo and Port Said area. Go to the main road near the Yacht Club for a bus or taxi into Suez city.

From the verandah of the Suez Yacht Club, visiting boats are seen at fore-and-aft drum moorings with the southern entrance to the Suez Canal top left.

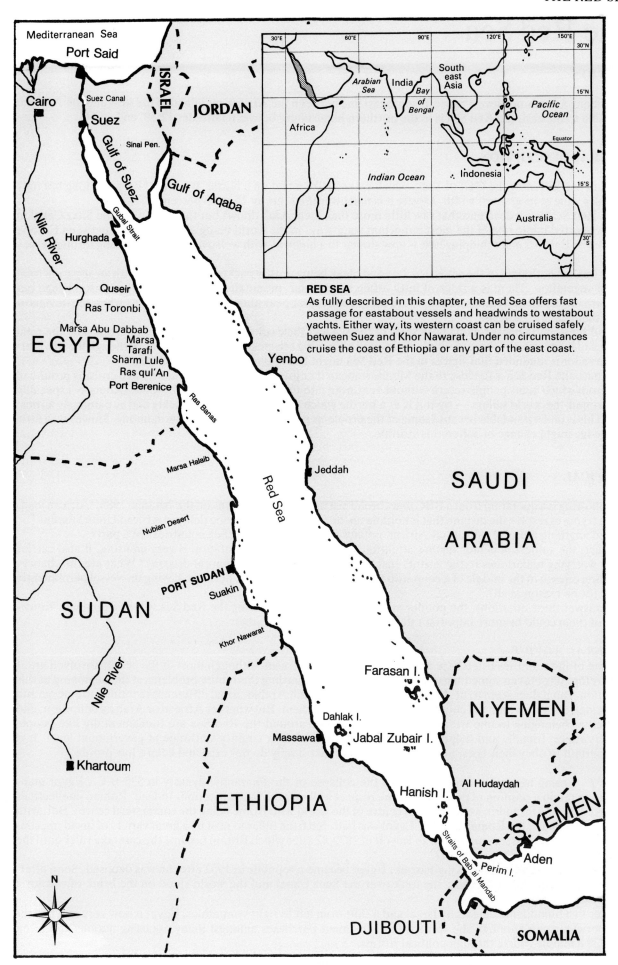

RED SEA

As fully described in this chapter, the Red Sea offers fast passage for eastabout vessels and headwinds to westabout yachts. Either way, its western coast can be cruised safely between Suez and Khor Nawarat. Under no circumstances cruise the coast of Ethiopia or any part of the east coast.

The Red Sea

POSITION

Lying along a north-northwest to south-southeast line between the African mainland to the west and the Arabian peninsula to the east, the Red Sea is in the northern hemisphere between latitudes 12°39′ and 29°56′.

GENERAL DESCRIPTION

The Red Sea including the Gulf of Suez, which extends like a teat on a bottle, is nearly 1400 miles long but only 200 miles wide at its greatest width. Mostly it is narrower than this by 25 to 90 percent.

The Red Sea was a dead end that saw little more than local Arab dhows but the opening of the Suez Canal in 1869 converted it into one of the most important waterways in the world being a vital short cut between Europe and the Far East. Its main shipping lane is now similar to a highway with well over 100 ships passing through every day.

The land on both sides of the sea is desolate and bleak being mostly packed sand or stone with an apparent total lack of vegetation. There is a ridge of lofty, often spectacular, mountains along much of the coastal fringe but these are mostly 10 to 30 miles inland where they readily disappear under dust and haze just when the navigator needs them, as will be seen.

Coral reefs are peppered along both sides of the sea and their colourful display seems to accentuate the total absence of living colour ashore. Fishing, diving and swimming are most enjoyable pursuits, although the Mediterranean sailor is reminded that sharks in the Red Sea might bite! Some caution is necessary.

Because the Red Sea is so close to the Mediterranean it enjoys considerable popularity as a cruising ground in itself from which many people return without venturing into the Indian Ocean and beyond. Others — especially those round-the-world sailors — treat it is as a hurdle which must be jumped as quickly and as painlessly as possible. This is understandable because some of the problems peculiar to the area can be daunting. However, a little knowledge might change or soften this attitude.

POLITICAL

The following is a quotation from a BBC news broadcast monitored in Cyprus on the 7th June 1983: 'African leaders are trying to resolve the dispute that is holding up the convening of the long delayed African Unity Summit.'

Need anything more be said about African politics of which many Red Sea countries are a part?

In fact, the subject demands further attention because, whilst the quotation is very amusing, it also carries rather worrying undertones to the visitor. Just how safe are nations in apparent disarray? What are the chances of finding oneself in the middle of a coup with very real bullets flying and, perhaps, having the vessel permanently seized for no reason at all?

To answer these questions, the politics of those countries surrounding the Red Sea will be examined. Knowledge of them could be more important than knowing about the weather.

GENERAL ADVICE

Some of the countries listed here are not, by definition, African, although most of the people involved are. I therefore have taken some liberty in using a quotation regarding their unity problems at the beginning of this section. But it does seem to fit. In all countries, except Saudi Arabia, tribal differences continue to emerge and threaten disunity within the countries as well as between them. But whether African or Arab by definition, and whether belonging to one tribe or another, the people around the Red Sea are fundamentally like people everywhere; friendly and helpful with no real thought of their country's attitude at government level. It is important to obey their laws, not to expect services that simply do not exist and keep a low profile.

EGYPT Losing her world dominance with the collapse of the Pharaonic dynasty in 525 B.C., Egypt managed to retain a position of power and some respect well into the Roman period. Indeed, Roman intellectuals looked upon Alexandria as the cultural centre of the world with Rome being the commercial centre. But, with the crumbling of the Roman empire, Egypt was battered from pillar to post by a great variety of invaders, conquerors and colonisers until the Arab Revolt of 1879-82 after which Britain became the caretake ruler until the granting of independence in 1922.

At first a kingdom under King Farouk, Egypt became a republic in 1952 after he was deposed. Soon after, in a fit of nationalistic fervour, she took over the Suez Canal and the world stood on the brink of war for a number of weeks.

After two humiliating defeats by Israel and a shift from left to right sympathies, Egypt is now very much in the American camp although she spreads her armament purchases amongst many opposing nations and often steers a middle course through political storms.

Today Egypt is very safe for visitors, the tourist dollar being welcome. This is often difficult to believe when passing through formalities aboard a small boat, but one must take heart in the knowledge that they put their own people through similar wringers when anything more difficult than a sneeze is anticipated.

Egyptian formalities are different for visiting yachtsmen than for normal tourists. A fact that is wonderful news for the normal tourist. The yachtsman is treated with respect and is often welcomed, but he must nevertheless play the bureaucracy game which is nothing short of awesome, the number of offices involved confusing. There is also the possibility of backsheesh (bribe payment) but this seems to be on the wane in government departments.

Egyptian visas are not necessary unless the nautical visitor wants to go ashore beyond the compound of the harbour or yacht centre involved and then they are available on the basis of each person wanting to venture ashore cashing no less than US$150 at the official rate. This is good for one month.

A ten day visa can be obtained in Suez only for the changing of US$50 per person.

An advance visa is obtainable from an Egyptian embassy or consulate outside the country for a payment of about US$12. This eliminates the obligation of changing a set figure into local currency upon going ashore, but it seems also to carry considerable doubt with it. Make sure you have the embassy official spell it out for it is true that some visas are issued on the assumption that the visitor will land in Cairo by plane. The yachtsman with the wrong advance visa then finds he or she must still change dollars before being allowed ashore to get to Cairo! That is about par for the course with Egyptian formalities.

Tourist police Apparently recognising the problems of the tourist, this band of men was formed to help prevent the blatant extortion of tourists. If you find yourself in any trouble whatsoever, threaten to call the tourist police. It usually works.

Currency in Egypt is the pound which is broken into 100 piastres. Prior to the American dollar's meteoric rise in the middle of 1984, it hovered at around 80 piastres to the dollar officially. On the black market it was worth over 120 piastres and at legal money dealers it was 115 piastres.

SAUDI ARABIA Opposite Egypt and Sudan, and occupying most of the Arabian peninsula which is formed between the Red Sea and the Gulf (ex-Persian Gulf), Saudi Arabia is a supporting, as against supported, country. Part of its immense oil wealth goes to other, less fortunate, Arab countries.

A benign form of Islam is followed here which tends to reject force, as a means of purity. As a result, tourists are not wanted — nor needed — for fear of cultural pollution. This rejection does not, however, prevent Saudi Arabia from importing brains and brawn from all over the world, for earning high wages in that country are labourers from Sri Lanka, dentists from Australia and oil experts from America.

Because the private yacht is given the respect of international maritime law, it is allowed to enter Saudi Arabia at either its main port at Jeddah or its secondary port at Yenbo. But under no circumstances will cruising the coast be tolerated whether a vessel has been legally cleared into the country or not. The nautical visitor must restrict activities to the port in question and may be obliged to return aboard before sundown. Travel inland is not permitted at all.

The attitude of officials in Saudi Arabia tends to be friendly towards yachtsmen but they are obliged to uphold local laws. One of these laws is the total prohibition of alcoholic drink. Any ship's stores of this nature must remain sealed for the duration of a visit.

Saudi Arabia is the world's biggest producer of oil at 6 to 7 million barrels a day, and prior to its discovery in 1938 a major source of income was generated by pilgrims flocking to Mecca. This trade still flourishes with many large Saudi Arabian car ferries connecting their country with Egypt and Sudan.

Considering Saudi Arabia's wealth and stability and her rather interesting coastline, it is a shame that the yachtsman is limited to just two ports and is subject to so many restrictions. In the face of these limitations it cannot be recommended, except as a single stopover of short duration. The warning is repeated here *not* to cruise its coast as vessels infringing the law are liable to be impounded.

SUDAN The largest country fronting the Red Sea at 2,505,813 square kilometres, Sudan is also the most relaxed when it comes to visitors in any form. Despite recent upheavals in its capital, Khartoum, there is no threat of its doors being closed.

Sudan is an independent republic reaching down into the very heart of Africa and bordered north and south by Egypt and Ethiopia respectively, she gained her independence on 1st January 1956.

For centuries subservient to Egypt, the latter was forced out during the second half of the last century. The British, covering the Egyptian retreat, were beseiged in Khartoum in 1884 during which time General Gordon was killed. The resultant Sudanese regime depended on force to retain control, a fact that made her independence a somewhat brutal one. The British therefore decided to occupy the country after the Battle of Omdurman in 1898. From that time Sudan was jointly governed by Egypt and Britain right up to her independence in 1956. Even today, the 70,000 strong Sudanese army and the 360,000 strong Egyptian army are under unilateral command with a hotline between command centres.

During the first half of 1984, President Gaafar Numeiri appeared to be losing control of his country. Riots in Khartoum and civil war in the south coupled with his failing health suggested that his 15 year rule was coming to its end. In 1985 a successful coup reduced the Islamic bias in home and foreign policy but the future seemed unclear. But whatever happens, the coastal fringe is unlikely to feel much effect from internal strife and should remain safe for the cruising boat.

As noted later under the heading, 'Can I anchor-hop?' it is physically and politically possible to seek anchorage every night along the Sudan coast. This is good news to all yachtsmen who prefer a cruise to a long spell at sea, but it is especially appealing to the northbound navigator who faces strong headwinds all the way.

Because Port Sudan is the only port of entry along the entire coast, international law obliges yachts to enter the country there first before actually cruising the coast. In fact, because this makes little sense physically, a blind eye is turned to those sheltering along the coast prior to, and after, clearing in at Port Sudan. It is recommended that this freedom not be abused by venturing ashore unless beckoned by army personnel.

Currency is the Sudanese pound which equals 100 piastres.

ETHIOPIA　Sudan's next-door neighbour to the south, on the western side of the Red Sea, Ethiopia is absolutely out as a cruising area. It is a country embroiled in constant civil war with its coast patrolled by gunboats; do not venture to within 12 miles of its coast or islands and a greater distance is recommended as the author was fired upon and apprehended outside this limit.

NORTH YEMEN　Sharing the southern tip of the Arabian peninsula with South Yemen, with nearly 300 miles of coastline on the Red Sea, this country is known as the Yemen Arab Republic and is governed by a people's assembly of 90 members. As is not uncommon in Moslem countries, the sympathies tend towards the left and the type of belligerent Islam practised in Iran seems to appeal, an American yacht being seized here during the hostage crisis.

Friendly towards visiting yachtsmen in the mid 1970s, the attitude has changed until now it is impossible to be sure of the reception to be expected. Under the circumstances it is best avoided, a fact that makes the entire southern portion of the Red Sea out of bounds to anyone wanting to anchor. The consequences of this will be dealt with later.

English yachtsmen wanting to establish what policy prevails in North Yemen before starting their cruise might write to the British ambassador, San'a, Yemen Arab Republic.

SOUTH YEMEN　Although not a country bordering the Red Sea, it is included here because of its usefulness as a haven before or after the Red Sea transit.

Sharing the border on the southern tip of the Arabian peninsula with North Yemen, the People's Democratic Republic of Yemen own the islands of Socotra (off the northeast tip of Somalia), Perim (in the Strait of Bab al Mandab — the entrance to the Red Sea) and Kamaran (in the Red Sea towards the north of North Yemen). None of these islands should be visited by the private yachtsman for they are definitely out of bounds.

The mainland coast of Southern Yemen, however, can be cruised on the condition that a cruising permit is gained whilst in the capital, Aden. And if the permit is not forthcoming, at least the harbour and facilities of Aden are definitely available as a haven as described under its own heading.

The People's Democratic Republic of Yemen came into being on the 30th November 1967 after a popular revolution ousted the British from their Aden Protectorate. The government quickly turned towards Russia for aid so that today most ships in Aden fly the Russian flag and the country is undeniably communistic.

Visas are not required in Aden but the nautical visitor is limited to the Aden area only. Sometimes, if Russian warships are in port, a limit of two days may be imposed on all visitors but this is rare, and officials are welcoming and very helpful. I do not suggest testing this friendliness to the point of touching on the coast without formalising entry at Aden.

Currency is the dinar which is divided into 1000 fils. It is roughly US$2.80 to the dinar.

DJIBOUTI　This tiny country lies in the westernmost corner of the Gulf of Aden with one corner reaching up into the Strait of Bab al Mandab. The name Djibouti is given to both the country and the main town and its only port is here.

Previously a French colony, Djibouti gained independence in 1977 and adopted a republican form of government with a president. Because the country is especially poor in natural resources, it remains heavily dependent on the French who use its port as a naval base. As a result, it is a perfectly safe country for the visiting yachtsman but the cost of living is geared to a sailor's pay and attitude, and can prove far more expensive than Aden for rest and recreation.

RED SEA WEATHER

The area is well known for its winds with their special names which breed dread in the hearts of many sailors but as violent as they can be and as blinding as the sand they carry really is, the fact is they are few and far between and do not deserve the attention they enjoy. They will be described later but here the everyday weather conditions are looked at.

As the four wind maps show, the most dominant wind is the northerly which is, in fact, a north-northwesterly following the direction of the sea itself. The wind as a whole is Force 6 and 7 but is also often absent, or present as a light to moderate breeze. Its uglier moods will only cause anxiety to the northbound yachtsman or to anyone anxiously seeking refuge against a coast that tends to disappear under dust haze.

During the northern hemisphere's winter, a south-southeasterly often encroaches upon the Red Sea creating two seasons which can be worked, or avoided, to advantage depending on the direction one is sailing. These are detailed here.

WIND — DECEMBER TO APRIL   Sometimes inclusive, but most often excluding December and April, the northeast monsoon in the Arabian Sea canalises down the Gulf of Aden and turns into the southern part of the Red Sea. When being compressed through the Strait of Bab al Mandab it can easily reach gale force and bring with it considerable seas.

This wind which tends to be south-southeast in the Red Sea, commonly extends north to the border of Ethiopia and Sudan but has been known to extend further north. Generally it can only be depended upon by the northbound sailor to take his vessel as far as the beginning of Sudan. Often it fails as early as the Hanish Islands.

During this time of year the north-northwesterly prevails north from the border between Ethiopia and Sudan right to the Suez Canal although where the two winds collide is often calm as noted under the subheading 'The Convergence Zone' later.

WIND — APRIL TO DECEMBER   Often inclusive of these two months, the northerly extends over the entire Red Sea from the Suez Canal to the Strait of Bab al Mandab. There tends to be less strength in the gusts during the middle of this period which is the northern hemisphere's summer.

THE CONVERGENCE ZONE   Not always agreeing exactly with the *Pilot's* illustrated definition, this is the collision area between the constant northerlies of the north Red Sea and the commonly occurring southerlies of the south Red Sea during the months December to April.

The cold north wind lifts the warm south wind and a heavy cloud layer results, sometimes obliterating the sun for days and creating yet another problem for the small ship navigator. Towards its northern fringe, around the Ethiopian-Sudan border area, the cloud can clear and close every few hours and then close down completely for days during which rain might fall inland and try hard, but usually fail, on the coast.

WIND SLANTS   When the wind is blowing with any force along the line of the sea, it holds a constant bearing. When southerly in the southern area it is south-southeast; when northerly in the northern area it is north-northwest. However, when the wind eases to a maximum of around 15 knots at its strongest, it can haul offshore during the night and very slightly onshore during the afternoon. Typically, on the east coast during a northerly wind, it will blow very light westerly after midnight, slowly increasing as it shifts to the northwest towards late morning then continuing its clockwise movement and getting into the north-northeast by mid-afternoon. It will remain in this quadrant until late evening after which it calms ready to start again after midnight from the west.

It should be emphasised that the above is a coastal phenomenon. At sea it rarely offers useful slants to the sailor. And even those coastal slants mentioned are difficult to use because of the danger of sailing close enough to the coast to enjoy them, especially the night breeze.

CALMS   The fact that calms are as common as strong winds is not realised by the northbound sailor who dreads remaining offshore, beating for days against strong headwinds. As a result, much of the coast can be anchor-hopped under engine, hiding in a secure haven during a blow. Broadly speaking, personal observation suggests that calms come in four-day segments after four days of strong northerlies. A calm in the Red Sea is a true calm, the sea being absolutely motionless and allowing a small boat under power to make good time.

SPECIAL WINDS   Localised thermal winds are possible anywhere within the Red Sea in the form of whirlwinds, waterspouts and dust devils. Mostly they are localised and can be easily avoided.

These winds are most common against the coast in summer. Otherwise there are only two special winds to beware of during a general cruise or passsage through the Red Sea. These follow.

Khamsin This is essentially a southern extension of the Sirocco which can blow with great enthusiasm up the Italian coast. The most common period of occurrence is between February and May and the direction is always south-southeast following the direction of the sea. They are seldom felt below the Gubal Strait (the entrance to the Gulf of Suez) and commonly blow at Force 6 from there north. Stronger gusts are recorded which bring a lot of airborne sand.

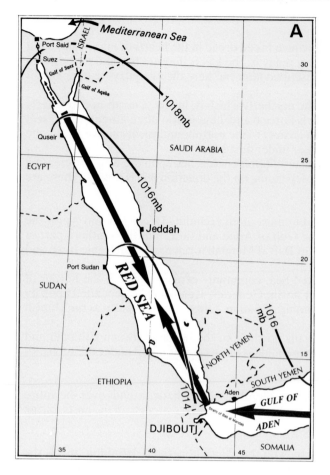

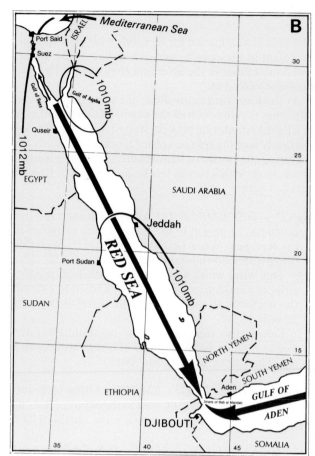

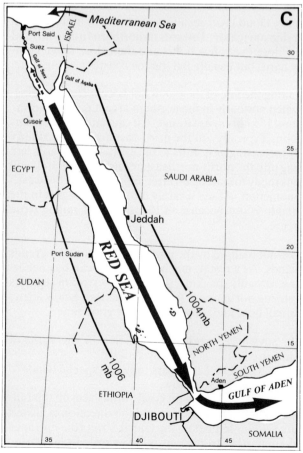

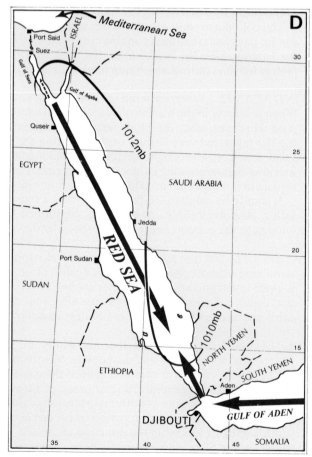

WIND SLANTS RED SEA

Along the west coast of the Red Sea wind slants are often experienced inshore when the prevailing wind eases below 15 knots.

RED SEA WINDS

A

During the months of December, January, February and March there is a good chance of experiencing strong southerlies between the Sudan-Ethiopian border and the Strait of Bab al Mandab. Northerlies prevail as always north to Suez. The curved lines show typical pressures for the period.

B

Spring in the Red Sea sees the prevalent northerly wind reaching the southern extreme where it meets the last of the Arabian Sea northeasterly monsoon.

C

During the summer months the northerly wind dominates the entire area and unites with the Arabian Sea southwest monsoon in the Gulf of Aden.

D

In autumn, the northerly wind of the Red Sea recedes slightly and occasionally in the southern extreme allowing the early northeast monsoon to enter. Mostly, the Gulf of Aden is a non wind area in both spring and autumn.

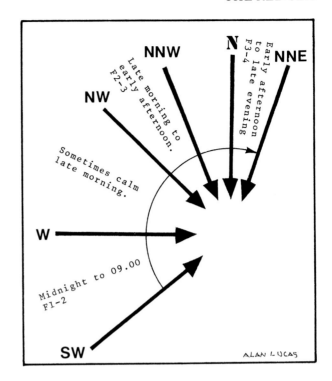

Haboobs are unique to the Sudan coast and especially to the Port Sudan area where they blow from the southeast through south to west. Force 8 is common and despite their short duration, they can cause havoc in crowded anchorages. Most common between July and September, whole seasons can enjoy complete freedom from them.

BAROMETER Casual observation seems to indicate that the barometer will rise slightly before a northerly wind as well as a calm, dropping slightly during either condition.

DESTRUCTIVE WINDS do not occur in the Red Sea. The strongest gusts of normal winds rarely reach 50 knots and more commonly peak at 30 knots.

HAZE The Red Sea is surrounded by thousands of square miles of barren land. There is scarcely a blade of grass to bind the soil together to prevent it from becoming airborne to every strong wind. And this is what it does to the dismay of the navigator:

When coasting, the mountains twenty-odd miles beyond the shoreline provide wonderful reference, their conspicuous peaks offering targets at which to aim the hand- bearing compass. Whilst this may be scarcely necessary when day-sailing hard against the coast, it is vital when making a landfall after standing off the coast for a night or two. Much of the coast, it must be remembered, has fringing or barrier reefs, or both, parallel to its low sandy featureless shoreline. When haze closes down, this strip of land is often all that can be seen which is tantamount to saying there are no identifiable marks at all.

As can be appreciated, dust haze is a child of the wind. It therefore occurs at the very worst time; when you are weary from being bounced around at sea and anxious to find anchorage. It is this desire for comfort at the wrong time that accounts for most small-boat losses in the Red Sea. The navigator tries to make a landfall on a featureless coast and puts his ship on an offshore reef that should not have been there.

The speed with which mountains can become lost behind haze is nothing short of spectacular, a phenomenon encouraged by the rapidity with which a calm can turn into a gale. I have seen thirty knots of wind pick up within an hour, after three days of total and absolute calm, during which time a curtain of dust obliterated the mountains before my very eyes and did not expose them again for twenty-four hours. And even then their outlines were hazy, impossible to identify unless one was keeping count.

Nothing can be done about dust haze beyond learning to live with it; when coasting it is of little importance, but once offshore, out of sight of land, it is folly indeed to try to make landfall unless absolutely sure of previous celestial sights.

THE HEAT The Red Sea can be suffocatingly hot during summer (May to November), being surrounded by desert, and not too far from the tropical belt. Those accustomed to tropical living will be unconcerned whilst those straight from a cold country might experience distress. However, the latter will have just travelled from a Mediterranean summer in which case a fair background of tropical living will have been acquired. Either way, it cannot be avoided if a cruise or passage is undertaken during summer.

During winter — and especially around January-February — temperatures are delightful with cool nights, and days that permit fair exertion in very light clothes without undue perspiration. At this time of year the dryness of the air is a tangible thing, cracking lips and creating a good thirst and it is said that conditions are perfect for those with respiratory problems.

During winter the sea water can actually be cold enough so that only the hardiest diver or swimmer will spend more than half an hour in the water.

THE SEA

It has been noted how totally calm the Red Sea can be when wind is absent. On the other side of the coin is its disproportionate behaviour to strong winds. Waves tend to be larger than life, rising as high as 5 metres in a Force 6 but more commonly in the 3 to 4 metre range. Even in the low range, they tend to be rather too short and steep to allow a boat beating to windward easy progress. There are too many 'brick walls'.

However, the seas are not especially dangerous when handled with common good seamanship and will rarely give rise to concern when sailing with free sheets.

CURRENTS   A northbound current can run up the southern part of the Red Sea during December to April, sometimes extending all the way to the Gulf of Suez where it turns about and joins a southbound current coming out of the gulf. For the remainder of the year any major current is dominantly southbound, especially towards the southern part of the sea. Rarely, however, does a current run at more than half a knot and mostly at half that rate.

A strange phenomenon of such a narrow sea is the undoubted existence of strong east and west currents emanating out from the mainstream and eventually completing a circle to rejoin it. This sympathetic eddying is normal, but the strength with which it can run here is not. A stream was discovered by the author off north Ethiopia which ran towards the coast at a speed of no less than one knot. Other yachtsmen have reported similar surprises along much of the Red Sea, but the Ethiopian one seems to be the most common of them all. It certainly needs special attention considering the political instability of the country and that being carried onto this coast can result in apprehension by gunboats.

TIDES   These tend to seesaw around the central area so that a spring rise of 0.9 metres is common in the south whilst in the north the range tends to be around 0.6 metres. At the centre, in the Port Sudan area for example, there is no appreciable vertical movement at all.

NAVIGATION

Let me start this section by saying that if you have a reliable satellite navigation set aboard, the following problems do not relate.

As noted under the heading 'Haze', wind-carried dust can suddenly 'shut you down'. Within minutes good shore reference disappears leaving only dismal, low and featureless strips of sandy coast from which to take bearings and this, of course, is impossible.

The foreshore land around the Red Sea is flat and very low offering few, if any, conspicuous objects from which to take sights. In conditions of light haze, the foothills are visible as seen here but the lofty mountains some twenty miles inland disappear altogether.

In those areas where the shore is relatively free of fringing or barrier reefs, the concern will be one of directional uncertainty. Which way is the anchorage? North or south of the landfall? But where reefs stretch offshore, making it dangerous to be close to the coast without being sure of the position, a crisis could develop. Where doubt prevails under these circumstances, the navigator should haul offshore and remain at sea regardless of the discomfort aboard ship.

Celestial navigation is also hampered by the dust haze, refraction easily throwing a sight out by twenty miles. Errors of this magnitude are acceptable when making passage but not when laying a course for a coastal anchorage or port with reefs offshore.

There is no magic elixir here. The navigator must exercise more caution than normal, that is all. And when in doubt *remain at sea*. Also, during those periods of good weather and therefore reliable celestial or coastal bearings, keep the sights coming. Remember that you can be closed down very quickly.

CAN I ANCHOR-HOP?   This is the casual question of the southbound sailor and the anxious question of the northbound sailor. The reason is that the former looks forward to fair winds all the way down the Red Sea whilst the latter faces hundreds of miles of hard beating to windward. If he can anchor-hop he saves himself and ship a lot of misery.

The simple answer is 'yes'. But only along those coasts politically safe and this narrows the field down to Egypt and Sudan. *Do not be tempted to coast along any other country.*

Because Egypt and Sudan are safe politically, most sailors favour that side of the sea, especially if anchor-hopping. When practising this rather pleasant form of cruising, an anchorage can be found at the end of every day from Suez right down to the Sudan-Ethiopian border with just a few difficult spots along the way in terms of distance between anchorages. It also presumes that the sailor is not opposed to motoring hard during calms here and there.

A typical Red Sea *marsa*

THE REEFS

Coral reefs fringe much of the entire coast of the Red Sea on both sides with a well-defined barrier reef along the Sudan coast. There are no mid-sea reefs except those fringing certain continental islands.

The coral is of good quality with some of the most splendid gardens to be found anywhere and diving is a very popular tourist sport with charter boats working out of Hurghada (Egypt) and Port Sudan (Sudan). In terms of general navigation, the reefs are well charted but those wanting information on a large scale for some of the coast involved will be frustrated and care should be exercised in reef waters.

FISHING

This is very good in all parts of the Red Sea but more especially in the southern area. Spear fishing is not allowed in most areas but hand lining is popular. The cruising sailor should get good results from trailing a heavy-duty line and spinner.

TRAFFIC

There is a well-defined shipping lane down the centre of the Red Sea. All through traffic adheres to this lane although occasionally one sights a ship taking a short cut across a long dogleg. The areas of greatest danger from shipping are in the narrow southern entrance (Strait of Bab al Mandab), and where the sea narrows in the north to become the Gulf of Suez (the Gubal Strait).

Cross-sea traffic is mostly in the form of dhows running between Sudan and Saudi Arabia as well as Saudi Arabian ferries carrying pilgrims to Mecca.

When out of the shipping lane it is possible to go for days without sighting a ship but a good watch should nevertheless be kept against cross traffic and the occasional freelancing ship.

SMUGGLING

This is a popular pastime for many Arabs whose *dhows* carry electronic equipment from Saudi Arabia to Sudan and backload sheep for sacrificial slaughter and meat. The sound of sheep being loaded into *dhows* in an isolated anchorage along the Sudan coast is not in any way unusual.

Association with smugglers when they are encountered cannot be recommended, however, they are not especially interested, nor intimidated, by your presence so a low profile kept all round seems the best policy.

THEFT

All ports described as being useful in this section are under armed guard, so there need be no fear of theft. At isolated anchorages, fishermen will occasionally attempt to barter but there appears to be no threat of theft. Only where a vessel is obviously abandoned might a thief be tempted so trekking inland overnight from isolated anchorages cannot be recommended.

OIL RIGS

These are confined to the Gulf of Suez and will be sighted at its mouth at the Strait of Gubal and around its central area. Rigs are well lighted although certain support structures close by — such as helipads and so on — might not be. It is important to hold the shipping lane whenever in doubt. There are no rigs in the part of the Red Sea under review in this book.

REPAIRS AND MAINTENANCE

Haul-out is possible in most ports but, as noted earlier, the mind boggles at the potential for bureaucratic harassment (benign but nevertheless maddening). The prices, also, are generally outrageous.

Odds and ends in the form of paint and shackles are often found but dependence should not be placed on finding the exact items required; best bring your own.

Try to avoid having equipment shipped or flown into any Arab country, their complete disregard for the duty-free rights of a boat in transit being legend.

ANCHORAGE

Many anchorages are unique to the Red Sea being inlets, or cuttings, into the fringing reef. Some only penetrate the reef proper whilst most continue into the actual land so that a small boat finds itself completely surrounded by low, hard-packed land with no trees or features worthy of mention. So low is the land that the mast of a small boat can be seen in such an anchorage from close offshore and in this way a lot of fleet sailors keep together. This type of anchorage is mostly referred to by the Arabic word *marsa* which actually means 'anchorage' or 'harbour'.

Whilst these classic inlets are called *marsas*, the Arabic word *khor* means inlet but is more often found associated with fairly conventional bays. A *ras* is a headland behind which anchorage is often found but is subject to the wind remaining constant from the one direction which north of Port Sudan is almost guaranteed.

Reef anchorages in the Red Sea are like reef anchorages all over the world and this subject has been discussed in the chapter 'Coping with Coral'.

PORTS AND ANCHORAGES

The following ports and anchorages are all those capable of offering shelter to a small vessel coasting along the accessible parts of the Red Sea. Not all are illustrated owing to the similar nature of many of them and the fact that the author did not personally visit each and every one. Acknowledgement to other skippers involved is offered where relevant. Many illustrations are from the author's sketch plans made in previously uncharted anchorages and because there is always the chance that important details may have been missed, caution is advised.

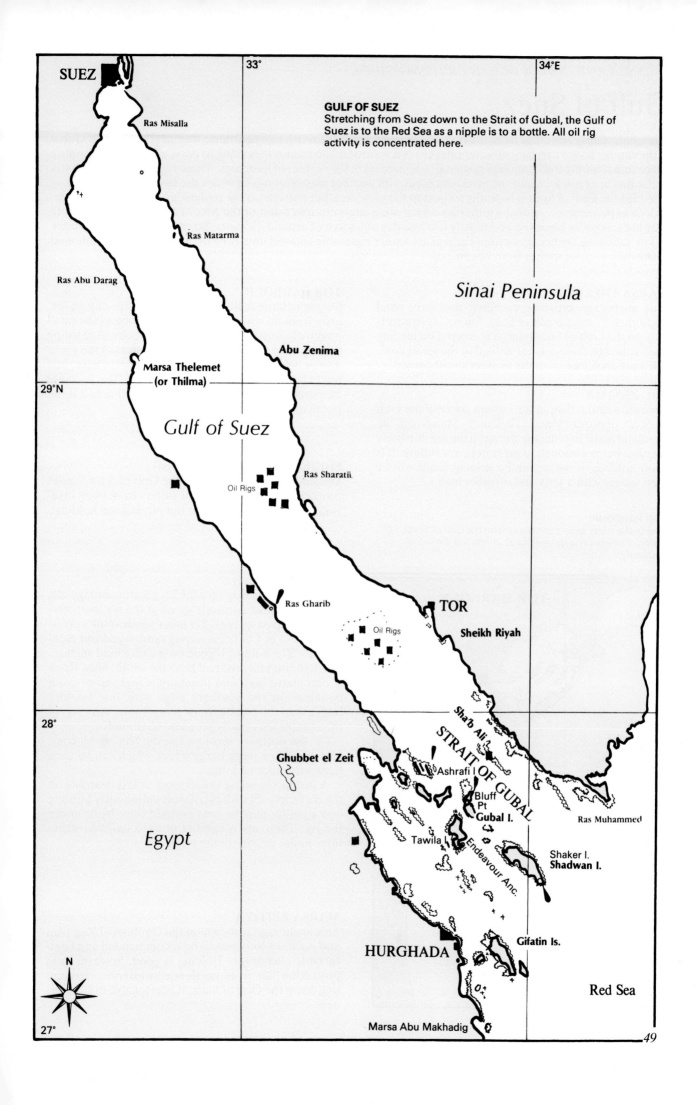

SUEZ

Ras Misalla

Ras Matarma

Ras Abu Darag

GULF OF SUEZ
Stretching from Suez down to the Strait of Gubal, the Gulf of
Suez is to the Red Sea as a nipple is to a bottle. All oil rig
activity is concentrated here.

33°

34°E

Sinai Peninsula

Abu Zenima

**Marsa Thelemet
(or Thilma)**

29°N

Gulf of Suez

Oil Rigs

Ras Sharatil

Ras Gharib

Oil Rigs

TOR

Sheikh Riyah

28°

Egypt

Ghubbet el Zeit

Sha'b Ali

STRAIT OF GUBAL

Ashrafi I

Bluff
Pt
Gubal I.

Ras Muhammed

Tawila I.

Endeavour Anc.

Shaker I.
Shadwan I.

HURGHADA

Gifatin Is.

N

27°

Marsa Abu Makhadig

Red Sea

Gulf of Suez

Stretching nearly 200 miles from the port and city of Suez in the north to its entrance through the Strait of Gubal in the south, this narrow strip of water offers very few worthwhile anchorages along its coast whilst it does promise maximum shipping traffic and navigational confinement in the regions of its oil rigs. These regions are dominantly in the Ras Sharatib area and the Strait of Gubal with another cluster of rigs between the two over Tor Bank.

Whilst the Gulf of Suez is basically subject to the same weather patterns as the remainder of the Red Sea area, it does experience occasional southerlies which are a southern extension of the Mediterranean *siroccos*. Here they are known as *khamsins* and mostly last one day at a force of around 25 knots. Stronger gusts are common.

The following anchorages within the gulf are rather miserable and will mostly be of interest to the northbound yachtsman seeking shelter from headwinds.

MARSA THELEMET
This anchorage provides excellent northerly wind anchorage 55 miles south of Suez. Shown illustratively only on the Gulf of Suez map, it is entered on leading lines although these are not critical to the small boat. The best anchorage is in the northernmost corner.

ABU ZENIMA
An insubstantial dent in the eastern shore of the Gulf of Suez opposite Marsa Thelemet. Shoals off the headland assist in reducing the swell during northerly weather but not enough to prevent heavy rolling. It is good holding, however, and a mining camp will be seen ashore with a jetty and offshore buoys.

TOR HARBOUR
One of the most secure anchorages in the Gulf of Suez, Tor Harbour offers security against all winds but the worst southerly.

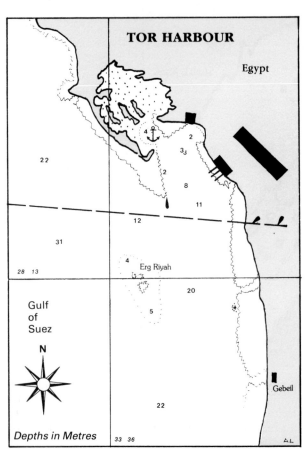

TOR HARBOUR
Shown in large scale here, this anchorage enjoys security from all winds except south as long as the small boat tucks into the so-called boat harbour. According to American yachtsman, Thomas Waters of the yacht *Tiama,* who weathered a severe dust storm here, fuel might be offered at absurdly low prices. This must not be expected and under normal circumstances it is not permissible to make a landing here.

SHEIKH RIYAH (not illustrated)
Situated on the east coast of the Gulf of Suez 5 miles southeast of Tor Harbour, it suffers from swell invasion during northerly winds but offers good holding.

SHA'AB ALI (reef)
As shown on the map on page 52, good anchorage can be found against northerly winds at the northern end of this complex of reefs 3½ miles south-southwest of Ras Kenisa in 4 fathoms having sand, weed and coral patches. The holding is good even with a mud anchor.

When rounding the reef from the south, Shag Rock is one metre high and in reality is a group of coral boulders on the southern edge with one boulder larger than the rest but none remarkable. All reefs in this complex are easily seen and identified.

On the northern most reef of the Sha'ab Ali complex there is a large barge wreck which can be seen from a distance of 5 miles.

A producing oil rig stands more or less centrally on the reef complex with two flares continuously burning and a tender may be seen berthed close by or under the rig. There are a number of miscellaneous structures in the vicinity of the oil rig.

MARSA ZEITIYA
This anchorage is shown on the Ghubbet el Zeit plan and is rather too open to be recommended as a comfortable anchorage. Holding is good, however, and protection fair from north-northwesterlies channelling down the Gulf of Suez. It is untenable in southerlies.

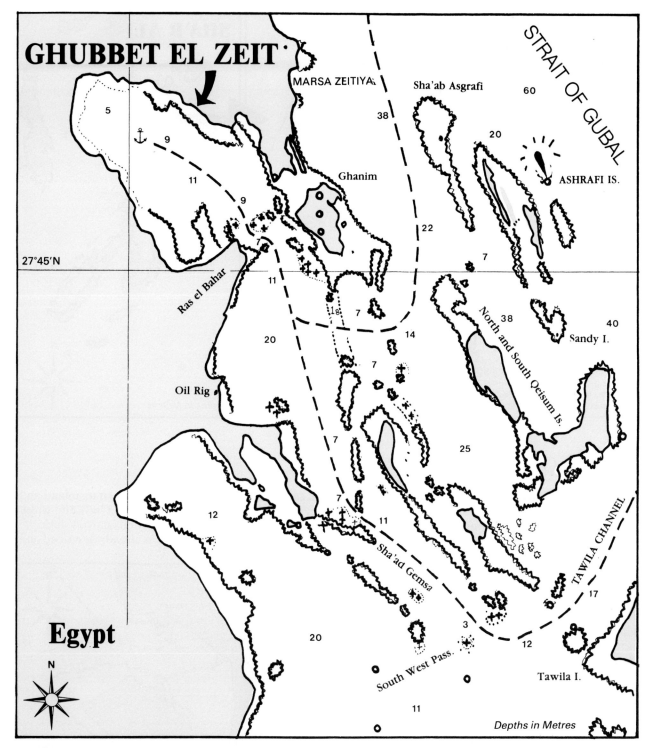

GHUBBET EL ZEIT

STRAIT OF GUBAL

MARSA ZEITIYA

Sha'ab Asgrafi   60

38

20

Ghanim   ASHRAFI IS.

5

9

11   22

9   7

27°45'N

Ras el Bahar   11   North and South Qeisum Is.   38   40

18   7   Sandy I.

20   14

Oil Rig   7

7   25

7   12

12   TAWILA CHANNEL

7   11   17

Sha'ad Gemsa

Egypt   3   12

N   20   Tawila I.

South West Pass.

11   *Depths in Metres*

GHUBBET EL ZEIT
The totally enclosed bay of Ghubbet el Zeit offers full security
against all winds but can prove a long way out of the way for
vessels drawing more than six feet. It lies on the western side
of the Strait of Gubal.

GHUBBET EL ZEIT

This large and totally enclosed bay in the northwest
extreme of the Strait of Gubal is recommended only
to those who wish to spend a little time at rest and
recreation. It is not an easily taken anchorage
because of the distance off course one must go unless
with a draught under 6 feet.

As the plan shows, a shoal neck extends south from
its eastern headland and fringing reef with a
maximum of 6 feet over it. A vessel of considerable
draught, therefore, is obliged to enter and exit via
Tawila Channel. Beacons and buoys will be seen in
the area but in the event of their absence or poor condition, eyeball navigation is recommended.

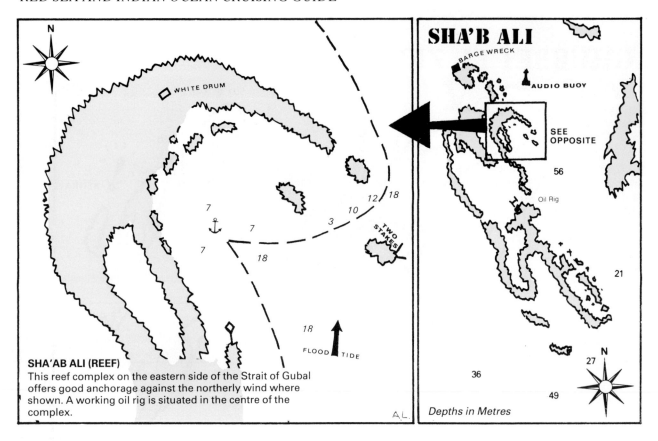

SHA'AB ALI (REEF)
This reef complex on the eastern side of the Strait of Gubal offers good anchorage against the northerly wind where shown. A working oil rig is situated in the centre of the complex.

SHA'B ALI

Depths in Metres

Strait of Gubal

This is the southern entrance to the Gulf of Suez being a 14 mile wide gap between the Egyptian mainland and the southern tip of the Sinai peninsula. It contains many reefs and islands which further restrict its useful width and experiences very strong north-northwesterlies owing to the extreme funnelling effect of its narrow neck.

Dominant amongst the anchorages it offers are Sha'ab Ali (reef) and Ghubbet el Zeit as already described and the next anchorage described, Endeavour Anchorage.

ENDEAVOUR ANCHORAGE (Tawila Island)
Lying near the southern extreme of the Strait of Gubal some 20 miles out of the Egyptian port of Hurghada, this magnificent anchorage promises total security from all winds. There is a cairn on the inlet's northern headland with abandoned buildings obvious to the west of the anchorage. This may have been an army base, a mechanic's pit apparent in one of the buildings.

The reefs off the entrance are easily identified being exposed fully half a metre regardless of tide. The most conspicuous natural object on approach is a plateau of raised coral vaguely shaped like a mushroom and standing one metre above the fringing reef which extends from the southern headland.

The best casual anchorage is where indicated on the map near the remains of a jetty and in an area free of fringing reef. The beach here is commonly speckled in crude oil globules.

Whilst in this area, a relatively new wreck will be sighted to the east of Sha'ab Abu Nuhas (reef). She is a large tanker or ore carrier which failed to make the turn into the Strait of Gubal.

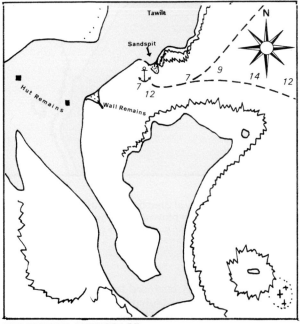

ENDEAVOUR ANCHORAGE
One of the best anchorages in the entire Red Sea, Endeavour Anchorage is also called 'The Fish Hook' and will be found in the Strait of Gubal on Tawila Island.

SHAKER ISLAND
This is an Egyptian army military base and under no circumstances may a private vessel seek shelter here.

HURGHADA
Lying on the southern lip of the mouth of the Gulf of Suez, Hurghada is often recommended as an ideal port where the vessel may be safely left so that her crew may trek inland to the fabulous ancient ruins at Luxor (Valley of the Kings). My personal recommendation is the port of Suez, however there are other reasons for stopping here, amongst them a visit to the ultramodern Sheraton Hotel.

Formalities are obligatory, this being an Egyptian town, and port dues of US$9 are demanded. A visitor may not venture ashore beyond the harbour compound without a shore pass.

Anchorage is in deep water over patchy coral demanding plenty of scope. Otherwise, the anchor may be laid so that the stern can be warped up to the quay where shown. This is a guarded area making it secure for leaving the vessel, but holding is not dependable and a swell commonly invades the harbour as a whole.

Victualling is possible in town as is money changing and other day-to-day functions, but the town is a long walk or taxi ride away from the harbour.

Literally an oasis in a desert, the modern Sheraton Hotel stands proud immediately south of the Egyptian port of Hurghada. To its south is a *Club Med* and anchorage is not permitted at either venue.

HURGHADA HARBOUR
Often chosen by those wanting to leave their vessel to visit the Valley of the Kings near Luxor, Hurghada cannot be recommended above Suez for this venture.

The harbour of Hurghada is formed by a slight indent in the land and protected from seaward by a huge reef. Swell often invades the area and facilities ashore are minimal. There is a US$9 port due payable here.

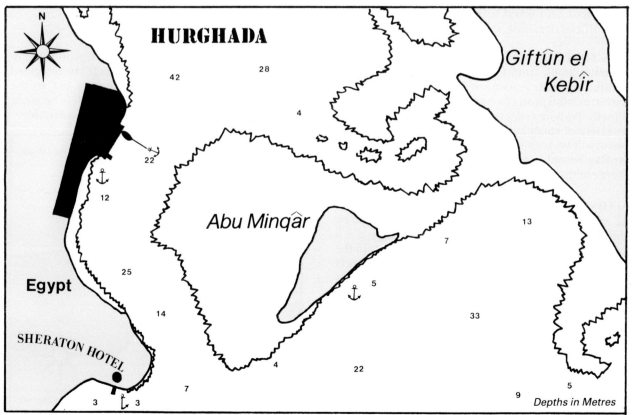

HURGHADA

Giftûn el Kebîr

42   28

4

22

12

Abu Minqâr

13

7

Egypt

25

5

14

33

SHERATON HOTEL

4

22

7

9   *Depths in Metres*

3   3

5

Fuel can be bought here by the drum but I caution against such folly, the local chandler once having a yachtsman jailed until his price was paid. This was an outlandish US$400 for one 44 gallon drum!

Immediately south of the harbour will be seen the new, circular shaped Sheraton Hotel. Anchorage is not permitted offshore but visitors may approach on foot from the harbour. The smorgasbord there is recommended.

RAS ABU SUMA (not illustrated)
Lying under the lee of the headland of the same name, this secure anchorage is recommended to those folk preferring solitude to port life. After reading the description of Port Safaga and considering the potential insecurity of holding in Hurghada, it is recommended before both those ports.

Ras Abu Suma lies 25 miles south from Hurghada and is immediately north of Port Safaga but is not subject to any formalities. The holding is good and water calm, albeit ruffled by strong winds.

PORT SAFAGA (not illustrated)
This is a major Egyptian port where it is not uncommon to see Australian wheat being unloaded under a cloud of choking dust. Being a port of entry the visitor must formalise his visit and for this reason the place is advised against. It is quite uninspiring with the extra penalty of being put through bureaucratic hurdles, agents and port dues.

QUSEIR (not illustrated)
42 miles down the coast from Port Safaga, Quseir is another port of entry with rampant bureaucracy and virtually no harbour. Unless you enjoy rolling gunwales-under whilst being continually bombarded with official demands, stay away afrom Quseir.

RAS TORONBI
31 miles south from Quseir, this apparently insubstantial and quite inadequate headland actually offers excellent calm protection from all winds except those directly onshore (very rare). To its north will be seen a variety of small buildings and one or more fishing boats will be seen snugged behind the fringing reef. At Ras Toronbi itself there will be seen a jetty under the lee of the headland and a couple of low buildings.

MARSA ABU DABBAB (not illustrated)
22 miles south of Ras Toronbi, this was not used by the author but those who did anchor here gave it a very poor rating during northerly winds. It lies in the southwest corner of a bay formed by offshore reefs extending out from the mainland 9 miles north of Marsa Tarafi.

MARSA TARAFI (not illustrated)
This is said to provide fair shelter but demands care when entering, its protection largely being provided by reef.

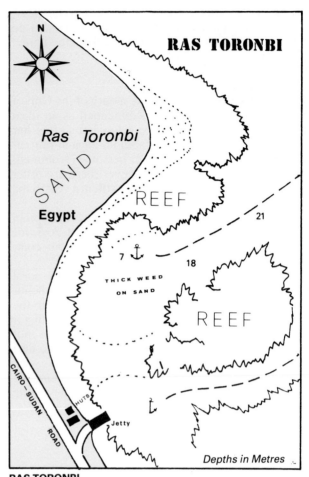

RAS TORONBI
Good protection is enjoyed here thanks to the fringing and barrier reefs.

SHARM LULE
This rather poorly defined dent in the Egyptian mainland provides better security than might be imagined thanks to the offshore reefs stretching out to the island, Gez Wadi Gimal. Passage can safely be made through this reef. Caution and lookout is advisable.

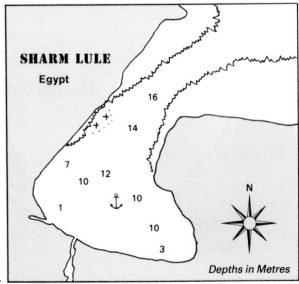

SHARM LULE
At latitude 24°37' north, fair anchorage will be enjoyed here.

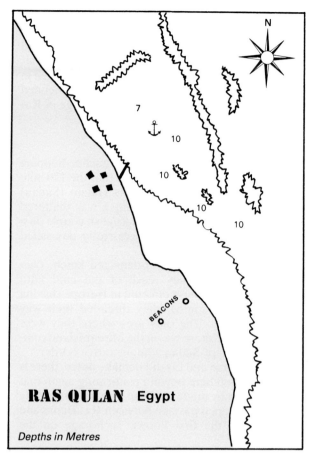

RAS QULAN Egypt

Depths in Metres

RAS QUL'AN
Swell invades this anchorage but it is secure enough in even the strongest northerlies.

RAS QUL'AN
24 miles south from Sharm Lule, this is a reef-protected anchorage offering good holding but some discomfort during strong north-northwesterlies.

RAS BANÂS
Position 23°53'N 35°47'E. This is a major headland on the Egyptian coast which forms Foul Bay and extends out from the small port of Port Berenice. Although easily identified from a good distance offshore by the two ranges of 180 metre high hills, the end of the headland itself cannot be seen until 4 miles off. It is low sand which gives a last minute hook to provide good protection from the prevailing wind.

A reef extends 3½ miles to the south-southwest from Ras Banâs. its southern edge becoming scattered coral heads with deep water between. This fact can cause some concern when trying to identify the true end when approaching from the south or when rounding from the north into Port Berenice.

The anchorage under the headland is over coral and demands an Admiralty Pattern anchor for absolute security, although a mud anchor usually grapples well enough.

Even during strong northerlies this anchorage remains essentially calm allowing the yachtsman to live in fair comfort. Reef viewing will be enjoyed here, there being some excellent coral outcrops fringing the headland.

Ashore is a small army outpost and further in towards Port Berenice is the village of Banâs whose lights will be seen at night. Anchorage is available off the village if required but the bay is full of scattered reef.

RAS BANAS
The anchorage under the headland (left) known as Ras Banas is comfortable in strong northerly winds and the reef viewing is outstanding.

55

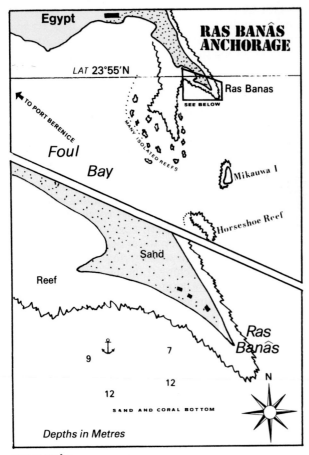

RAS BANÂS
This is the most southerly of the useful anchorages on the Egyptian coast.

PORT BERENICE (not illustrated)
This is Egypt's most southerly port and is not a port of entry. Being an army base visitors are not permitted ashore although there have been cases where locals have willingly rounded up essentials for yachtsmen in a most friendly manner. It cannot be recommended above the easier and more isolated anchorage of Ras Banâs.

FOUL BAY (no large scale details)
There is a popular belief that anchor-hopping through Foul Bay is impossible and that the 120 mile passage from Ras Banâs to Marsa Halaib (Sudan) must be made in one hop. This myth was shattered when George and Liz Purkis, an English couple on a vessel bought in Australia, successfully day-sailed through this much feared area.

Anxious to keep their reef-damaged ketch, *Quo Vadis*, within emergency reach of the land until repairs could be properly effected in Europe (having hit a reef further south), they threaded their way through Foul Bay. The only area where they were obliged to haul offshore was in the Mirear Island complex near the Egypt-Sudan administrative border.

Because George and Liz did not take notes, there is little to be added here beyond confirming again that the passage can be made by those who prefer holding the coast to an open passage between Ras Banas and Marsa Halaib, the first known anchorage on the Sudan coast.

The Sudan Coast

Before continuing south into the Sudan coast, it will be looked at overall here.

Unlike the Egypt coast, there are so many anchorages all the way down to the southern border that a small boat can find a snug haven every night without fail and in all cases they are in totally secure inlets unless otherwise chosen. So many are the inlets along here that many a sailor has spent a day or two in a particular place only to realise later that he was not where first thought. This may smack of appalling navigation but such is the similarity of inlets and such are their numbers in places that a mistake in identifying the location could be made by anybody.

The foreshores along the Sudan coast fit the general description of the Red Sea already given whilst the reefs form a barrier for much of the distance. As a result, a vessel may be taken along an inner or outer route depending on circumstances or may find anchorage immediately offshore under the lee of an actual reef. When coasting it is better to remain between the barrier reefs and the land as long as a sensible watch is maintained.

A fringing reef extends off the land along the entire coast and this, like the barrier reefs, is well noted on all charts but an eye should be kept for small isolated patches off the fringing reef. These only endanger a vessel so close-in as to be dangerously near the fringing reef anyway.

Army trucks are commonly sighted on the coastal road as are camel trains or individual nomads. Army bases are placed strategically along the coast with a few small bases on the banks of inlets. Papers may be called for from a small boat at anchor but molestation of any form is unknown. Local fishing and cargo *dhows* are occasionally seen but are far less common than one might presume; their crews take little interest, most attempts to barter being experienced on the Egyptian coast.

Most reef beacons shown on Admiralty charts are in place and are maintained, but reliance should never be placed on them. Red marks differ in top shape between vertical oblong or 'T' whilst black marks are all triangular. As yet there is no attempt to change to the IALA 'A' buoyage system of red and green and topmark shape: *Pass red to port and black to starboard heading for Port Sudan regardless of direction.*

The following description does not include every potential anchorage, however, it will prove comprehensive enough for day sailing by those who prefer this type of cruising. Those choosing to sail direct will find the offshore approach lights and marks for Port Sudan substantial and in place.

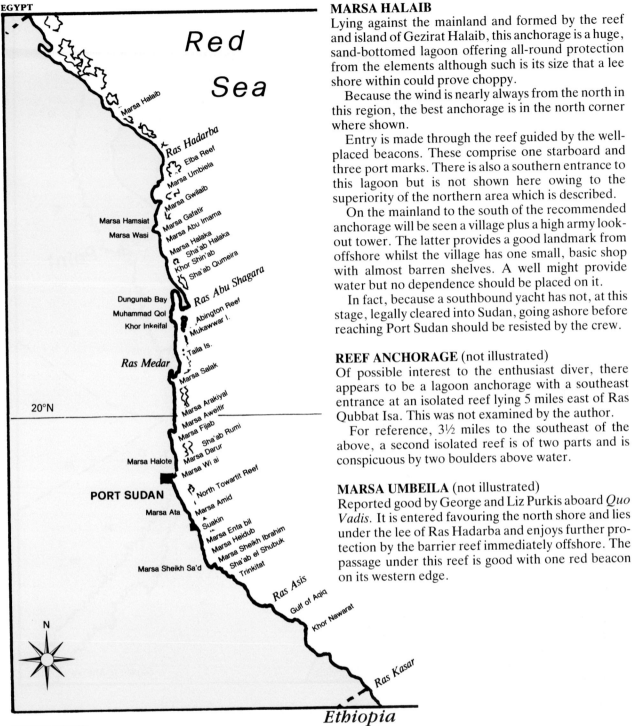

SUDAN COAST
From Marsa Halaib in the north to Khor Nawarat in the south there are anchorages every few miles along the Sudan coast.

MARSA HALAIB

Lying against the mainland and formed by the reef and island of Gezirat Halaib, this anchorage is a huge, sand-bottomed lagoon offering all-round protection from the elements although such is its size that a lee shore within could prove choppy.

Because the wind is nearly always from the north in this region, the best anchorage is in the north corner where shown.

Entry is made through the reef guided by the well-placed beacons. These comprise one starboard and three port marks. There is also a southern entrance to this lagoon but is not shown here owing to the superiority of the northern area which is described.

On the mainland to the south of the recommended anchorage will be seen a village plus a high army look-out tower. The latter provides a good landmark from offshore whilst the village has one small, basic shop with almost barren shelves. A well might provide water but no dependence should be placed on it.

In fact, because a southbound yacht has not, at this stage, legally cleared into Sudan, going ashore before reaching Port Sudan should be resisted by the crew.

REEF ANCHORAGE (not illustrated)

Of possible interest to the enthusiast diver, there appears to be a lagoon anchorage with a southeast entrance at an isolated reef lying 5 miles east of Ras Qubbat Isa. This was not examined by the author.

For reference, 3½ miles to the southeast of the above, a second isolated reef is of two parts and is conspicuous by two boulders above water.

MARSA UMBEILA (not illustrated)

Reported good by George and Liz Purkis aboard *Quo Vadis*. It is entered favouring the north shore and lies under the lee of Ras Hadarba and enjoys further protection by the barrier reef immediately offshore. The passage under this reef is good with one red beacon on its western edge.

KHOR EL MAR'OB (not illustrated)

Not tested by the author, this large, double-headed inlet is reputed to offer fine haven and easy entrance. 2 miles east-northeast from the entrance there is an uncharted reef in mid passage which may carry less than 7 fathoms over it. The barrier reefs beyond display many large boulders.

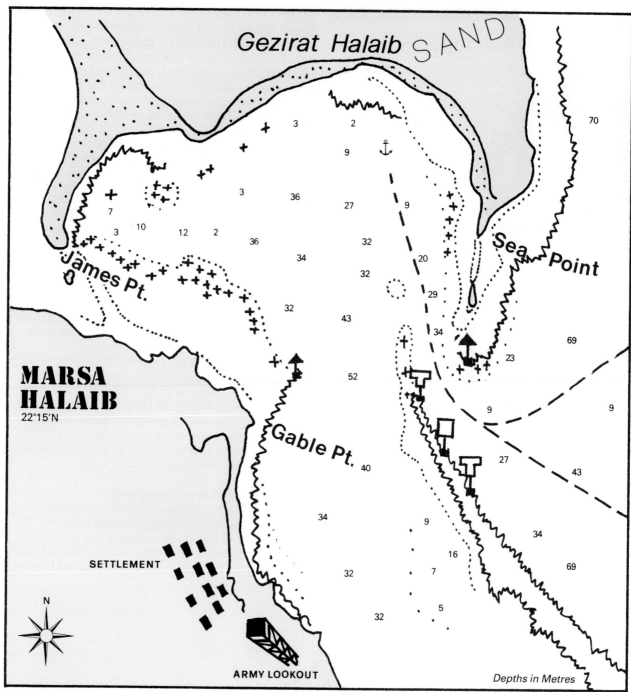

Gezirat Halaib S A N D

James Pt.

MARSA HALAIB
22°15'N

Gable Pt.

Sea Point

Depths in Metres

SETTLEMENT

N

ARMY LOOKOUT

MARSA HALAIB
The most popular anchorage in the Red Sea, good anchorage,
diving and swimming will be enjoyed here.

MARSA GWILAIB
With eroded cliffs marking the south head and a slop-
ing beach with a white hut marking the north head,
this inlet lies 16 miles south from Ras Hadarba and
only 3 miles from the last anchorage. For minimal
depth go right to the head of the inlet but beware of
possible isolated patches of reef in the vicinity.

KHOR ABU ASAL AND MARSA HAMSIAT
(not illustrated)
Within 6 miles of the last inlet, these are said to provide easily entered and secure havens. Khor Abu
Asal is the better of the two.

MARSA WASI (not illustrated)
This is a deep and easily entered inlet 6 miles south
from Marsa Hamsiat. It branches into two inlets and
anchorage can be found more or less centrally in 10
fathoms and excessive depth is the only problem
here.

MARSA ABU'IMAMA
8½ miles from Marsa Wasi, the entrance to this fine
inlet is well advertised by a date palm on its north
shore which can be seen 7 miles away. On final
approach there is a starboard-hand beacon and a
stake on the fringing reef to port. Anchorage can be
taken in 14 metres towards the head after clearing
around two reef patches; or off a sandspit projecting

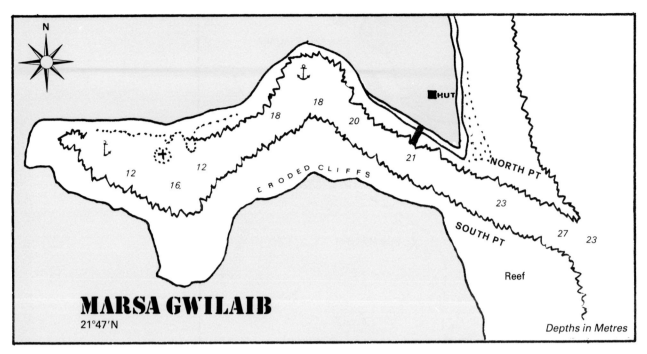

MARSA GWILAIB
21°47′N

Depths in Metres

MARSA GWILAIB
A hut marks the northern headland of this marsa.

southwest between the inlet and a lagoon to its north-west. Although deep water prevails, the anchor can be dropped literally onto this sandspit during steady northerly winds. Otherwise there is a 1.8 metre patch immediately east.

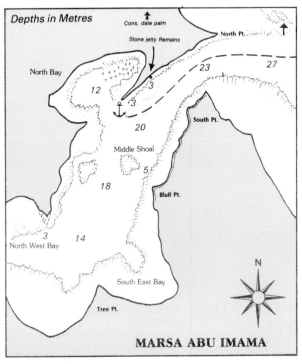

MARSA ABU IMAMA

MARSA ABU'IMAMA
Although tempting, the lagoon here is too deep for secure anchorage. When the wind is steady from the north-northwest the anchor can be dropped on the sand spit where shown.

MARSA HALAKA
South from the last anchorage by 5 miles is this inlet which is especially narrow but is clear of midstream obstacles. Totally secure, if it proves difficult to swing a vessel might be berthed fore and aft across the inlet towards its head away from possible — though unlikely — traffic.

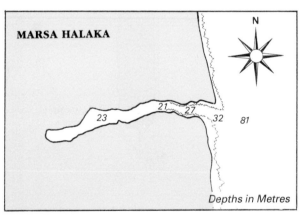

Depths in Metres

MARSA HALAKA
A very narrow inlet it is possible to berth fore and aft across its width.

REEF OFFSHORE (not illustrated)
Less than 4 miles southeast from Marsa Halaka there is an unnamed reef shown as two crosses on small-scale charts. It is actually one single reef enclosing a huge lagoon which is wide open to the west. On the reef is a conspicuous tower whose purpose is unknown.

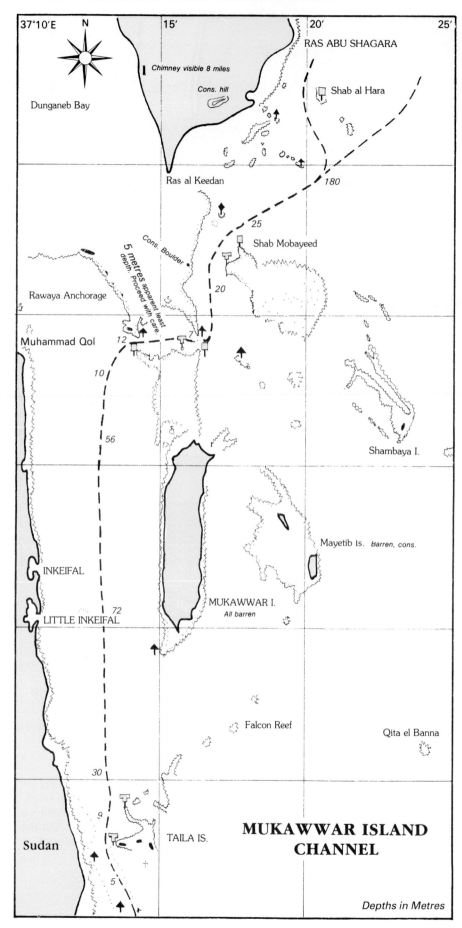

37°10'E   N   15'   20'   25'

RAS ABU SHAGARA

Chimney visible 8 miles

Cons. hill

Dunganeb Bay

Shab al Hara

Ras al Keedan

180

Cons. Boulder

25

Shab Mobayeed

5 metres apparent least depth. Proceed with care.

20

Rawaya Anchorage

Muhammad Qol

12   7

10

Shambaya I.

56

Mayetib Is. *Barren, cons.*

INKEIFAL

72

LITTLE INKEIFAL

MUKAWWAR I.
All barren

Falcon Reef

Qita el Banna

30

9

Sudan

TAILA IS.

MUKAWWAR ISLAND
CHANNEL

5

Depths in Metres

**MUKAWWAR ISLAND
CHANNEL**
The short cut through the
Mukawwar Island area is free of
swell and well beaconed.
Inkeifal is the best anchorage
and is shown separately in large
scale.

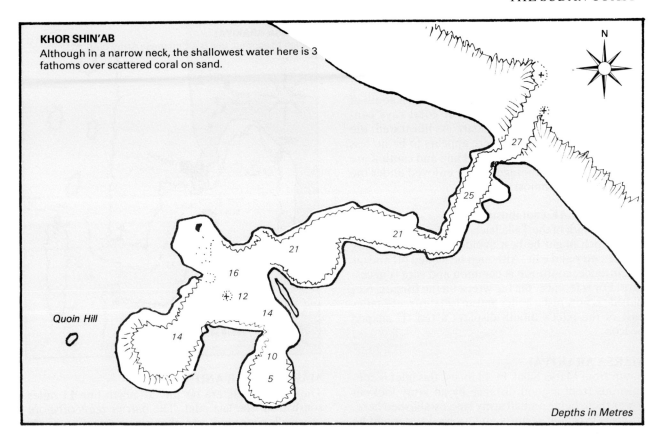

KHOR SHIN'AB
Although in a narrow neck, the shallowest water here is 3 fathoms over scattered coral on sand.

Depths in Metres

KHOR SHIN'AB

4½ miles from Marsa Halaka, this inlet is narrow and clear for much of its length and provides absolute protection as always. When leaving here, two reefs 3½ and 5 miles east and southeast of the entrance are conspicuous by the fact that they always break. Further along the coast a high and dry shipwreck rapidly rusting through will be seen on the outside edge of the reef, Sha'ab Quneira. There is a deep, beaconed passage between this reef and the mainland.

MUHAMMAD QOL

According to Canadian yachtsman, Andy van Herk, anchorage is fine here in the north peak of the reef-formed bay towards a settlement. The Arab fort and many buildings are obvious on approach and the passage in from the headland, Ras Abu Shagara, is clearly beaconed with ample water for deep-keeled yachts. The fishing through the reefs can be excellent by lure.

MUKAWWAR ISLAND

Rising to a little over 90 metres, this long, narrow island is totally barren and uninspiring whilst offering no anchorages around its perimeter. However, because of its disposition and the reefs around, an area of semiprotected water is created between it and the mainland as well as to its north where huge Dungunab Bay provides total protection for anyone wishing to venture off the track.

Those remaining on the track will find no trouble navigating the Mukawwar Island area thanks to clearly defined channels and ample beacons.

INKEIFAL

A south-seeking inlet on the mainland opposite Mukawwar Island surrounded by low, broken and overhanging sandstone cliffs, Inkeifal provides a perfect haven. It is entered between two beacons.

KHOR INKEIFAL
The handiest anchorage in this small inlet is shown.

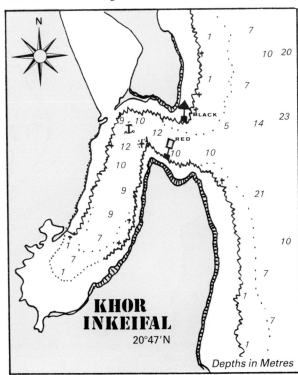

KHOR INKEIFAL
20°47'N

Depths in Metres

LITTLE INKEIFAL (not illustrated)
Not as good as the previous anchorage but useful nevertheless.

TAILA ISLETS
Standing across the inshore passage 6½ miles south of Mukawwar Island is this group of coral cays connected to the mainland by shoals. As illustrated, the channel is beaconed and there appears to be no less than 5.4 metres within, but lead line and caution are suggested. Fair anchorage will be enjoyed under the less of the westernmost islet.

MARSA SALAK (not illustrated)
13 miles south of the Taila Islets, this is a rather messy inlet which might be best avoided by those wanting simple entry and exit. Although beaconed off and, at its entrance, confusion is common and care is necessary. For reference, the tug wreck on the fringing reef outside is now just a boiler and an isolated reef 2 miles east of the inlet's mouth displays a red 'T' shaped beacon.

MARSA ARAKIYAI
South from Marsa Salak by 14 miles, this inlet is conspicuous from a good distance by an army lookout tower there being a small army base established here. It offers excellent security and a camel trip might be possible at a price.

MARSAS FIJAB AND ARUS
These two inlets are on the 20° north line 11 miles south from the last inlet. The barrier reefs offshore are well beaconed and the fringing reef is easily sighted except in reflective, calm conditions.

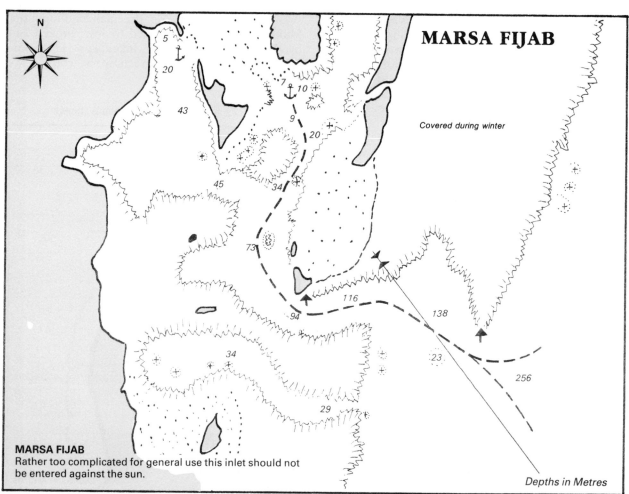

MARSA FIJAB
Rather too complicated for general use this inlet should not be entered against the sun.

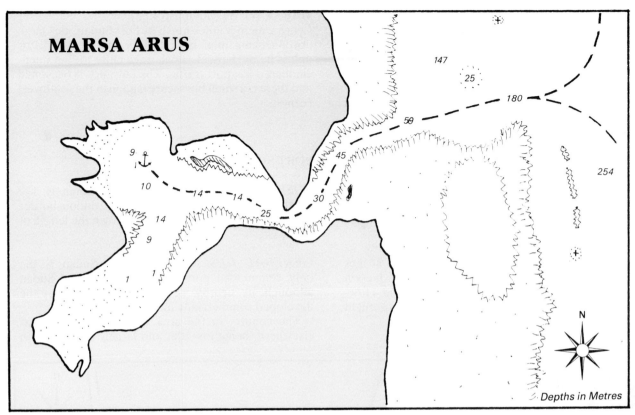

MARSA ARUS
Immediately south of Marsa Fijab, this anchorage is to be recommended as by far the better of the two.

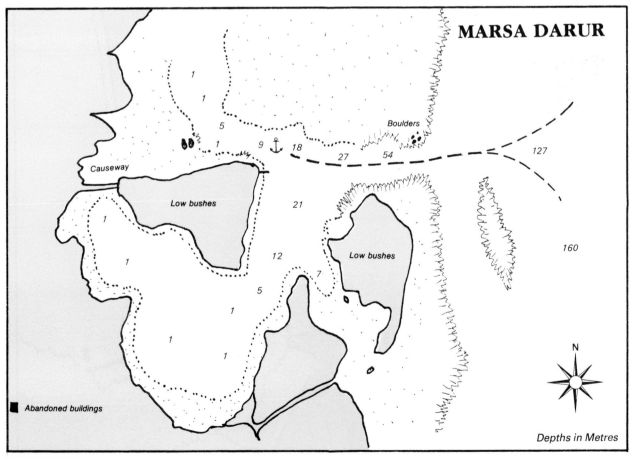

MARSA DARUR
Appreciated for its minimal depths, there is good holding here.

SHA'AB RUMI (Reef) (not illustrated)
Lying 13 miles southeast of Marsa Fijab, this reef
lagoon offers excellent diving to the enthusiast and
might be considered a point of pilgrimage for scuba
diving exponents, it being the site of Jacques Cous-
teau's early experiments. He actually lived underwater here for many weeks and his house can still be seen
12 metres down.

MARSA DARUR
Now only 15 miles north of Port Sudan, this inlet has
good holding, is well protected by reef, land and
shoals, and has a clear entrance identified by a few
boulders on its northern edge. There is an isolated
reef immediately offshore to the south of its entrance.

MARSA HALOTE (not illustrated)
12 miles north from Port Sudan, this inlet strikes
south into fringing reef and opens up to a lagoon
which may be too shallow for deep-keeled use. However, *dhows* will be seen within and the visitor might
care to test it.

MARSA WI'WI (not illustrated)
Lying a mere 3 miles north of Port Sudan, this large
north-seeking inlet is of little value to the visitor
unless he or she seeks anchorage close to, but unen-
cumbered by, port traffic. The entrance is beaconed
and there is a small but secure lagoon in the southwest
corner.

PORT SUDAN (Shaikh Barghuth)

POSITION 37°14'E 19°37'N Approximately 150
nautical miles north from the Sudan-Ethiopia border
which is almost exactly two thirds down the length of
the coast.

GENERAL DESCRIPTION Port Sudan is the
only commercial port for the Republic of Sudan
although its nearby neighbour, Suakin, may be
developed commercially in the future.
The country in the area is exactly the same as
elsewhere, being low, flat and largely desolate with

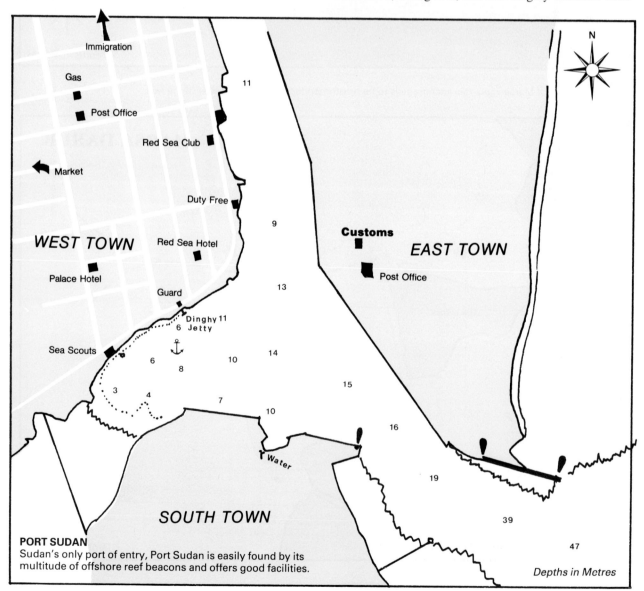

PORT SUDAN
Sudan's only port of entry, Port Sudan is easily found by its
multitude of offshore reef beacons and offers good facilities.

PORT SUDAN
Approach into Port Sudan. The lighthouse, left, stands on the edge of a large fringing reef and is passed to port.

PORT SUDAN
Charter boats based in Port Sudan often anchor too close for comfort. About twelve operate out of here, the majority being Italian.

mountains in the distant background. The harbour is the mouth of a relatively long inlet and the town embraces it in three sections, these being South Town, East Town and West Town. These are looked at here.

South Town is dominated by fuel tanks and is of little interest or use to the visitor.

East Town has most of the main shipping wharves with associated support systems. Customs and immigration will be found in this area when clearing out of Port Sudan.

West Town is where it all happens, having hotels, cafés, the main shopping centre, market and many government offices.

A railway links Port Sudan with the country's capital. Khartoum,   400 miles inland on the banks of the river Nile.

APPROACH   Under no circumstances should the navigator find himself in this region without a larger scale chart, there being a barrier reef close inshore

and scattered isolated reefs offshore. Under the circumstances the following is brief and in no way complete, it presumes approach is made from seaward, coastal approach being by logical progression.

From the north   This is a clearer approach than that from the south there being fewer offshore hazards and those which do exist are much closer to land. The logical orientation point should be the light tower on Sanganeb Reef lying nearly 14 miles northeast of Port Sudan. From there clear water will be enjoyed until Wingate Reefs which are well charted and marked by two lights.

From the south   Lying some 48 miles east-southeast from Port Sudan is Owen Reef which is unlighted making it something of a hazard, the first lighted offshore danger being Hindi Gider Reef which has a cay atop standing some 4 metres above sea level. This lies nearly 8 miles further west from Owen, with a smaller reef known as Peshwa, en route. Great caution should therefore be exercised in making up to Port Sudan from seaward when sailing from the south. It is best to make Masamirit Islet your first orientation point. This low cay lies nearly 60 miles southeast of Hindi Gider and be wary lest a west to northwest current experienced by the author in the region should prove normal at all times of the year. There is a major light on Masamirit Islet visible fifteen miles but is sometimes out.

ANCHORAGE Visiting private boats are limited to the western spur immediately inside the harbour towards its north shore. This is also a favourite area for berthing smallish ships which have been temporarily or permanently decommissioned. As a result, it can be crowded and occasionally threatened by ship movement.

Adding to the congestion and sometimes causing confusion are the dozen or so charter yachts and motorboats working out of this anchorage. Their skippers tend to covert a certain spot as being 'their' anchorage and will drop anchor virtually alongside if they return to find you there. This is not an act of aggression so much as necessity and, generally speaking, they are welcoming and helpful to visitors.

As shown on the map, the anchorage is divided into two areas by one or more derelict ships lying across the bay to fore-and-aft buoys. To the west and north of these ships is the best anchorage but to their east is more than acceptable with the proviso that a good distance is held off the derelicts to allow for their lateral wandering. Also, in this position, beware of anchoring too far to the south in which position you might obstruct safe ship movement into the so-called coal wharf (this is now a container wharf).

The bottom is excellent holding mud and as long as sufficient cable can be ranged out a vessel will not drag in the fiercest gusts.

FORMALITIES Upon anchoring in Port Sudan remain aboard until cleared by health officials. A doctor will come aboard with a single form to be filled out and signed and he will require a single crew list. He may or may not demand health clearances from previous ports and he may or may not insist on injections on the spot if not up to date. Mostly he is very relaxed on this subject. It is best to arrive with cholera, typhoid and yellow fever inoculations up to date, but apparently not obligatory.

Having cleared health formalities, the visitor may now go ashore to finalise other formalities. This will go as follows:

Armed with all passports and ship's official papers, go to the port office where the ship's papers must be surrendered for safe keeping against payment of port dues before leaving. You will also be obliged to fill out three crew lists, two of which, together with another form from the port office, must now be taken to immigration. Here, all passports and paperwork are held except for a single, signed crew list. You are now free for a while but should return to immigration the next day when passports are returned in exchange for a fee of three Sudanese pounds per passport.

The passports should now be taken across the harbour to East Town immigration office where shore passes are issued. This final formality is often ignored by visitors to no ill effect, but I would suggest you get local advice at the time before flouting what is, after all, an obligation.

On clearing out, go to the port office and receive paperwork which is then taken across to Ports Corporation at East Town where US$10 is paid (in hard currency only) for port dues. Two forms will be received after payment, one to be taken to the customs at East Town, the other back to the port office in West Town on the receipt of which your ship's papers will be returned. You are now free to depart.

Having cleared customs and whilst still in East Town, duty-free cigarettes may be purchased. Otherwise, duty-free tobacco, toys, clothes and some wines are available in the other duty-free shop at West Town. Experience suggests that these services are available whether legally cleared out or not, the local foreign-owned charter vessels often use them for alcohol (before the imposition of strict Islamic law) and tobacco supplies. Certainly the duty-free store in West Town can be used at any time during your stay.

TIDES There is virtually no vertical or lateral movement of water in Port Sudan this part of the Red Sea being almost tideless.

WEATHER This subject is covered fully in the Red Sea general description. Here it should be emphasised that Port Sudan experiences dominantly north to northwest winds throughout the year which often blow at gale force for two day periods before settling back and eventually dying leaving calm periods of many days in duration. The south-south-easterly can reach this far north in the months December to March but mostly it fades some one to two hundred miles further south.

FACILITIES It should be emphasised that Port Sudan has a number of private agents who can act as purchasing agent for any item required aboard ship. Some specialise more in the formal side of easing the entry and exit pains for charter boat guests whilst others specialise more in straight victualling. The visitor should discover who is who upon arrival lest he finds himself with the wrong agent for the job. They all seem to be honest men eager to perform their task efficiently but a man specialising more in formalities may not tell you that he cannot get diesel fuel as cheaply as a man specialising in victualling. Most speak English, Italian and Arabic.

Fuel Petrol must be carted from town service stations whilst diesel is only available in 44-gallon drums through an agent. Depending on the quality of the agent's contacts, this costs from between US$55 and US$75 per drum in early 1983. The business of siphoning it into demijohns at the dinghy landing, then carrying it out to the vessel at anchor, is tiresome but inescapable. Some charter boats have their own pump aboard and warp their stern

PORT SUDAN
The town of Port Sudan is everyone's idea of an Arab town and provides a remarkable variety of facilities to the visiting boat including a fabulous market and a number of shipping agents specialising in assisting small boats.

in close enough to pump direct from drums. If you can rig a similar system a lot of tiresome mess will be avoided.

Paraffin is available from the Shell service station in West Town but is often scarce owing to demand. Methylated spirits must be purchased through the black market at an outrageous price.

Gas is easily obtained from a station behind the post office in West Town. It is reasonably priced and there is no trouble connecting up to western bottles.

Oil suitable for petrol engines is readily available at the Shell service station but diesel oil can be difficult. An agent is often necessary here. Hydraulic gearbox oil is simply not available.

Water can be hosed aboard from the port office jetty in West Town, with permission, or it can be demijohned across from the coal (container) wharf to the south of the anchorage. All tap water appears to be excellent with no stories of water-induced illness amongst the charter fleet.

Communications are unreal in Port Sudan with trunk phone calls being very difficult and expensive and mail being rather slow. One month should be allowed for incoming foreign mail and then there is a fair chance of it being routed to the wrong place in Port Sudan. For example, a letter sent to me

care of the post office was collected in the Red Sea Club by a friend two months later! My best advice is to avoid the need of any communications in the area, however unimportant mail might be directed to: Post Office, Port Sudan (West Town), Republic of Sudan. It will be found, if you are lucky, in a pile of dusty, dog-eared mail on the counter.

Transport Taxis are definitely not cheap and should be avoided unless a price understanding is reached in advance. Train and plane connect Port Sudan with the outside world.

Traffic drives on the right-hand side of the road. It is a busy town but traffic jams are a long way off yet.

Currency is the Sudanese pound which is broken into 100 piastres. The rate to the US dollar in early 1983 was officially 129 to 135 piastres, but a black market existed where the rate went as high as 170 piastres. It is best to arrive with US dollars in cash. It is possible but very difficult to obtain hard currency in Sudan.

Shops in West Town are mainly grouped around the market area where many items will be found. Recognising the potential market in the charter business, a few shops have a good range of such items as toilet paper, tinned food and so on. Victualling is no trouble and local feta cheese is superb.

The Market in West Town is fabulous, having a great variety of fresh food and vegetables at good prices. Mangoes and grapefruit are especially recommended in season with the latter being of a remarkably pink flesh which is sweet. Some fruit is imported such as apples from France but otherwise most items are locally produced being from the fertile river Nile area.

In little alleys around the market will be found herbs and spices overflowing out of bulging sacks and the whole area offers some unusual smells and sights. The donkey wagons and camels are especially fun to see.

Commercial hours The market seems to be open all the time whilst many government offices open only for the mornings. Shops close for much of the afternoon but open again in the evening. Being an Islamic country, all activity ceases on Friday.

Souvenirs There are a number of shops selling tourist items in West Town with the heavy silver and typically Arab jewellery being the most likely items to appeal. Some of this jewellery is fabricated from old Arab coins.

Also of interest are the locally manufactured swords. Very few visitors leave the area without at least one hanging from the bulkhead. If you can find an old model, used but not too abused, the steel will be found to be far superior than that used in the tourist models.

Duty-free has been noted under the heading 'Formalities'. Here it should be noted that those keen on pipe tobacco or cigars will find the West Town duty-free the only source of supply.

Clubs There are a few clubs still functioning from the colonial days with the Red Sea Club being the most famous. However, all insist on the old formality of entry meaning that a visitor can only enjoy a meal or a drink at these establishments if introduced by a member.

Hotels These are surprisingly clean, well run and affordable and are available to anyone wanting a room or a meal or both. The service and quality of food tends to be good.

Milk Bar Reminding one of the United States in the mid 1950s, the Palace Hotel has a milk bar attached where one can enjoy a *cappuccino* coffee, hamburgers and other western snack foods. It is not cheap but is fun for its oasis-like quality.

Eating out All clubs, hotels and cafés offer meals at fair prices; a typical top-of-the-line meal costing, for one, about US$4 (1983). Arab cafés are much cheaper with the cheapest being the so-called Sea Scouts Café on the waterfront near the anchorage. Here a tin plate full of beans and liver, fish, or shish kebab cost less than one dollar including excellent, large bread rolls. Being very much a Moslem show, no utensils are supplied, the diner being expected to eat with his *right* hand. (Note the emphasis, the use of the left hand for anything other than menial tasks is an insult to a Moslem.) See page 3 for notes on behaviour.

Garbage There is no collection service near the harbour. Research this first in the event of things changing.

Dinghy must be landed at the small concrete quay near the conspicuous guard house. Nothing is stolen from here.

Fishing would appear to be worthwhile in the harbour during calm days, schools of large fish often entering and chasing small fry amongst the anchored boats.

SIGHTSEEING Those persons wanting to see something of the Nile and the capital, Khartoum, in particular, can leave their vessels in the capable hands of an agent and trek inland. The train runs once or twice a week and buses run more regularly but both services tend to be rather basic, the latter taking two days over the journey.

A direct Port Sudan-Khartoum flight is available costing a little over US$100 return.

Minibuses connect Port Sudan with Suakin daily offering an opportunity to see this marvellous, falling-down town which is still used as a main venue for camel trains.

Other sights are in the town of Port Sudan itself from the groups of camels and goats wandering aimlessly all over the place to the heavily robed women, or sword-carrying desert men in town for a milkshake or a spot of banking.

I would warn the visitor against aiming his camera at people, especially women. This invasion of privacy is not appreciated, although in Suakin it is different, the people there rather enjoy having their photograph taken.

Egyptian Embassy Those sailing north will enjoy full facilities here for the acquiring of advance visas if considered necessary after reading the section 'Formalities' in the description of Egypt earlier in this chapter.

TOWARTIT REEFS (not illustrated)
This complex of barrier reefs spreads down the coast from a point 7 miles south of Port Sudan to a point 23 miles south. There is a well-defined and deep passage between them and the mainland, and ships awaiting entry into Port Sudan will be seen at anchor near the northern tip. Beacons will be seen in this region also.

Anchorage is possible near the northern part but cannot be recommended because of the bothersome depths and general exposure.

In the area south of Towartit Elbow, on the mainland, will be seen hundreds of *dhows* stranded on the fringing reef. These are government-confiscated smuggling vessels and do not suggest harbourage.

MARSA ATA
This is a fringing reef inlet which strikes north and reaches the land by virtue of shoaling water. Anchorage is possible during northerlies at its entrance which is marked by a red and black beacon to port and starboard respectively.

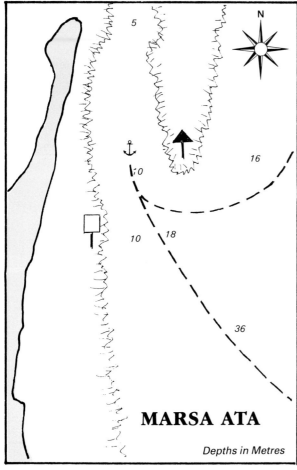

MARSA ATA AND SH'AB DAMATH
Both reef anchorages, beacons assist in locating them.

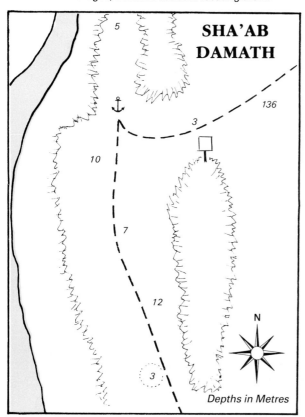

SHA'AB DAMATH
This is a reef close against the mainland's fringing reef just north of Suakin and 24 miles south of Port Sudan. It combines with a small inlet to create fair haven tucked up under the hook of the fringing reef in 5 metres.

SUAKIN (not illustrated)
About 30 miles south of Port Sudan, Suakin provides good shelter in an interesting environment, this being a town mostly in ruins but still visited by camel trains. The market is excellent and swords can be purchased there.

It is not a port of entry and members of the army based here may ask for papers. The entrance is well beaconed and an army tower on the land is conspicuous.

MARSA HEIDUB (not illustrated)
Just 11 miles south of Suakin, this inlet is used by a fleet of local *dhows*.

MARSA SHEIKH IBRAHIM
4 miles beyond the last anchorage, this provides better shelter where shown on the map. Holding is outstanding.

MARSA SHEIKH SA'D (not illustrated)
Only 3 miles south from Marsa Sheikh Ibrahim, this inlet offers superb anchorage also but has three reef patches in its entrance which make entry against the afternoon sun rather hazardous.

SHA'AB EL SHUBUK (reef)
This is a collection of reefs which form an effective barrier along the coast for the 18 miles between Marsa Sheikh Sa'D and the headland, Melita Point. In fact, protection extends beyond there, remaining effective right to the tiny abandoned harbour of Trinkitat during northerly weather. The passage between the reefs and the mainland fringing reefs is very well beaconed and the water is affected only by wind and there is no swell here.

Because the southbound yacht is effectively still leaving Port Sudan it is important to remember that red beacons will be passed to starboard and black to port.

Anchorage can be taken within the reef complex, a suitable place being indicated by the weather of the time. Otherwise it is an easy matter to sail the full distance and take anchorage at the other end.

TRINKITAT HARBOUR
(not illustrated on a large scale)
According to Steve and Marja Vance on the American yacht *Twiga*, anchorage within the bay is good although subject to slight swell at times. Not used commercially, there will be seen the remnants of a jetty and building on the southern shore.

The beacon on the reef outside (Qita Kanasha) is in place and can be passed to either side depending on approach. A submerged patch of rocks in mid entrance has less than 6 feet over it and must be eyeballed on entry.

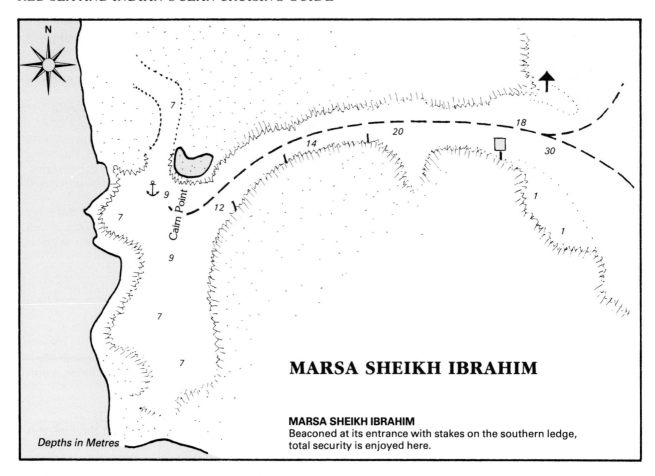

MARSA SHEIKH IBRAHIM

MARSA SHEIKH IBRAHIM
Beaconed at its entrance with stakes on the southern ledge,
total security is enjoyed here.

Depths in Metres

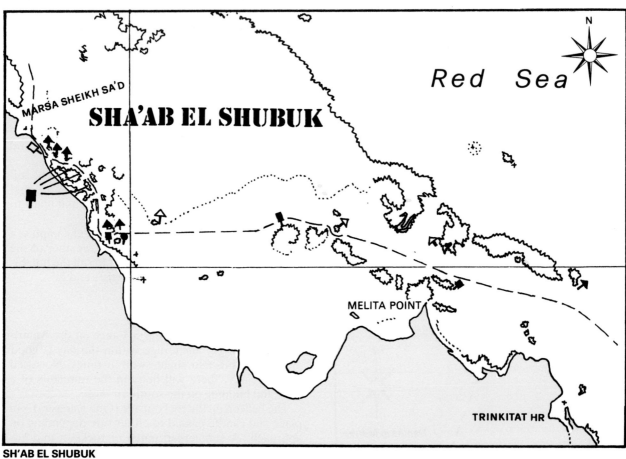

SH'AB EL SHUBUK
A well beaconed calm water passage lies between the reef Sha'ab el Shubuk and the Sudanese mainland.

GULF OF AQIQ (not illustrated)

There is a small settlement and army base in the south-west corner of this bay known as Aqiq and two islets lie towards the southeast corner. During northerlies, fair protection is enjoyed under the lee of the headland Ras Asis, tucked up as close as possible.

KHOR NAWARAT

Being the last, or first, mainland anchorage in the Red Sea this bay is looked at in detail here.

POSITION 18 miles north of west from the Sudan-Ethiopia border, approximately 120 miles southeast from Sudan's main port, Port Sudan.

GENERAL DESCRIPTION Khor Nawarat is an island-studded bay with most islands stretching across the mouth forming a barrier. This line of islands extends northwest to overlap the northern headland. As a result, good security from any weather can be found within the bay or fair anchorage can be enjoyed around its mouth.

All islets stand on coral reefs and are low and sandy in nature with some stunted growth and in places very low but distinct cliffs are formed by hard-packed sand. The foreground mainland is similar in essential character with a fringing reef extending right around the bay. This reef scatters in places to present a navigational hazard and anyone scouting around within should stand a good lookout.

The only indication of habitation in the area is a small and sometimes deserted fishing village on the western end of Bahdur Island plus the appearance of two or three fishing *dhows* around the reefs. A camel and rider will sometimes be seen ashore. No one seems to take much interest in a visiting boat although an army detachment from Aqiq, in the next bay north, may request your identification.

During clear weather the background hills and mountains provide good reference during a landfall but are mostly under cloud, this being the convergence zone.

APPROACH The person making for Khor Nawarat from the south will, in all probability, be experiencing his first landfall in the Red Sea since the islands 400 miles to the south. It is thus important to remind the navigator, yet again, that the author — and many others — experienced a very strong west-setting current in the region. Allow for the possibility of this current setting you on and if a fair breeze is being experienced then there is little to recommend coming in for anchorage.

If convergence zone cloud exists the background hills may not be visible until close-in and then only in brief glimpses. In this event, watch for the low-lying coastal fringe which is often not obvious until three or four miles off. In fair visibility the location of Khor Nawarat will be obvious by taking bearings off Quoin Hill. I should warn, however, that the two hills constituting Quoin Hill are duplicated further south. The true Quoin Hill(s) is the lower of the two groups. Also, its southern hill is higher and more rounded than its mate.

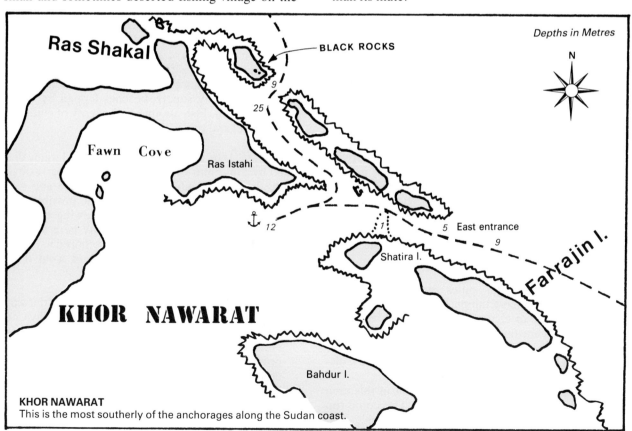

KHOR NAWARAT
This is the most southerly of the anchorages along the Sudan coast.

Where overcast skies deny long-distance identification, move in as close as you dare to the coast and watch for the obvious gap between Farrajun Island and the islets to its north. This is *East Entrance* and may be used with safety. Beware, however, of a shallow reef area extending northeast from Shatira Islet. Hold to starboard and watch the ground for the best water. The *Pilot* refers to a minimum of 6 metres in this fairway; I found considerably less but may not have located the best depth.

Vessels approaching from the north should use the northern entrance which is shown on the map and use Black Rocks as a reference point. These rocks are stated by the *Pilot* as being visible from 5 miles although from the deck of a small boat the figure is closer to 3. In fact, the better landmark is the islet on which Black Rocks are situated. This appears, at about the same time, as a low dome with a fringe of grass reminding one of a bald head.

Pass Black Rocks to starboard from where the course into recommended anchorage will be obvious.

ANCHORAGE can be taken just about anywhere depending on weather. Many yachts remain outside the bay proper under the lee of a suitable islet so as not to arouse the interest of anyone ashore. Otherwise, the best and most convenient anchorage against the prevailing northerly is under the lee of the headland, Ras Istahi, where shown. Seven fathoms, excellent holding, will be found here well off the fringing reef and no rolling will be experienced. In heavy southeast weather it would be better under the lee of Bahdur Island.

WEATHER During the months of June to October it is possible to experience a *haboob* which can blow from the east to south in gusts up to 40 knots. According to the *Pilot,* they are mostly preceded by a thick atmosphere, the hills disappearing from view. I would point out here that the hills often disappear from view owing to the common convergence zone cloud layer. This, in itself, is not the precursor of a *haboob.*

The weather in the Khor Nawarat area is otherwise mostly northerly throughout the year with a good chance of southeasterlies reaching this far north during the months December to April. Because of the precipitation that can occur with the convergence zone cloud layer, rain is not uncommon inland from here and it can sometimes drizzle on the coast although this is rare.

WARNINGS Not 20 miles south from Khor Nawarat is the Sudan-Ethiopia border. The latter is in a constant state of civil war and must not be visited under any circumstances. Shape all courses to remain outside their 12 miles limit and triple that distance to be certain. Gunboats roam the coast and one's distance off is not necessarily respected.

The warning that an onshore current in this area might prevail year round is repeated. This could run west or northwest at a rate as fast as one knot.

Because of the unfriendly Ethiopian coast from here down to the bottom of the Red Sea there is a natural temptation to seek anchorage on the other side amongst the Farasan Islands. This is not permitted nor may anchorage be safely taken anywhere on the east coast.

Under the circumstance, only the island anchorages noted next may be considered as politically safe havens but the word 'haven' is in doubt as we will see.

JABAL ATTAIR ISLAND (not illustrated)
Dramatically obvious against the surrounding deeper water is a shallow patch under the lee of this island at Yellow Bluff on the south side. Suitable only in northerly winds, the holding is good but comfort poor. From Khor Nawarat the distance is 270 miles.

ZUBAIR ISLANDS (not illustrated)
35 miles south of southeast from the last island, this group offers very little in the way of fair anchorage. However, those anxious to rest from boisterous seas might find the rolling under the lee of Centre Peak Island preferable during northerlies only.

HANISH GROUP AND JABAL ZUQAR ISLAND
70 miles southeast from Zubair Islands and 70 miles northwest from the southern entrance to the Red Sea (Strait of Bab al Mandab) and stretching for some 25 miles in those directions, these islands are uninhabited and safe politically. Anchorages are not outstanding but certainly pleasant enough, although a sudden and complete change of wind direction is possible from December to April. An anchor watch may be necessary.

The largest islands in order of size are Jabal Zuqar, Great Hanish and Little Hanish. To avoid confusion here it should be pointed out that both this group and the Zubair Islands have an island named Haycock.

The entire group is treeless, volcanic in origin and rugged in appearance with mountains rising to 624 metres and many superb beaches lapped by water clear and clean. Fish abound with plenty of evidence of mackerel and tuna.

ANCHORAGE around the group will be largely dictated by conditions of the moment, a northerly obviously driving you under the southern lee and vice versa during a southerly. But it is the possibility of either a southerly or a northerly blowing that can cause the greatest sense of insecurity here and the sailor should watch for a change if anchored to one or the other wind; or an introduction of wind if he anchors there during a calm.

The potential will be looked at here:
Great Hanish Island really offers nothing in the way of good bays in which to anchor but I have no doubt a person weary from battling to weather in either direction will find something that should prove better than nothing. The greatest problem is depth and the closeness to land one must get to find bottom. This places one rather too close should the wind swing.
Tongue Islet lies between Great Hanish and Jabal Zuqar Islands, favouring the latter, and has an

JABAL ZUQAR
Jabal Zuqar Island offers the best anchorages in the Hanish Group. Beware of changing winds during the winter.

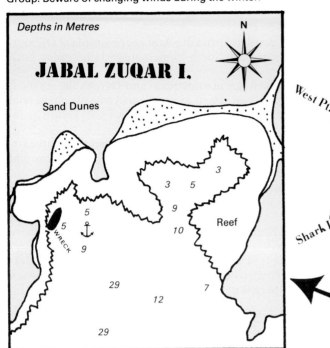

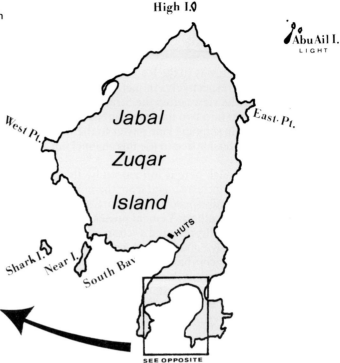

interesting lagoon that was not tested by the author. However, it could be worthwhile to the person cruising the area, as against the person rushing through, and entrance will be found on its eastern side where the bottom shoals to three metres before dropping away again to depths that are rather too excessive for successful anchoring.

Jabal Zuqar Island is easily the largest of the group, lying to the north where its few bays offer the best anchorage for various winds. If blowing from the north, the south bay is good close to the obvious wreck as indicated on the map.

The lagoon formed by coral reef here suggests good all-weather anchorage, but in fact the entrance is extremely difficult to identify and once in there would be no tolerance for a dragging anchor.

South Bay, just around the corner from the above area, offers anchorage in its northeast corner, where will be seen a couple of fishermen's huts, or in its northwest corner which is formed by Near Islet. This bay offers potential in winds from northwest, through northeast, right round to southeast, although towards the latter extreme conditions would be anything but comfortable.

One and a half miles west from Jabal Zuqar's North Point there is anchorage from southerly winds which cannot be described as comfortable but is nevertheless suitable. There is an opening in the fringing reef giving entrance to a lagoon which can be used but with the same qualifications as those noted for the south lagoon. Quite a few boats have experienced distress here after a southerly has swung to the north and it should be emphasised that winds in this area can introduce and change rather rapidly between November and April.

JABAL ZUQAR ISLAND
This view of Jabal Zuqar Island typified the type of country to be found amongst the Hanish group.

73

Strait of Bab al Mandab

POSITION 12°40′N 43°22′E

This the southern gateway to the Red Sea separates the African mainland from the Arabian peninsula at Djibouti and North Yemen respectively. In fact, South Yemen is right alongside North Yemen at this latter point, both countries sharing the view across the Strait.

The Strait is split into two navigable areas by Perim Island which lies in midstream and favours the Arabian peninsula. The main shipping lane passes to the west of the island leaving the eastern channel free of commercial traffic. The private boat is free to use this channel but the main channel is recommended if only for its known quantity.

The weather through here is influenced by the Arabian Sea, monsoons being dominant from the southeast, December to March inclusive, and from the northwest for the remainder of the year. Its canalising effect can add considerably to a wind's speed and its short, steep seas are legend during strong winds.

Perim Island is a Southern Yemeni possession which is inhabited by fishermen and a small army unit. Despite the attraction of its well-protected anchorage on the southwestern side, the visitor is warned away. Doctor Dale Huber and his family, aboard the American cutter *Hornet*, anchored there but were requested to leave immediately; other yachts have been fired upon for anchoring. They were probably warning shots only but there is no doubt that the army at Perim Island does not want visitors.

As a matter of passing interest, according to English yachtsman, Jack Richardson who was based in Aden during the Second World War, an English Class 'K' destroyer was rammed onto the south point of Perim Island when one of her torpedoes spontaneously ignited. From a distance, there is no evidence of this vessel today.

The Gulf of Aden

This ever widening gap between the bottom of the Arabian peninsula and the African mainland is the funnel from which eastbound boats will pass en route to India and beyond. Often dominated by calms, it is subject to the northeast monsoon between December and April at which time the dominant wind is east, and the southwest monsoon between May and November at which time the dominant wind is west. In fact, this is often the calmest period, the southwest monsoon not being properly felt until clearing the African mainland.

The useful ports in this gulf which are described in this book are, in order of appearance, Djibouti, Aden and Salalah.

DJIBOUTI

POSITION 11°35′N 43°09′E

Noted in the general section on the Red Sea, Djibouti is repeated here as a reminder that it offers an alternative, or an addition, to Aden.

Djibouti is a tiny African independency surrounded by Ethiopia and having a small section of its border with Somalia. It is at the head of the Gulf of Aden and overlooks the Strait of Bab al Mandab, the southern entrance into the Red Sea.

The port is secure but uninteresting and, according to friends, the cost of living is exceptionally high being tailored to the French navy who use Djibouti as a base. There is also a rather stiff port due payable and it is said that friendliness at official level is often lacking.

All in all, from comparisons made by the author, it would seem that Aden is vastly superior on all counts to Djibouti. However, its more strategic position related to the Strait of Bab al Mandab cannot be denied giving it some attraction for the passing boat.

ADEN

POSITION 12°47′N 44°57′E.
Nearly 100 miles east of the southern entrance to the Red Sea.

GENERAL DESCRIPTION The area known as Aden is divided up into a number of towns, the largest being Crater and the closest to the harbour being Steamer Point. The harbour is a very busy bunkering and refinery port which offers nothing in the way of scenic interest to the yachtsman. However, strategically placed as it is, between the Mediterranean Sea and India, Aden makes an excellent revictualling area and in this respect it is recommended.

With a population of around 300,000 people who range from coal black Africans to snow white Europeans, Aden is the main centre for the People's Democratic Republic of Yemen (South Yemen), and despite communistic leanings, welcomes the seaborne visitor.

APPROACH From the Red Sea is by logical progression along the coast. From the east, Aden is very often the first landfall after the passage from India, Sri Lanka, or the Maldives in which case its high, bald

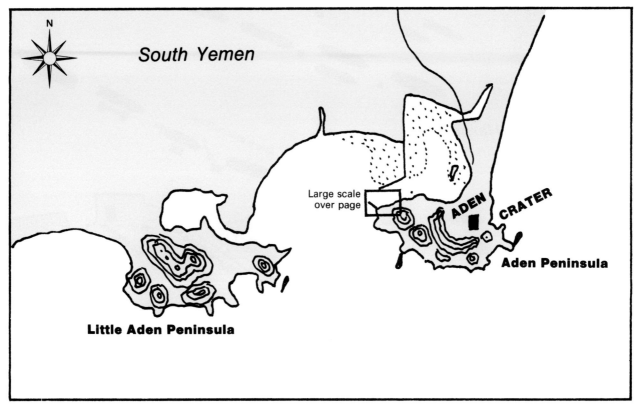

ADEN
The harbour of Aden is tucked under the Aden Peninsula.

and very rugged East Head is appreciated. This appears as an island from a good distance offshore even in dismal, overcast conditions. On final approach the harbour is entered carrying a short breakwater to starboard. Ships will be seen anchored in the bay immediately outside.

ANCHORAGE There is no choice here, all boats being obliged to anchor where shown on the map, near the Customs Wharf. Upon entering the harbour, a port control launch will meet and lead the visiting private boat. This service is brief and friendly.

The holding is good with enough cable laid out and the harbour slop is reduced by the line of ships at fore-and-aft moorings.

FORMALITIES Despite the impoverished appearance of the buildings ashore and the propaganda disseminated by Aden television, the whole world could take a lesson from Aden's formalities. They are efficient, pleasant and demand a minimum of paperwork. All such work is carried out aboard after which visitors are allowed ashore. Passports are taken and exchanged for shore passes which must be shown at the customs gate.

When departing Aden buy a 100 fil duty stamp from the post office before walking out to port control where a form is signed before passports are returned from immigration. Failing to get this stamp could prove the only nuisance in an otherwise smooth operation.

TIDES These occur normally twice a day with a maximum range of a little over one metre.

WEATHER The climate is very comfortable in the December to April northeast monsoon period and on rare occasions good falls of rain can occur at night which further cool the atmosphere.

The southwest monsoon often fails in Aden leaving the area with a stifling climate broken sometimes by violent local thermal-induced winds.

FACILITIES In all probability, a chandler's launch will heave alongside soon after clearing into Aden. These companies appear to be scrupulously honest in their dealings and represent the only way of organising duty-free grog. They cannot compete with the bowser on the customs wharf for fuel prices and admit as much.

Diesel fuel is bowsered on the eastern side of the customs wharf. The price tends to be slightly cheaper than Cyprus and half the price of India.

Petrol must be carted from the nearest service station. It is more than double the price of diesel.

Oil is found at service stations but gearbox oil is not available anywhere.

Paraffin and methylated spirits can prove hard to find. A chandler's advice should be sought.

Gas also proves difficult making it advisable to stock up in advance. It is available, but connectors are not universal.

Water is plentiful and of high quality. It is piped to the customs wharf and is available free of charge.

Engineering facilities match the needs of such an important port but are not available to the private person. This is also true of haul-out and hull repairs. An emergency may, however, be met.

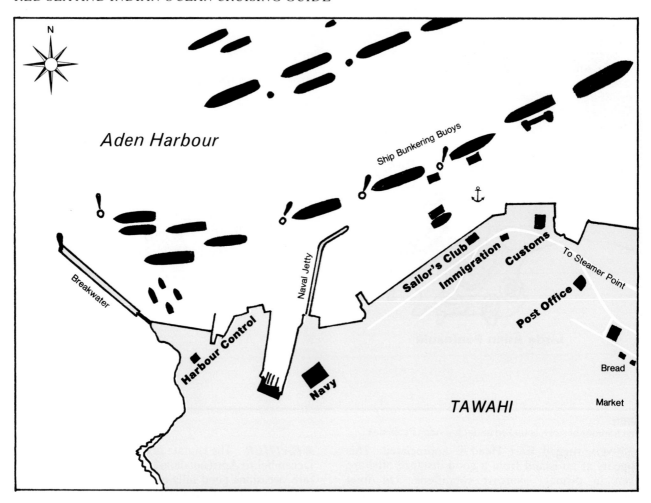

ADEN
The only small boat anchorage within Aden harbour is immediately west of
the customs wharf.

ADEN
Customs Wharf from the anchorage in Aden harbour. The arrow shows the best landing for the dinghy.

Shops are dismal and poorly stocked although one often finds surprises in the form of gift foods from supporting nations at giveaway prices (they should not be sold at all of course!). Nevertheless, victualling along basic lines is definitely possible. The fresh fruit and vegetable market at Steamer Point is poor by any standards and rather expensive. The best day is on Friday. There is a supermarket near the new Aden Hotel.

Communications are outstanding by Middle Eastern standards. Mail should be kept simple using, Post Office, Steamer Point, Aden, as the address and telegrams are cheap and reliable. Worldwide trunk calls can also be made.

Transport is good in the Aden area, a fleet of buses running continuously from the base at Steamer Point near the anchorage to all other local centres. Buy your ticket before boarding and cancel it in a machine on the bus. Taxis are plentiful but expensive.

Eating out is rather poor and expensive unless a local dive is patronised but sidewalk eating is definitely the cheapest and can be rather fun; try the roasted corn. For a cup of coffee or a drink, the top floor lounge of the Rock Hotel is recommended.

Sailor's Club This worthy establishment is on the waterfront next to the anchorage. It is very expensive for both drinks and food but its showers are free.

Commercial hours. Being a Moslem country, Friday is a holiday with most establishments being open every other day. Banks open mornings only whilst shops open morning and evening.

Currency is the dina which is divided into 1000 fils. The English habit of shillings prevails with 20 shillings making one dina. Thus, 50 fils is one shilling.

Aden's banking system is reliable and fast and there is no trouble getting hard currency.

WARNING Cameras are not permitted ashore in Aden and the visiting of other boats requires permission from the customs officer on the wharf. In fact, a blind eye is mostly turned to the practice but do not risk visiting a commercial ship in port as this can lead to a jail term.

CRUISING PERMIT It is sometimes possible to obtain a cruising permit for the coast of South Yemen. Customs and immigration should be approached. Do not cruise the South Yemen coast without explicit, written permission.

ADEN
Snapped illegally by the author before being advised that cameras were not permitted ashore, this shows Steamer Point and the customs wharf, centre.

The Arabian Sea

POSITION

The northwest extreme of the Indian Ocean lying between the Arabian peninsula and the subcontinent of India. Approximate southern boundary, 8° north.

NOTE

In the interest of clarity, this description takes the attitude that the Arabian Sea extends down to the Equator. Thus, the island group of the Maldives is included here and not in the later general description of the Indian Ocean.

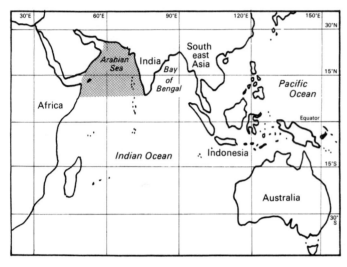

The Arabian Sea spreads between the Arabian peninsula and India and reaches south to the Equator here for simplicity's sake.

GENERAL DESCRIPTION

Most cruising folk recall their Arabian Sea crossing with a degree of affection because it tends to be a quiet stretch of water for most of the year. Only during the thick of the southwest monsoon — specifically June, July and August — are seas somewhat rumbustious and then only for an area a few hundred miles east of Socotra.

During the northeast monsoon, there is virtually no swell of any consequence and the wind rarely tops Force 5, bringing a maximum wave height of around 3 metres with a more general height of 2 metres. When there is swell evident it rarely exceeds 2 metres and is mostly from the ENE until Socotra where it moves slightly south of east.

During the southwest monsoon, when easterly passages are best made from the Gulf of Aden to Sri Lanka and beyond, the winds commonly reach Force 7 and hold at that speed for three days at a time before easing back for a week or so then increasing again. The seas at this time are normal for such winds and cannot be called comfortable. To the east of Socotra, waves tend to stack up and become very uncomfortable but not dangerous to a seaworthy hull handled properly.

Destructive winds occur during the southwest monsoon but are very rare at any time of year in the extreme western side of the sea and are virtually unheard of down the Gulf of Aden. The northeast monsoon months, January, February and March are safe from cyclones. The transitional months, December and April are also generally safe; albeit, there is little useful passage-making wind.

PASSAGE PLANNING

This has been already noted in a general form earlier in this book under the heading 'The Best Routes'. The navigator need only be reminded of the following basics:

Eastabout Use the southwest monsoon's safest period of July, August, September, favouring August which is a totally cyclone-free month. If in the area during the dangerous months of May, June, October and November, stay as close to the Equator as the continuation of useful winds allows. Remember, cyclones do not occur over the Equator at any time of the year.

Because the entire west coast of India is a hot, wet and potentially dangerous lee shore at this time of year, the passage is best planned for Sri Lanka or beyond to Singapore. Alternatively, the Maldives make a pleasant destination although lacking in secure anchorages for a time of year that could bring severe winds.

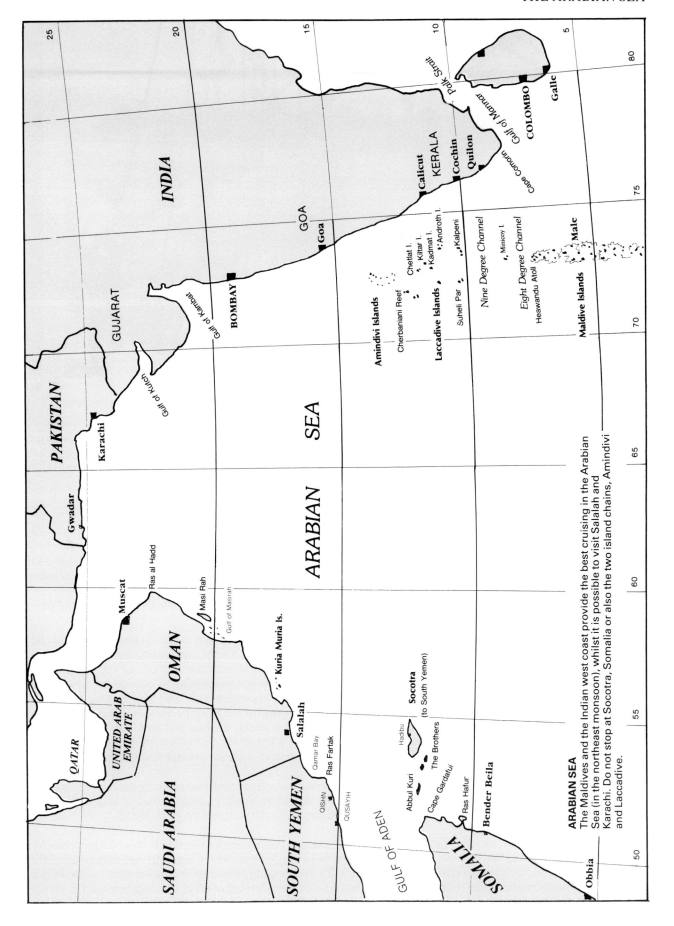

ARABIAN SEA
The Maldives and the Indian west coast provide the best cruising in the Arabian Sea (in the northeast monsoon), whilst it is possible to visit Salalah and Karachi. Do not stop at Socotra, Somalia or also the two island chains, Amindivi and Laccadive.

ARABIAN SEA
Of the many countries around the Arabian Sea, India is the most cruisable with sights like this fishing net awaiting the visitor.
Note the crude but effective use of stones as a constantly increasing or decreasing counter-weight system.

Westabout The months of January, February and March are unbeatable because of the dry northeast monsoon wind and the total freedom from destructive tropical cyclones. This is the logical time to visit the Maldive Islands and to cruise the west coast of India at which time it is in a windshadow offering a benign onshore-offshore wind pattern.

CRUISING AREAS

The best cruising area in the Arabian Sea for those who delight in reefs and coral cays is the Maldives, and for those who thrill to incredible new sights, the west coast of India. Both have their problems, of course, as noted later under their own descriptions, but at least both are politically welcoming.

The following is a roundup of countries around or in the Arabian Sea starting from the Gulf of Aden and moving clockwise.

OMAN   This is a wealthy, independent sultanate occupying the eastern extreme of the Arabian peninsula end-to-end between the country of South Yemen and the Gulf of Oman which is the entrance to the oil-rich Gulf.

With a population of less than one million and the capital town of Muscat the only one of any significance, Oman practices a gentle form of Islam which is neither belligerent nor welcoming to outside influence. As a result, tourists are not admitted but right to enter port is granted to private craft. The best port by far to exercise this right is at Bandat Rayzut which is a new and modern port for the town of Salalah, 7 miles distant.

A night curfew may be imposed on visitors here but English is widely spoken and hundreds of English soldiers are based in the area. Many have resigned their commission to join the Sultan's army at much higher pay.

In the rather charming town of Salalah there is a modern American-style supermarket where most processed items will be found as well as a market.

Generally speaking, the country in this area is green and productive and there is a temptation to coast hop along its length. This, regrettably, is not possible owing to the Sultan's policy towards tourism and the fact that guerilla skirmishes still occur in various parts of the country and safety cannot be guaranteed.

PAKISTAN   With Iran to its west, India to its east and besieged Afghanistan to its north, this Moslem country has a coastline of about 500 miles in the northern extreme of the Arabian Sea. Originally one of two successor states to British India, it received independence in 1947 and now comprises only the western part of those two states. This and complex tribal tensions has been the cause of considerable conflict which culminated in a coup in which the army chief of staff, General Mohammad Zia ul-Haq ousted the civilian government of Zulfikar Ali Bhutto (who was executed) to establish a type of dictatorship. Right or wrong, the country seems to be enjoying stability for the time being.

Like so many Islamic republics, cultural purity is pursued by religious teachings which even pervade the banking system, a fact that might prove economically suicidal if overseas investors see it as an eventual seizing of funds. Meanwhile, cultural purging denies me the ability to say whether the coast of Pakistan can be cruised or not, but its capital, Karachi, is often visited by European yachtsmen who give it a high rating on friendliness.

INDIA, SOUTHWEST COAST Although ports may be hundreds of miles apart, the west coast of India is well worth the effort of cruising if only to enjoy the remarkable cultural contrasts and to experience the friendliness of the people. Also, the cost of living is very low, allowing the visitor to take a financial breather whilst continuing to cruise.

Seasons The only time of year to seriously consider cruising India's west coast is during the northeast monsoon. This is at its best during the months of January, February and March with the transitional months of December and April often proving suitable also.

During the northeast monsoon the weather is dry and sunny and for a one hundred mile wide band along the coast a windshadow occurs for most of the time. As a result the sea is mostly calm with just a modicum of swell and the winds tend to be offshore at night and onshore during the afternoon; the mornings are mostly totally calm. Because of the wind-shadow effect, it is possible to anchor off the coast without seeking shelter of any kind, for although the afternoon breeze might prove uncomfortable for an hour or two in the evening, its rapid replacement by an offshore wind makes for tolerable conditions. In most areas it is possible to move into two or three fathoms of good holding mud or sand along the coast.

To identify the coastal breezes more accurately, the offshore wind during the night commonly favours the southeast quarter whilst the afternoon onshore breeze often follows the coast from the northwest. Rarely does either wind bring a sea with it of any consequence.

Currents The northeast monsoon should produce a south setting current along the coast of about one knot. In fact this current is often absent or flows at about half that rate and rarely presses hard against the coast. Close in, there is a countercurrent setting north along the coast at rates of up to one knot and this can, under certain circumstances, produce an initially uncomfortable windward-tide situation when anchoring off the coast in the evening.

The Coast The foreshore tends to be one of long beaches capped in coconut palms and dense scrub with evidence of large villages at regular intervals. In the background is a ridge of mountains which are often hazy owing to the countless cooking fires; it should be remembered that many of India's three quarters of a billion people live at subsistence level without electric or gas stoves and the situation is not unlike that of London before private coal fires gave way to cleaner fuels and ended her famous smogs.

Temperatures These are similar in every way to those given in the section 'Cochin' later in this book.

Fishermen Owing to the absence of reefs along the coast, navigation at night is possible but not recommended because of the huge fleets of fishermen spreading from close inshore to as far as twenty miles offshore. The thickest band tends to be around three to ten miles off.

Fishermen use a great variety of craft from one man sailing dugout canoes to outboard powered stitch-planked canoes measuring fully fifty feet and also, the more modern diesel trawler will be seen. Very few carry lights and as a result the quality of lookout aboard the cruising vessel must be high indeed. Collisions are not uncommon.

Ports of call It is beyond the scope of this book to describe all ports in detail and only Cochin harbour is dealt with thus because of its relatively good position for those passing through without actually cruising the coast. It is also an ideal alternative to Sri Lanka should the latter's port dues prove excessively high. Cochin will be found at the end of this section.

Generally speaking, Bombay and Goa will prove the most interesting alternatives, and advice regarding other ports can be gained from the cruising fleet as you go. Bombay has a fine Royal Yacht Club with a rather nasty anchorage whilst Goa tends to be the visitor's favourite being very cheap (even by Indian standards) and with an obvious Portuguese hangover which is very attractive culturally.

Formalities Noted in detail in the description of Cochin harbour, formalities are excessive in terms of paperwork but are mostly relaxed and dealings should be conducted with patience. As a general rule Indian officials are courteous and helpful but do insist on the same madness in every port.

Visas are not necessary for most friendly nations although at the time of going to press it is unknown whether American citizens continue to require advance visas. Regardless, most visiting yachtsmen are granted a landing pass anyway which restricts one to a certain area. However, many a visitor has toured India on such a pass without raising any eyebrows.

LAKSHADWEEP ISLANDS   Comprising the two groups, Amindivi and Laccadive Islands, these low, coral cays and reefs lie 200 miles off the extreme southwest coast of India. It is said that Russia has a missile base on one of the islands, but this is shrouded in mystery.

Also shrouded in mystery is whether or not the visiting boat may cruise the area. Many officials questioned personally by the author suggested that there is no problem but permits are never forthcoming when applied for. I know of no one who has ever received permission at higher official level.

Under the circumstances the yachtsman is warned away from these islands. However, the uninhabited cay of Suheli Par offers fair anchorage between its two cays and might be used should anchorage be necessary during passage across the Arabian Sea. I emphasise that this is not permitted at official level and the yachtsman would need good reason for stopping there if discovered.

MALDIVE ISLANDS   This group enjoys a full description after this section as does the Indian port of Cochin and the Sri Lankan port of Galle.

SOCOTRA   This island lies off the northeast tip of Somalia and is owned by South Yemen. Having no useful port and being peopled by a mixture of folk who tend to make their own rules regardless of their government's policy, the visiting yachtsman is warned away. Vessels have been grappled and towed into shore for looting in the past. Under no circumstances find yourself becalmed close in without means of steaming offshore.

SOMALIA   Completing our clockwise tour of the Arabian Sea, Somalia is another country in political upheaval and should be avoided. It is safe, however, to pass between Somalia and Socotra as long as there is no likelihood of being helpless in the area.

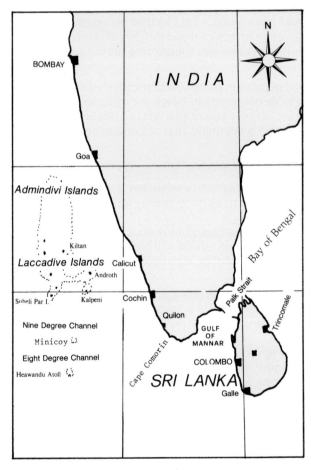

INDIA SOUTH COAST
The southwest coast of India offers a number of interesting ports including Bombay, Goa and Cochin.

COCHIN (India)

POSITION 9°58′N 76°15′E.   400 miles from Galle, Sri Lanka and 670 miles south of Bombay on the southwest coast.

GENERAL DESCRIPTION   Cochin is the commercial port for the Indian state of Kerala and is one of the major ports for the entire country. But despite the constant movement of ships and areas of heavy industry, the harbour also provides a non-commercial atmosphere for the visiting yachtsman eager to see at least a part of India. In fact, such is the natural security of the anchorage here and the facilities, that Cochin is seriously recommended as an alternative to Galle, Sri Lanka, should the latter's port dues prove too much of a financial burden.

Being the outlet to a system of shallow coastal lakes, the country surrounding Cochin harbour is low and featureless. It is occasionally inundated during the southwest monsoon season although this problem has largely been solved by reclamation works in and around the harbour.

Cochin, or Fort Cochin, is the name of the town on the harbour's southern headland. In fact, the major city area is called Ernakulam and the anchorage, recommended later, lies closer to Ernakulam than to Cochin. The whole area is clean and apparently prosperous and the inhabitants are, in the main, gentle and friendly.

APPROACH   During the December to April northeast monsoon, when the west coast of India tends to be dominantly calm, the position of Cochin is well advertised by the presence of many large ships lying at anchor offshore awaiting wharf space inside the harbour. These lie to the immediate north of the channel approach line.

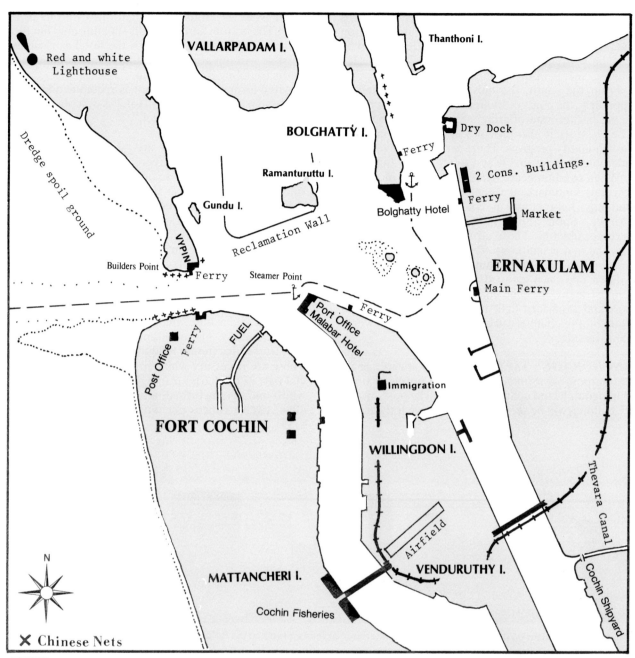

Red and white Lighthouse

VALLARPADAM I.

Thanthoni I.

Dredge spoil ground

BOLGHATTY I.

Dry Dock

Ferry

Ramanturuttu I.

2 Cons. Buildings.

Gundu I.

Ferry

Market

Bolghatty Hotel

VYPIN

ERNAKULAM

Builders Point

Reclamation Wall

Main Ferry

Ferry

Steamer Point

Ferry

Port Office
Malabar Hotel

Post Office

Ferry

FUEL

Immigration

FORT COCHIN

WILLINGDON I.

Airfield

Thevara Canal

Cochin Shipyard

MATTANCHERI I.

VENDURUTHY I.

Cochin Fisheries

N

✕ **Chinese Nets**

COCHIN
The best anchorage for private vessels in Cochin is where shown off the Bolghatty Hotel. Formalities must be carried out at Steamer Point first.

The Malabar Hotel as seen from the obligatory first anchorage in Cochin harbour. There is a jetty nearby on which the visitor can be served tea or hard drinks but landing is not permitted before clearing customs.

83

During heavy southwest monsoonal weather ships will remain at sea eliminating this valuable location aid. Under these circumstances navigation should be spot-on so that one is not obliged to claw off a lee shore in search of the harbour.

From the south, the most common direction of approach, the coast of India rises to mountain ridges in the background offering a few useful landmarks. The coast itself also provides enough landmarks to easily identify progress. There can be, however, considerable haze, probably as a result of cooking fires.

When conditions are hazy, the first and most conspicuous landmark at Cochin is a large six storied building, light stone in colour and sprawling in attitude. Soon after, the lighthouse to its north becomes obvious. Those using old charts are warned that the major lighthouse for Cochin now stands on the *north* shore, not the south shore.

Final approach up to the harbour is made via a long, straight, dredged channel which is marked by port and starboard light buoys. According to your draught, this channel can be entered from somewhere along its side.

ANCHORAGE The first obligatory anchorage for the purpose of formalities is off the northern tip of Willingdon Island at Steamer Point. The port authority building will be seen here with its own jetty as well

as the Malabar Hotel to its right, also with its own jetty. The bottom here is rapidly shoaling mud but the visitor should move in towards the hotel as close as possible without going aground to avoid commercial traffic rounding Steamer Point.

After formalities the visitor is recommended the anchorage off the Bolghatty Hotel as described under the heading 'Bolghatty Hotel.'

FORMALITIES These are straightforward but rather formidable. However, officials are pleasant enough and are obliged to operate according to their rules and regulations so the visitor should exercise patience and it pays to make up a list of all removable items on the boat. This list should include all electronic gadgetry, stove, musical instruments and so forth. Leave nothing out, for India is anxious to prevent the sale of such luxury items on the street.

Upon anchoring off the Malabar Hotel port trust area, customs will board (do not go ashore until boarded) from a launch to check against items that might be sold ashore, then allow the skipper ashore. The skipper, or his representative, should go to the port trust office (hours 1000 to 1700) to pay port dues. These are necessary whilst in the dredged, commercial part of the harbour in which, of course, you are whilst undergoing formalities. Port dues cost, in early 1984, twelve rupees per day which was then about US$1.20.

The city of Ernakulam on the eastern side of Cochin harbour as seen en route to the Bolghatty Hotel anchorage.

Cochin ferries are narrow and ancient but provide an excellent service to all parts of the harbour.

Dating back to the Kubla Khan period, these lift nets line both sides of the entrance to Cochin harbour as well as certain upharbour parts of the shoreline. A similar system of netting is used in Italy.

Having secured a receipt for payment of port dues, now go diagonally across the road to the customs building where no less than eight forms will require your attention including a letter that you must write to the fellow announcing and explaining the attached forms!

From customs, now go to immigration down near the Willingdon Island railway terminus for the issuing of a restricted shore pass. Passports are not surrendered here and the shore pass obliges you to remain within four miles of Cochin. In fact, many a visitor has toured India on such a pass without question.

India is paperbound at government level like so many ex-English colonies. However, it is heartening to know that a local lawyer-boating enthusiast was anxious to start a yacht club in Cochin. He is aware that formalities might frighten away the visitor so had started action to have private boat formalities simplified so the serious user of this book may, or may not, enjoy the fruits of his labour.

BOLGHATTY HOTEL Having cleared customs and immigration, and having paid for the inevitable fact that you must pass through a dredged part of the harbour, the visitor is recommended the free anchorage off the Bolghatty Hotel. This will be found at the southern end of Bolghatty Island after negotiating the shallow channel which approaches from the south-southeast as indicated by the dotted line on the accompanying plan.

The bottom is outstanding holding being sticky mud and the only problem may be in windward-tide activity if anchored too close to another vessel. Usually there is plenty of space unless determined to be as close to the hotel jetty as possible.

When anchoring in this area be sure to leave a channel between Bolghatty Island and anchored craft for the large sailing-poled cargo canoes which work along here.

TIDES Occuring twice daily, the range is very low at around 0.6 metres maximum. Currents in the harbour easily attain a speed of two knots during the ebb but tend to maximise at one knot at the Bolghatty anchorage.

WEATHER This has been covered under the relevant heading in the previous section but to recap briefly and to make local notes: the dry northeast monsoon occurs from December to April, inclusive, with peak sailing months being January, February, March. The wet southwest season fills the remainder of the year and can bring typhoons, more particularly towards the end of its season.

The Bolghatty anchorage would be highly suitable in a typhoon season layover in terms of protection, but I have no reason to doubt that problems could be caused by freshwater runoff during excessive rains and onshore winds.

In the prime visiting time of December to April the nights in Cochin are mostly calm with only an occasional offshore breeze followed by calm mornings with an afternoon seabreeze. This afternoon breeze is not felt at anchor because of the total protection offered by the hotel and its surrounding trees and as a result there is little daytime relief from the heat.

Temperatures in Cochin are as follows: southwest monsoon, 35°C maximum, 22.5°C minimum; northeast monsoon, 32°C maximum, 20°C minimum. Most rain falls from June to October with an annual average of 254 cms.

FACILITIES Despite Cochin having a very large and industrious shipbuilding yard the private boat owner should not presume that boat hardware, as he knows it, is available. There is no trouble finding shackles, chain, paint and rope, but anything of a more specialised nature would have to be imported and I recommend that the Indian parcel mail is *not* tested to this extent. Otherwise, facilities in Cochin are fairly well represented, as shown here.

Fuel Petrol is available from any of the many service stations and cost slightly under US$3 per imperial gallon in early 1984. Diesel fuel is bowsered on the quay at Fort Cochin under the sign *Indianoil* and cost slightly over US$2 per gallon. Illicit diesel is apparently available at half that price but details were not discovered by the author.

Paraffin is available in one litre lots only from hardware shops, bulk being impossible to obtain without a licence from the courthouse. Inquire at customs, but better still, avoid needing kerosene in bulk.

Methylated Spirits is of good quality and no trouble finding it at a hardware store near Ernakulam market.

Gas I regret that the full story was not researched. However, gas is definitely available in Cochin but there is nearly always trouble connecting up with foreign bottles.

Water There is the usual paranoia amongst Westerners about hygiene but those who have used local water report no troubles. This could very much depend on the season so the visitor is cautioned to boil drinking water. There is a tap outside the staff toilet and shower at the Bolghatty Hotel. Seek permission from the manager.

Hauling out is possible in Cochin but the yards are not geared for the modern yacht. The slipway at Vypin, opposite Fort Cochin, is said to have successfully hauled out two yachts in its time but I understand there were a few problems. It is best to avoid hauling out here unless the small dry dock, north from the Bolghatty anchorage, can be afforded. The manager seems to have a rather inflated idea of its worth but his price might be negotiable.

Rubbish There is nowhere to deposit rubbish. I regret that the local habit of using the harbour itself as a dump cannot be avoided.

Fresh food in the form of a wonderful range of excellent quality fruit and vegetables, meat, chicken and fish, will be found at the Ernakulam market on the banks of an old Dutch canal. This can offer a way of bulk cartage should victualling prove too tiresome by taxi and ferry. The dinghy could be easily taken up the canal.

Chickens are guaranteed fresh, birds being weighed live and then killed before your very eyes!

Processed food will be found in abundance but lacking the appeal of cheap pricing. Certain locally produced tinned food is excellent value but, in the main, western prices and range will not be matched. The shopping centre around the market area is excellent and a few shops along MG Road are outstanding.

Drinks both soft and alcoholic are produced in India with softdrinks being of good quality and low price. The Indian beer is excellent as are a few spirits, grog shops being dotted around the town. A range of pure fruit drinks is worth buying and if thirsty whilst shopping try a fresh lime soda from a sidewalk stall — superb and unbelievably cheap.

A cargo canoe sails up Cochin harbour. They are poled or towed to windward.

COCHIN
One of the many huge cargo canoes of Cochin is poled through shallows.

Transport There are many systems in and around Cochin. The railway services the area but does not offer transport in the local sense. This leaves buses and taxis ashore and ferries and rowboats on the harbour.

Harbour ferries run frequently to all major points and are cheap, if overcrowded. Rowboats are available as a sort of short distance watertaxi service although some folk have hired them for tours of the whole harbour.

There are two types of taxis; the Indian built Ambassador four wheeled car or the three wheeled tritaxi. The latter has obvious capacity and speed limitations but costs one third of the former making it ideal for the average person returning from a shopping spree. Thirty cents seems to take you anywhere.

There is an airport at Cochin with regular flights to Bombay and other major centres.

Engineering can be done at various small shops in the area and as well there are casting facilities. Many engineering bits and pieces will be found by searching, with many shops apparently specialising in just one field. For example, a shop may sell only 'V' belt pulleys, another only brass and aluminium sections and so on. I suspect the yachtsman will find everything he wants with a little perseverance and a lot of legwork.

Brass and stainless steel ornaments and containers are locally made and sold in a number of shops near the market. They offer a spectacular sight as well as high quality goods.

Communications are excellent from Cochin, but there can be a problem booking a long-distance call owing to the language barrier. Telegrams are no trouble and mail seems to flow well enough although the dispatching and receiving of a parcel is an experience we can all do without. Try not to use this function whilst in India.

The best address in Cochin is: Poste Restante, Head Post Office, Fort Cochin, Kerala, India. Those wanting mail closer to the recommended anchorage could use: Post Office, Ernakulam etc.

Prawns and fresh fish are often offered by harbour fishermen at very reasonable prices from their dug-out canoes. There appears to be no basis for fear of theft from these men who will often be heard chanting and banging the side of the canoe to chase fish into their nets.

Eating out in India is very reasonable with a vast array of eating places. It is hard to beat an Indian snack and a glass of fruit juice from one of the coffee houses and the top quality food from the most hygienic of kitchens; try the Mughal Durbar on the front at Ernakulam, being a moslem restaurant no alcohol is served but this is more than compensated for by their excellent fresh squeezed fruit juices. A meal of juice, fried rice, garlic prawns, soup and sweets cost in early 1984 US$2.50.

Watchmen are not absolutely necessary when the boat is left unattended, theft being rare, however, those found offering their services at the Bolghatty Hotel can be trusted and they should charge about US$1.50 per day or night.

Labour can be hired for around US$3 per day for a good tradesman boatbuilder. Repairs and even a complete refit can be effected through the dry-dock manager.

Banks and currency There are dozens of banks in and around Cochin as well as a few money changers along MG Road. Service is generally good with no delay on telex transfers. Hard currency is not easily bought and it is best to take in either traveller's cheques or US cash.

The Indian currency is the rupee which is one hundred paise. The exchange rate hovers around 14 rupees to one American dollar.

Local currency is issued in 2, 5, 10, 20, 50, 100 and 1000 rupee notes whilst coins of 10, 25, 50 and 100 paise are available.

Mosquitoes And now the bad news. Mosquitoes represent the only real qualification when advising a person to visit Cochin. They are mostly absent during the days and nights but can be bad at dawn and dusk. Their intensity varies for I understand that whole weeks can go by without a single insect being sighted.

Cigars An unusual heading in any of my cruising books, this is included here to advise that king-size Havana cigars are available in Fort Cochin, near the post office, for around fifteen cents each. The same product costs two and three dollars in other countries with one Belgian tourist telling me that they cost six dollars in his country. I'm not sure why there is such a dramatic difference but it could be part of a special deal from Cuba.

SIGHTSEEING The Bolghatty Hotel, set on its fifteen acres of lawns and trees on Bolghatty Island is, in itself, a sight, being originally built as a palace by the Dutch in 1744. It later became the seat of the British resident.

Mattancherry Palace This historic building is maintained by the government and is open for public viewing between 0830 and 1230 hours and again between 1400 and 1700 hours every day. Built by the Portuguese, it was presented to the Cochin Rajah in 1555 who used it for coronations and other functions. In 1663 the Dutch, replacing the Portuguese as the colonial power, carried out extensions and repairs and it has consequently become known as a Dutch Palace. There are many interesting relics and murals to be viewed within.

Chinese fishing nets Believed to have been introduced by the Chinese as far back as Kubla Khan's period, these cantilevered nets can be seen in operation along each side of the harbour entrance as well as upstream from the Bolghatty Hotel anchorage. If used at night, the light fitted to attract fish makes an attractive sight.

Synagogue This reminder that there are Jewish Indians was built in 1568 and is situated close to Mattancherry Palace at Mattancherry. Open between 1000 and 1200 hours and again between 1400 and 1700 hours daily except Saturdays and Jewish holidays, the Great Scrolls of the Old Testament and the grants of privilege recorded by Cochin rulers on copper plate are of great interest.

St Francis Church Fort Cochin, was built by the Portuguese in 1510 and is believed to be the first church built in India by Europeans. Vasco da Gama, the first European to reach India (via Africa), died in Cochin in 1524 and was entombed here. His remains have since been returned to Portugal.

Cochin Museum, Durbar Hall, Ernakulam, is low key but worth a visit having paintings, coins, sculptures and a collection from the old Cochin royal family.

Dutch canals will be found everywhere around the Cochin area which are not especially interesting in themselves but are a reminder of the Dutch influence.

SOUVENIR BUYING There will be found wonderful tourist shops with everything from Burmese knives to some of the finest carpets to be found outside of Persia (Iran). Some of the wood carvings are nothing short of spectacular whilst the glorious silk carpets are

COCHIN
The New Zealand yacht *Mainstay,* left, and the author's yacht *Tientos* lie serenely off the Bolghatty Hotel, Cochin.

COCHIN
Part of the market area of the city of Ernakulam, Cochin.

so reasonably priced that quite a few visitors buy them to resell later. Most companies dealing in these wares will pack and ship to any address provided and their service has proven very reliable and honest.

Some of the best shops will be found on Willingdon Island near the Malabar Hotel and close to the immigration office.

THE MALDIVES (No large-scale plan)

POSITION Scattered along longitude 73° east and between the Equator and nearly 8° north.

GENERAL DESCRIPTION With a population of 160,000 the Maldives form Asia's smallest country and probably the only one not having known colonisation, although it was a British protectorate from 1887 to 1965. For this reason English is widely spoken although the local language is closer to Sinhalese (Sri Lanka). The religion is Islam and certain parts of the island group are out of bounds on religious grounds to visiting boats. The attitude here waxes and wanes but the yachtsman must not stop anywhere before being properly cleared in nor after proper clearance out. The only port is Male which is on the eastern side a little north of midway along the chain.

The chain of islands consists only of low coral cays, there being no continental types at all. For this reason a landfall on the area can be critical with land not being sighted until about 10 miles distant.

With the advent of tourism in the early 1970s and the building of many fine hotels around the Male atoll, the country's economy moved from one based entirely on fishing and trading to one dominated by the tourist dollar, and I mean *dollar*, the US dollar being the only currency accepted at all resorts.

A very beautiful area for its dozens of atolls, sparkling clear sea, fine white beaches and excellent

fishing; there can be an anchorage problem when entering and leaving at Male, the water immediately off the reef being 140 feet with no shelving. The small-boat harbour in the reef is not available to yachts.

FORMALITIES No visas are required but the visiting boat must report to Male before exploring elsewhere. This is the only clearance port and, as stated, can prove harrowing during strong winds owing to the depth of water.

CURRENCY The Maldivian rupee is closely tied to the Indian rupee in relative value to the US dollar. It is divided into 100 larees.

APPROACH The group is low on the horizon and is rarely seen much before 10 miles off in fair weather. Being scarcely more than 8 feet high, with the additional height of a fully grown coconut palm. Because Male is the only entry port, there is no alternative to planning a landfall here.

WEATHER Trade winds cannot be expected as the islands are mostly in the calm area of the equatorial belt. Often the southern hemisphere's southeasterly reaches the Maldives whilst the northern hemisphere's northeasterly does likewise and in between there are variables and calms. However, in trying to establish a pattern it must be said that the climate conforms mostly to Arabian Sea behaviour and as a result knows southwesterlies and rain from May to October and northeasterlies from November to December. In either season a vessel should carry fuel enough for the calms.

FACILITIES Water wells are scattered throughout some of the islets and it is available at the only town, Male. Fuel and food can also be purchased here but prices are high because everything except a few tropical fruits, vegetables and fish is imported. Try to stock up in other areas and only top up here.

GALLE (Sri Lanka)

POSITION 06°01′N 80°13′E Off the southeast coast of India between the Arabian Sea and the Bay of Bengal.

GENERAL DESCRIPTION Sri Lanka is like a teardrop running down the cheek of India and is almost attched to that subcontinent by an umbilical cord of shoals which carry only two or three fathoms of water over them.This is known as Adams Bridge but of course is a bridge only in legend and not in fact.

Measuring approximately 450 kilometres long by 240 kilometres wide and occupying 65,610 square kilometres, its southern two thirds are mountainous whilst its northern section levels off to plains country. This is the so-called Tamil area where about 20 per cent of Sri Lanka's total population of about 15 million people live.

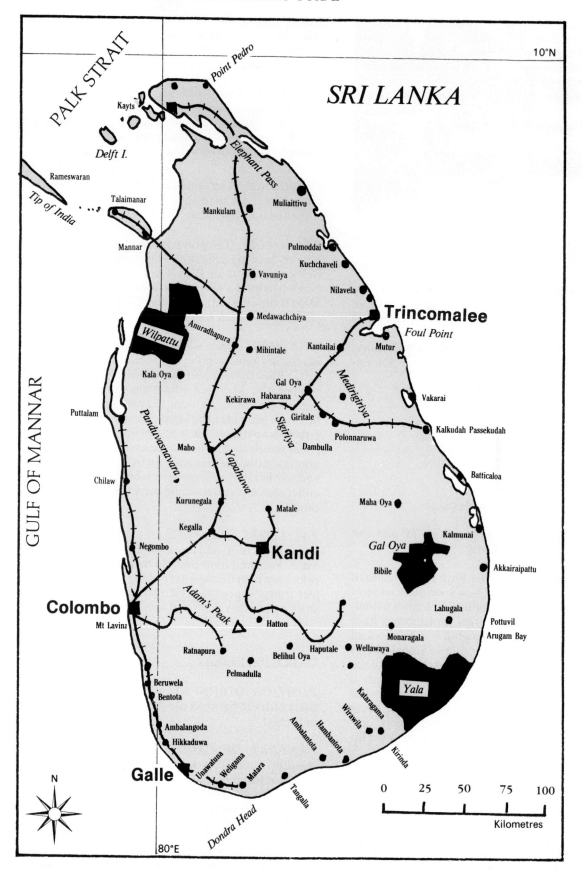

SRI LANKA
Densely populated with magnificent hinterlands, Sri Lanka is well recommended. Galle is the best port of call.

The mountains of Sri Lanka rise to as high as 2524 metres (Mount Piduratalagala) creating a region of towering peaks and splendid gorges; waterfalls tumble in thin streams from lofty clefts to gurgle down narrow, deep valleys into crystal clear and cool creeks. Slopes are planted in rich green tea and everywhere are dotted villages and plantation mansions of imposing proportions reminding us that this was once a wealthy British outpost.

Good beaches surround much of the island and the water is clean and clear. All arterial roads are sealed and a railway services all major centres and has some very pretty branch lines wandering into the mountains.

For reasons which will become apparent, Galle harbour is recommended to all cruising people and will be found on the southwest corner some 110 kilometres south from the country's capital, Colombo.

Not far to the east of Galle is this huge sitting Bhudda which can be climbed to the top of the head. Bhuddism is the main religion of Sri Lanka.

APPROACH   Because all vessels sailing between the Red Sea and Singapore are obliged to pass under Sri Lanka, Galle harbour is centrally placed making any diversion into its protection inconsequential in terms of extra miles travelled. It is also in a reef-free area allowing vessels to make up to the coast in safety. The following are typical approach paths.

From India and the Arabian Sea During the southwest monsoon, those approaching direct from the Arabian Sea after passage across from the Red Sea or Aden will come upon a coast largely smothered in rain cloud, this being the wet season for the west coast of Sri Lanka. Sights should be grouped up more regularly as the destination becomes closer and whilst clear days permit them prior to landfall.

Those coming from the Indian mainland depart from Cape Comorin and steer in a southeasterly direction for Galle. A landfall should not prove troublesome as the distance is only 250 miles across the Gulf of Mannar. Beware, however, the canalising effect of the Gulf of Mannar which can increase wind speed considerably and deflect it from its normal direction.

From the Maldive Islands This is a common approach for those private and charter vessels going to port for victuals. Because the Maldives tend to be in a calm area, it is not uncommon to find light winds and sometimes calms prevailing for much of the passage except during the thick of the southwest monsoon. A direct course from Male to Galle is recommended.

From Singapore Logically, the December to March northeast monsoon will be used for this east to west crossing. Winds can be expected to be boisterous as the Sri Lankan coast is closed and some rain may be encountered close in as this is the wet season for the east coast of Sri Lanka.

Because most yachtsmen making this trek are anxious to enter the Red Sea before March, Galle should be visited as early as the season allows and Christmas in Galle is recommended.

From Cocos (Keeling) Islands The following advice applies to any vessel approaching from the south Indian Ocean by way of Cocos Islands, Sunda Strait or Christmas Island.

The southeast trade wind of the southern winter should survive at a useful strength until late November and possibly into late December. It is therefore recommended that a vessel leave any of the above noted places no later than early November. In this way a fair wind is assured at least as far as the Equator and from the Equator to Galle the navigator must presume the wind will be either variable or non-existent with occasional thunderstorms likely from any direction.

An Equatorial Counter Current running east across the Equator should be allowed for but it was reported by many skippers in 1982 to be non-existent. It may therefore be possible to sail direct rather than 'beyond the current' in a curving track.

Final approach to Galle harbour Regardless of the direction from which the visitor comes, the final approach is identical and a simple matter of following the chart so that shoals hard in against the land will be easily avoided.

A conspicuous lighthouse and mosque, and soon after a fort wall, will be seen whilst offshore a bell buoy will be found. From this bell buoy into the inner breakwater harbour the buoyed channel should be followed but many buoys were not in

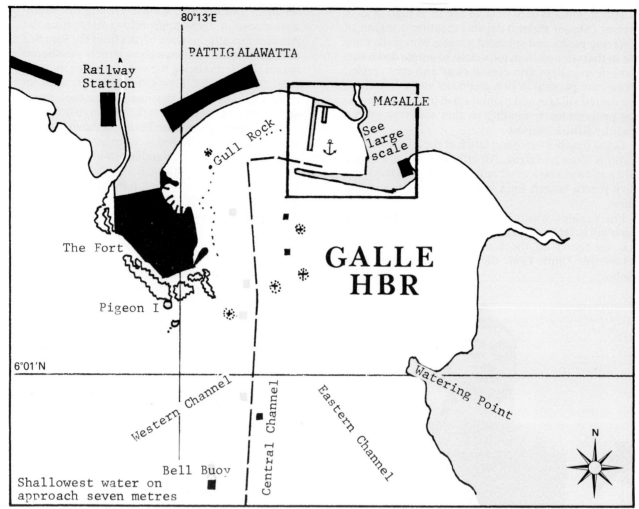

GALLE APPROACH

Galle harbour is a natural bay on the southwest tip of Sri Lanka. It is entered by a number of channels, the best being Central Channel via a large offshore bell buoy.

Taken from the seaward corner of Fort Galle, the mosque and lighthouse are seen left whilst the main entrance channel into Galle Harbour is indicated by a long arrow. The small arrows point to port and starboard channel buoys.

place during my survey. The chart and a little common sense will find the best water which is generally deep right across the mouth of the bay constituting the natural part of Galle harbour. The inner breakwater harbour offers no difficulties in approach and entering.

NAVIGATION AIDS The major lighthouse on Point Utrecht. Galle harbour's western bastion, is painted plain white and is manned but being electric it suffers from town power failure occasionally and is rather weak at the best of times. It is, however, conspicuous enough when singled out from the background.

The inner harbour should carry a red light at the end of the northern breakwater and a green light at the end of the southern breakwater. Beware of the possibility of a dredging light being left in place on the southern breakwater.

The leading beacons over the market area are down and many buoys are missing as stated earlier, those buoys still in place showing red to port and black or green to starboard. Most display a weak light: red to port and white or green to starboard.

ANCHORAGE Towards the northeast corner of the bay known as Galle harbour is an inner harbour protected by two breakwaters, one projecting south, the other west. Contained within are commercial shipping wharves, warehouses, fisheries and boatyards as well as buoys for use by private vessels which are obliged to use this harbour.

Anchorage is possible where space permits but the visiting vessel is best laid fore and aft between drum buoys or between anchor and buoy depending on congestion. It is advisable to maintain an east-west line when mooring so that the vessel does not roll during excessive swell.

A swell of up to one metre high enters the harbour during well-developed monsoons regardless of direction and despite the fact that the wind may not be felt in the immediate area. This is typical of the northeast monsoon whilst the southwest monsoon is mostly evident as a wind in the harbour. This swell is not constant and as long as the vessel is not beam on it is surprisingly comfortable.

Berthing alongside is not permissible unless taking on fuel or water at Ceylon Fisheries.

One of over twenty visiting yachts, the author's vessel *Tientos* lies fore and aft to buoys in Galle harbour. The obligatory port dues and agents include the cost of mooring.

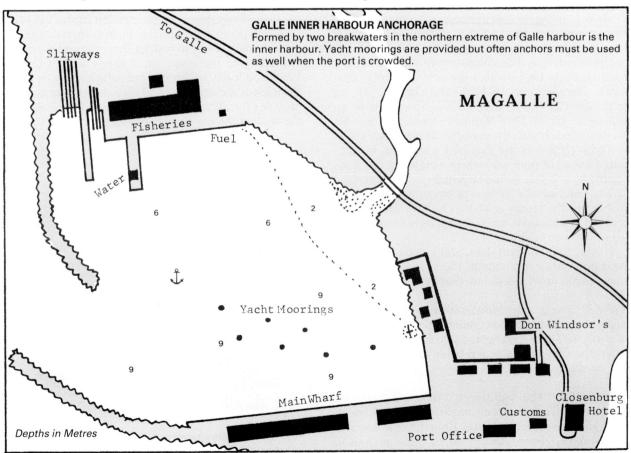

GALLE INNER HARBOUR ANCHORAGE
Formed by two breakwaters in the northern extreme of Galle harbour is the inner harbour. Yacht moorings are provided but often anchors must be used as well when the port is crowded.

PORT DUES AND AGENTS' FEES The Sri Lankan government, in all its misguided wisdom, convinced that all cruising yachtsmen are both drug runners and wealthy, introduced Section 37, Act 51 in 1979 which obliges all private boats to pay port dues amounting to 1000 rupees per month. The same amount is also applicable for any part thereof and furthermore, it must be paid in US dollars cash. This amounts to $66 per month.

The visitor is also obliged to hire a shipping agent costing as much as US$200 more unless the right agent is chosen. And herein lies another reason for choosing Galle as the best harbour in Sri Lanka; it has the best agent.

Local gem dealer and entrepreneur, Don Windsor, established himself as a yacht agent. He charges US$50 for the first month and half that per month thereafter and included in the price is the use of his home as a place to shower, buy a drink or meal and organise trips inland. Don's daughter also hires bicycles whilst his son can find the best place in town for mechanical repairs.

Considering the advantages of Galle it is difficult to find reason for going elsewhere. However, for those wishing to formalise their entry in Sri Lanka elsewhere, the following ports are legally recognised: Colombo, Trincomalee, Jaffna and Kanesanthurai.

It should be emphasised here that there are no circumstances under which a yacht might stop at Sri Lanka without paying the above fees. Those without the wherewithal will find Cochin an ideal alternative.

FORMALITIES These can be rather sluggish in Galle depending on how persuasive the agent can be. Most people are cleared within an hour whilst others have been kept waiting for two days.

Upon entering it is obligatory to remain aboard until cleared. This involves the port authority, customs, immigration (police) and health. If an unreasonable wait is involved it is acceptable to go ashore as far as Don Windsor's house to use his facilities and, hopefully, expedite formalities.

Three crew lists are required which can be prepared ahead of time, and where a crew intends leaving the vessel, this should be noted.

The granting of *practique* seems to be a mere formality but the visitor is advised to have cholera and typhoid inoculations up to date if only to safeguard his or her own health.

Having paid the port dues, and as long as they are paid promptly every month, the visiting yachtsman may remain in Sri Lanka indefinitely.

TIDES These are normal with two lows and two highs every 24 hours. Maximum spring high is under one metre. There is no appreciable current in the harbour, the only lateral action being caused occasionally by surge.

WEATHER The southwest monsoon, during which time tropical storms might occur, is between May and November inclusive. Rain in Galle harbour is guaranteed during this period for those anxious to

GALLE
The mosque immediately inside the walls of Fort Galle competes with the nearby lighthouse as a conspicuous landmark when locating Galle harbour.

catch their own drinking water. The dry northeast monsoon which is free of cyclones is between December and April inclusive.

On the northeast coast of Sri Lanka, the wet season occurs during the northeast monsoon owing to cloud precipitation against the land. Trincomalee is therefore wet when Galle is dry and vice versa.

Temperatures are tropical holding constantly in the high 20s and low 30s throughout the year. There is no such thing as a cold day or night along the coast, but high in the mountains pullovers are necessary at certain times.

FACILITIES There is a modern supermarket near the Galle Face Hotel in Colombo but its stock is very basic and prices unreasonably high. Generally speaking it is much better to restrict shopping and eventual victualling to the many small shops around Galle. Processed foods are limited but sufficient whilst local fresh foods are excellent and very cheap. The market provides for all such needs and this will be found at the head of the bay outside the fort.

GALLE
A Sri Lankan snake charmer.

Red meat and poultry is killed daily and is very cheap but is displayed without refrigeration and is often covered in flies. Definitely only for determined meat eaters! Frozen poultry imported from Germany seems good and cheap.

Duty-free items can be purchased from a special shop in Colombo but an entrance fee is applicable and the attendance of a customs officer is required. It is not worth the effort.

Alcoholic drinks can be had with meals in most cafés and hotels with the local *arrack* being the cheapest spirit. This distillation of coconut sap makes an interesting long drink mixed with the local, and very cheap, soda water. Otherwise spirits are expensive and local beer is almost undrinkable; duty-free imported beer is about twice European prices even when purchased duty-free.

Eating out is mostly good value and ranges from reasonable in good-class hotels to unbelievably cheap in local dives. The best value for money is in Don Windsor's home where quality is very high and price sensible.

Diesel fuel is bowsered at Ceylon Fisheries and is about on par with Cyprus prices per gallon.

Petrol and paraffin must be carted from town. Petrol tends to be twice as expensive as diesel whilst paraffin is about two thirds the price.

Methylated spirits should be avoided. It is mixed with paraffin and burns similarly.

Gas is a problem, the only universal connector in the country being at Colombo. Don Windsor plans to obtain a connector so that filling in Galle will become possible.

Hauling out at the Ceylon Fisheries cost, in 1983, US$38 for the first day then US$20 per day standing. Power and water are extra and prices may have risen with the recent takeover of the slipway section by Colombo Dockyards. There are two cradles capable of hauling 300 tons and 50 tons and both are flatbeds with reference posts; chocking and wedging is necessary.

Freezer repairs and regassing can be undertaken at Ceylon Fisheries. Labour charges are very low but the cost of Freon 12 gas is astronomical.

Bullock carts are still used in Sri Lanka, some being rigged to work as taxis.

Engineering Engineers are good around Galle or Colombo with engine rebuilding being possible in Colombo.

Electrical repairs can be farmed out by Don Windsor's son. Price and workmanship seem fair.

Ice from Ceylon Fisheries.

Water can be hosed aboard from a single outlet at Ceylon Fisheries where it is said to be properly chlorinated. Some doubt here. Best to catch rain water. Do not risk water from park near dinghy landing or any other general outlet.

Dinghies are best left in the southeastern corner of the harbour belayed alongside the concrete quay. They can be hauled ashore during a heavy surge.

Banks are crowded but efficient in essential services. Galle banks are only able to change currency; major transfers must be handled in Colombo. Take your passport regardless of how inconsequential an exchange may seem.

American dollars in cash or traveller's cheques are the best currency and arrange for further funds with a Colombo bank or American Express.

Currency in Sri Lanka is the rupee. It stood, in 1985, at 25 to the US dollar.

Best address is c/o Mr D. Windsor, 6 Closenburg Road, Magalle, Galle, Sri Lanka. Don Windsor will hold all mail until claimed or advised otherwise.

Communications are excellent in Sri Lanka, most parts of the world being on direct dialling. Don Windsor can assist here being able to place an international call within minutes. For this service he charges double normal rates but it is often worthwhile considering the crowds sometimes found at a post office.

Mail services are fair to middling with no post lost in my experience. All parcels are held at Colombo post office for customs clearance. They may be collected personally but the time spent in Colombo is often prohibitive. Best to fill in the advisory papers and have all parcels transferred down to Galle post office, but this can add as much as ten days to delivery.

Trains Services to most parts of Sri Lanka with the Galle-Colombo express being most useful to a visiting yachtsman. It leaves Galle every day at 0745 hours and Colombo, for the return trip, at 1545 hours. It costs US$1 each way and takes about 75 minutes for the journey.

Labour can be hired independently or through Don Windsor. A good hand with sand paper and paint brush costs 60 rupees (US$2.50) per day. Morning and afternoon tea should be provided, and a tip, if the man is good, should be considered mandatory.

Don Windsor a Sri Lankan in his mid-fifties, is a most jovial host who opens his home to visiting yachtsmen, his shower being available free of charge and his veranda being offered as a place to relax and enjoy a drink between town and boat. Don sells beer and *arrack* plus many very cheap locally made soft drinks, the best being soda water which complements *arrack* rather well.

Fishermen work from dugout canoes in Galle harbour using drop or cast nets.

Also available through Don is a laundry service, hire bicycles and labour hire. His son can assist wherever special problems are encountered in the mechanical field.

VILLAGE INDUSTRIES Sri Lanka is world famous for its gems. Don Windsor himself is a gem dealer with a large store near his home, and having once had shops in Singapore and Hong Kong, his advice should be sought before buying.

The carving of superb colourful wooden masks is another Sri Lankan industry and there are a few major carving centres along the Galle-Colombo road with retail outlets all over the country.

As well as masks, beautiful model fishing canoes are available but are rather expensive, if irresistible. A crew member on one of the Galle tugs is an exponent of this art.

SIGHTSEEING Once again, Don Windsor is the best contact as he can arrange a minibus and driver for a very reasonable sum inclusive of everything less food money for the driver. The accepted standard here is 50 rupees per day. Allow three days and two nights to see the mountain areas, Kandi and other centres. In Kandi, the Temple of the Tooth, and one of the better dance groups is a must. If you wish to view the ancient cities of Polonnaruwa and Anuradhapura, in the central north, as well as the Tamil area of Jaffna, allow four to five days.

Trains cover the above district and are much cheaper than road transport but not as convenient.

GALLE HIGHLIGHTS Historically, Galle is the most interesting of the still-functioning old towns. Up until the building of the Colombo Harbour breakwa-ters in the middle of the last century the natural bay at Galle was the nation's main harbour. It is hoped that the new breakwaters forming Galle's inner harbour might recapture a little of that trade.

Galle's commercial centre is divided into two districts: that within the old fort walls and that without which is on the other side of a canal to Galle railway station.

The Galle fort was built, in part, originally by the Portuguese then enlarged by the Dutch, and later the English in 1873 added its main gate to handle the increasing flow of traffic. The main gate area and the wall stretching away to each side was once further protected by a moat of considerable depth. Many of the Dutch additions consisted of grey granite which came to Galle as ballast in visiting ships and the ramparts were built by negro slaves under Dutch military supervision; Dutch soldiers also found themselves breaking rock as a form of punishment.

One of the most brutal administrators during colonial rule was the Dutch governor, Petrus Vuyst (1726-1729). He was eventually sent to the gallows in Batavia for the torture he meted out to others.

A walk around the fort walls is recommended as well as a wander through the many narrow streets within. Contained here will be found banks, post office, hotels, gem dealers, wood carvers, law courts and so on. Also recommended is a visit to the Closen-burg Hotel, once a shipmaster's private home, on the harbour's inner headland.

THE PEOPLE It is believed that a race known as the Veddahs originally inhabited Sri Lanka and their descendants survive today, although they were largely displaced by Sinhalese people arriving from India in, probably, the 6th century B.C. During the following centuries, the Veddahs settled in the area of Anuradhapura in the dry northern lowlands forming a kingdom; other kingdoms developed in the south and west regions. In the 3rd century B.C. Buddhism was imported from India and spread rapidly; it remains today as Sri Lanka's principal religion.

Over the centuries, Sri Lanka suffered countless invasions from China and Malaya but mostly from India, the capital moving to Polonnaruwa as a result. By the time Polonnaruwa was abandoned, there were a number of kingdoms throughout the land, including a powerful one at Kandi and another at Kotte, near Galle. During this period, a Hindu race known as the Tamils migrated across from southern India and settled in the far north at Jaffna.

Many centuries later, during British colonial rule, more Tamils were imported to work the tea plantations and considering their different religion, language, attitudes and status as cheap labour, it was inevitable that the Tamils would become a group within the country calling for some autonomy from the Sinhalese majority. In recent years this demand has at times been the cause of near civil war in Sri Lanka, 300 people dying in an uprising in Colombo in 1983. It should be said that those knowing Sri Lanka well suggest that more unrest comes from the ancient, rather than plantation labour, Tamils.

Sinhalese and Tamils constitute the dominant race but descendants of Portuguese, Dutch and English colonists form a notable minority. These people are generally half-caste, and were known as Burghers, their mixed blood being mainly of Portuguese and Dutch heritage. They became disproportionately powerful in the economy of the country and since independence many Burghers have left Sri Lanka in the wake of Sinhalese dominance.

HISTORY It has been shown how Sri Lanka was stocked primarily from mainland India with the first kingdom being created in the north, at Polonnaruwa, and later moving to nearby, but safer Anuradhapura after which other kingdoms blossomed in other parts of the country.

The first European incursion came with Portuguese Lorenço de Almeida in 1505 who was said to have been blown off course en route for the Maldives. He fetched up in Colombo, won the confidence of the king of Kotte, and established the important spice trade from Sri Lanka to Europe. The Portuguese eventually ruled the entire land with the exception of the kingdom of Kandi whose kings over the years always defeated attempts at annexation.

An attempt by the rulers of Kandi to enlist Dutch assistance in ridding their island of the Portuguese backfired; eventually the Dutch ousted the Portuguese but then effectively took their place in 1640 continuing an often brutal form of colonisation. They, too, failed to annex Kandi.

Not long after the French Revolution, the British took advantage of the general unrest in Europe and with little difficulty took the place of the Dutch in Sri Lanka, taming the kingdom of Kandi, they became the first power to control the entire island. The British ruled from their seat of government in Madras in India but in 1802 Ceylon (Sri Lanka) was made a full crown colony and the administration was moved onto the island.

Toward the mid 1800s, English settlers established themselves and developed coffee, coconut and cinnamon plantations, tea not being introduced until later after a disastrous leaf blight all but wiped out the coffee plantations. Rubber was also planted. It was as cheap labour that the British introduced the Indian Tamils to the plantations.

English colonialism left a good legacy in the shape of the excellent network of roads and railways; a legacy inherited by Sir Lanka when she peacefully won independence in February, 1948; changing her name from Ceylon to Sri Lanka, she became a member of the British Commonwealth of Nations. A series of governments including the first woman prime minister have run the country through civil strife and economic depression since then.

With a population density of about 200 people per square kilometre and a total population of over 14 million, it is difficult to imagine Sri Lanka being self-reliant in the near future. But, in the meantime, despite the conspicuous gap between the haves and have-nots, the unrest of the Tamils and thoroughly discouraging port dues and agents' fees, the country can be recommended to anyone passing that way by boat.

Sri Lanka still enjoys England's legacy of an excellent railway network. The single track between Galle and the capital, Colombo' is seen here.

Bay of Bengal

POSITION

Between the Indian subcontinent and the Malaysian peninsula.

GENERAL DESCRIPTION

The Bay of Bengal is not unlike a small version of the Arabian Sea and experiences similar weather patterns. It contains two groups of Indian-owned islands that are out of bounds to the visiting boat: the *Andaman Islands* and *Nicobar Islands*. However, passage between the two groups, or between Nicobar and Sumatra, is safe enough.

Between May and November, specially during November, the southwest monsoon commonly produces cyclones and unlike the Arabian Sea there is no month during this time that is completely safe. Passage planning is therefore hazardous to eastbound navigators who are advised to move before November and to favour the Equatorial area without losing the southwest wind.

The most important country in the area from the cruising point of view is Sri Lanka in the southwestern corner of the Bay.

Around the Bay of Bengal is the east coast of India, Bangladesh and Burma, an area that enjoys only brief mention in this book (see page 5).

Forming the eastern side of the Bay, other than Burma, is Thailand and Malaysia, the latter enjoying a brief description later. It should be emphasised here that whilst Thailand is a politically and physically acceptable cruising area, it is gaining a reputation as a place of pirates, especially around the Thai-Malaysia border.

Poking its northwestern tip into the southeastern corner of the Bay of Bengal is the Indonesian island of Sumatra which is part of a fine cruising country but clearance should not be expected without being in possession of an Indonesian Sailing Permit (detailed under the section 'Indonesia').

To recap; the navigator is advised to look upon the Bay of Bengal as an area across which to make passage rather than as a place to cruise. Generally speaking, passage direct from Galle to the tip of Sumatra is recommended to eastbound boats and an exact reciprocal course to westbound boats.

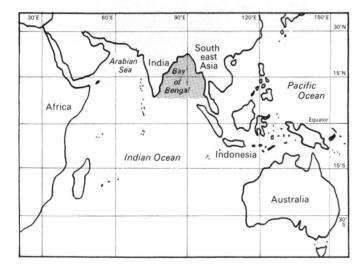

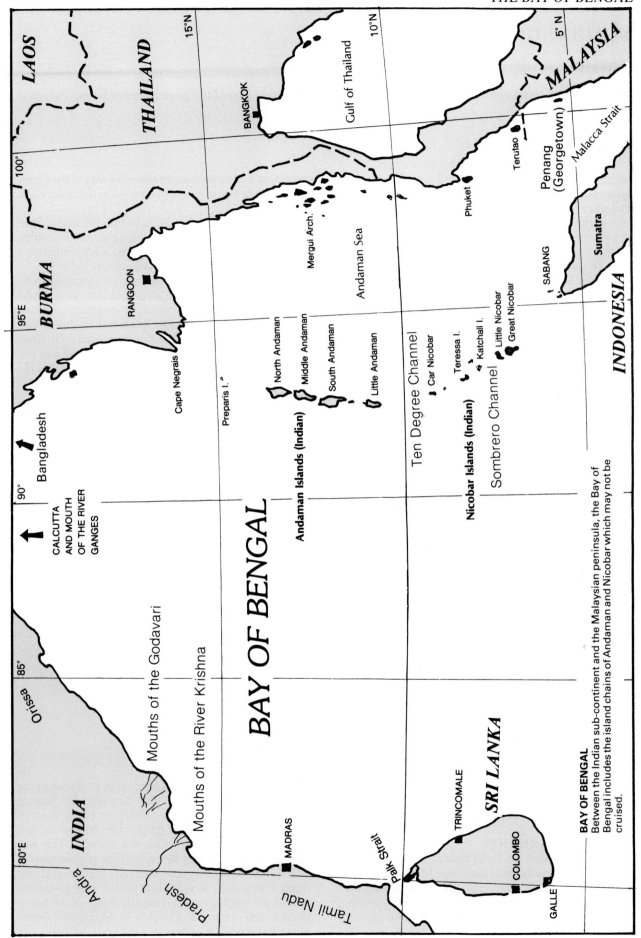

THE BAY OF BENGAL

LAOS

THAILAND

15°N

100°

95°E

BURMA

BANGKOK

Gulf of Thailand

10°N

MALAYSIA

Terutao

Malacca Strait

Penang
(Georgetown)

Phuket

Sumatra

SABANG

INDONESIA

RANGOON

Mergui Arch.

Andaman Sea

5° N

Cape Negrais

Preparis I.

North Andaman

Middle Andaman

South Andaman

Little Andaman

Ten Degree Channel

Car Nicobar

Teressa I.

Katchall I.

Little Nicobar

Great Nicobar

Sombrero Channel

Nicobar Islands (Indian)

Andaman Islands (Indian)

Bangladesh

90°

CALCUTTA
AND MOUTH
OF THE RIVER
GANGES

Mouths of the Godavari

Mouths of the River Krishna

85°

80°E

Orissa

INDIA

Andhra

Pradesh

Tamil Nadu

MADRAS

Palk Strait

TRINCOMALE

SRI LANKA

COLOMBO

GALLE

BAY OF BENGAL

BAY OF BENGAL
Between the Indian sub-continent and the Malaysian peninsula, the Bay of Bengal includes the island chains of Andaman and Nicobar which may not be cruised.

Malaysia

POSITION

Occupying the bottom end of the Malay peninsula and the northwest part of the large island of Borneo which it shares with Indonesia.

GENERAL DESCRIPTION

Comprising the eleven states of the former country, Malaya, and now a constitutional monarchy within the Commonwealth of Nations, Malaysia came into existence in 1963. Singapore was originally included in the federation but withdrew to become a separate country in 1965.

From the cruising point of view, Malaysia can be rather frustrating in the sense that while its officials and people are very welcoming and its coast offers wonderful anchorages there is the fear of piracy along its northwestern coastline. However, pirates notwithstanding, the island Penang, with its city of George Town, is recommended for its vibrancy and general interest whilst the port of Swettenham offers good repair and haul-out facilities.

The person anxious to cruise the west coast of Malaysia can do no better than to seek information from westbound sailors whilst in Galle, Sri Lanka. The threat of trouble with pirates will, in all probability, prove mild with no recent cases involving private vessels.

That part of Malaysia situated along the north coast of Borneo and known as Sarawak and Sabah is often raved about by cruising folk. Indeed, I know of one English yachtsman who returned there on two occasions from Australia before leaving the area finally. There are rivers, anchorages and ports dotted along the coast and the locals are friendly, living life at the village level. To date there are no reports of piracy having reached this far making it an interesting start to a passage from Singapore to Hong Kong.

Advance visas are not necessary for visitors from friendly nations.

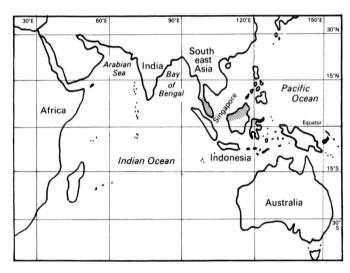

Malaysia occupies the bottom tip of the Malaysian Peninsula and the northwest coast of Borneo.

Singapore

POSITION

01°16′N 103°50′E Immediately off the southern tip of Malaysia peninsula separated by the Johore Strait.

GENERAL DESCRIPTION

Singapore has been an independent republic since 1965 although briefly federated with Malaysia and is a member of the Commonwealth. Comprising 54 islands, the island of most significance is that of Singapore itself which is of approximately 230 square miles.

Her ideal position to capture most of the shipping passing from the South China Sea into the Bay of Bengal and beyond and her ability to refine most of the oil coming out of her neighbour, Indonesia, has made Singapore a huge economic success. This was assisted in no small way by the attitude of government which cleaned the city up to such an extent that at one stage a bearded, long-haired visitor was given the option of turning around and leaving or of being shaved and trimmed! Hippies in Singapore disappeared overnight.

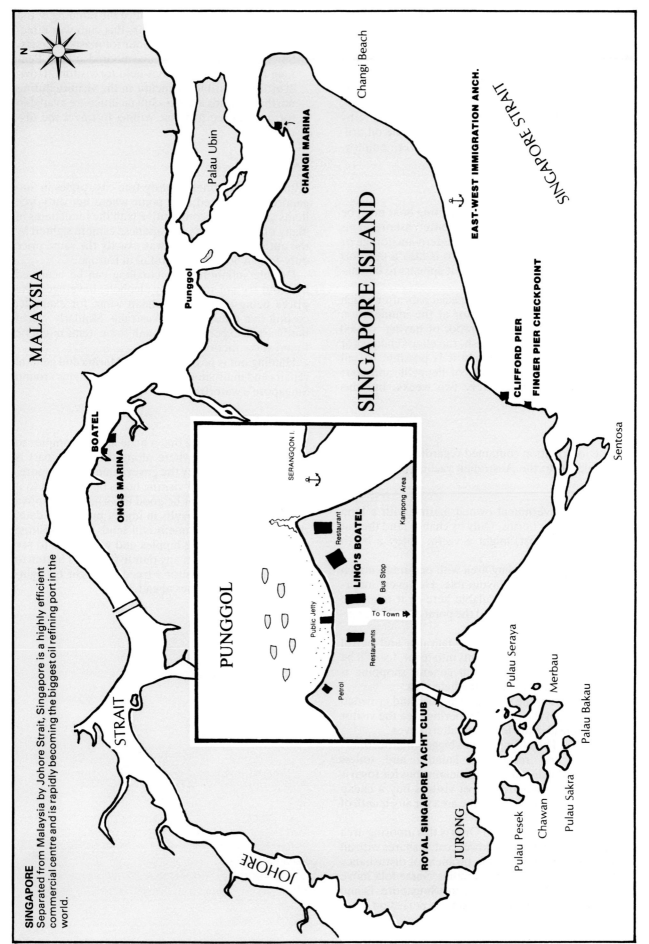

SINGAPORE

Separated from Malaysia by Johore Strait, Singapore is a highly efficient commercial centre and is rapidly becoming the biggest oil refining port in the world.

MALAYSIA

JOHORE STRAIT

Palau Ubin

Punggol

BOATEL

ONGS MARINA

ROYAL SINGAPORE YACHT CLUB

JURONG

Pulau Pesek

Chawan

Pulau Sakra

Pulau Bakau

Merbau

Pulau Seraya

SINGAPORE ISLAND

Changi Beach

CHANGI MARINA

EAST-WEST IMMIGRATION ANCH.

SINGAPORE STRAIT

CLIFFORD PIER

FINGER PIER CHECKPOINT

Sentosa

PUNGGOL

SERANGQON I.

Restaurant

LINQ'S BOATEL

Public Jetty

Bus Stop

To Town

Restaurants

Petrol

Kampong Area

Interestingly enough, the most commonly levelled criticism of Singapore nowadays is that it has become too clean and efficient and in so doing has lost its charm. Much of old Chinatown, for example, has been replaced by high-rise apartments and miles of beaches have given way to six lane highways, industrial estates and general expansion.

The yachtsman is often attracted to Singapore by its occasional promise of employment in the oil drilling and associated industries. However, employment must not be depended upon.

FORMALITIES

Visas are not necessary but the visiting boat must be cleared before her crew are permitted ashore. This can be achieved at the eastern-western anchorage or at Finger Pier checkpoint. There is also a customs office at Changi Yacht Club but it appears to be unavailable as a point of first entry.

Crew are given a two week special pass after which extensions must be applied for at the immigration office. Extensions demand proof of having S$5000 (about US$2500) in either cash, traveller's cheques or funds available. Alternatively it is possible to sail across to the Malaysian port of Pengelih and start entry formalities again every two weeks, but this proves tiresome.

ANCHORAGE

For the information contained regarding anchorages my thanks go to the Australian yachtswoman, Kate Reagan.

Changi is a government-owned marina with a long waiting list for berths. Only by chance, and then at considerable cost, might a visitor enjoy a berth here.

Punggol is a pig breeding area with odours to match when the wind is unfavourable. However, moorings are sometimes available here or it might be possible to anchor around the point close to Serangoon Island.

There are boat hiring, restaurants and petrol available here and a bus runs into town. Ice will be found at the boat shed but general shopping is severely limited in the immediate area.

Considering the general exposure and crowded conditions of the Punggol mooring area the visitor might consider the following alternatives.

Ongs Marina This is Singapore's biggest marina offering bar and restaurant, laundry and toilets although the distance to the nearest bus for town is about two kilometres. Most visitors buy a cheap push-bike if remaining in the area for any length of time.

Boatel Just half a mile from Ongs is this mooring area with a few facilities and lower cost, it shares with all areas so far discussed the problem of disturbance by passing traffic and northerlies. Some folk move around to the south shore of Singapore Island when the latter became rather too persistent.

Royal Singapore Yacht Club Since the building of the bridge over the Jurong river, this club was effectively cut off from the harbour for masted vessels. Since then, such vessels have moored at Pasir Penjang but moorings are not held for visitors. However, it is possible to anchor in the vicinity during northerly winds and the club facilities are available for a small fee to those willing to travel the distance.

FACILITIES

Although traditionally a duty-free city, prices in Singapore have soared to a point where her duty-free items are only just competitive with the retail items of many other countries. A Japanese camera sighted by the author, for example, was exactly the same price duty-free in Singapore as retail in Europe.

Despite inflation, all victualling can be achieved here but try not to buy any alcoholic beverages, the prices being outrageous: cheap wine, for example, costing five times that of Australia. Similarly, yacht hardware is expensive although some items might be found at competitive prices.

Hauling out is possible at Ongs Marina and general repairs and maintenance present no problems around Singapore's waterfront.

THE FUTURE

It is worth noting here that a huge marina complex to be established somewhere along the south coast is under consideration by the government of Singapore. It is proposed that all visiting boats be confined to it which may or may not be good news because captive clientele inevitably results in higher prices. To date, the Singapore government still tends to see visiting yachtsmen as floating hippies and would like to see them contained, not in any punitive sense, I hasten to add; certainly the visitor's freedom might be tightened if this project goes ahead.

Hong Kong

POSITION

22°18′N 144°10′E Against the Chinese mainland at the bottom of its Kwangtung province, 400 miles west of Taiwan at the northern extreme of the South China Sea.

GENERAL DESCRIPTION

An island and peninsula nation of only 404 square miles, yet with a population of 5,300,000, Hong Kong has often been called the shopping centre of the world. There is no disputing such a claim; her economy is bolstered by many overseas companies and her population has a merchant mentality that puts even the United States in the shade. Yet the visitor can only be enthralled by the vibrant pace and swinging scene that is especially Hong Kong and, as any sailor who has bought sails from here knows, the service is fast, the product good and the ethics scrupulous.

A British crown colony now enjoying considerable autonomy Hong Kong was first occupied by Britain in 1841 and was formally ceded by China in 1842 in the Treaty of Nanking. A lease was secured for the New

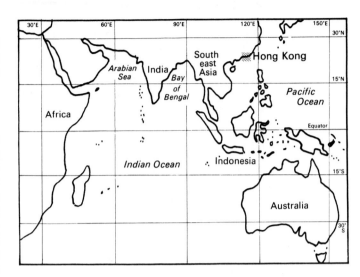

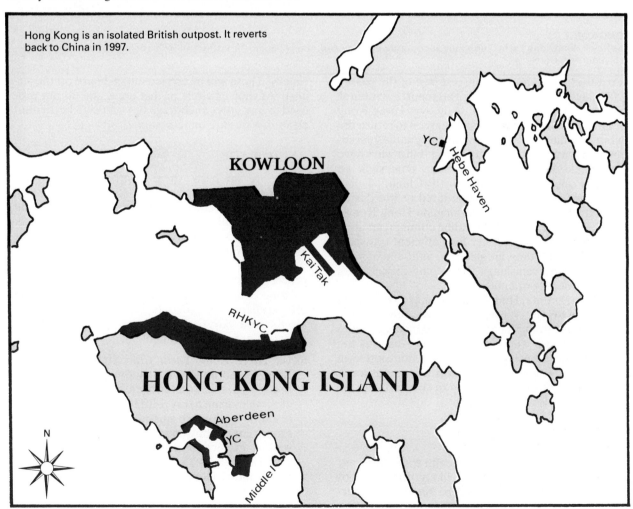

Hong Kong is an isolated British outpost. It reverts back to China in 1997.

HONG KONG
The Royal Hong Kong Yacht Club's moorings are always crowded, often obliging the visitor to limit his or her stay before moving to an alternative area.

Territories which form the largest part of the colony in 1898 and that expires in 1997. This report is written at a time when clouds of doubt hang over Hong Kong for although Britain has formally agreed to return the colony to China in 1997 and many safeguards guaranteeing the future of Hong Kong's capitalist ways have been made it remains to be seen how such an economy can be absorbed happily by China.

Whether agreements are honoured or not during the next century, it is hard to imagine Hong Kong's countless skyscrapers, her bustling commercial port, her international flights, her fast, efficient transport system, her museums, art galleries, amusement parts and yacht clubs vanishing. These things, surely, will continue one way or another.

In the meantime, Hong Kong remains a fascinating destination for any cruising boat whose crew prefer to sail northeast from Singapore instead of southeast to Australia. Those wanting to go on to Australia are reminded that by using the southwest monsoon from Singapore to Hong Kong, the northeast monsoon is then available from Hong Kong to Australia via the Philippines. It is worth a thought.

FORMALITIES

As in most British territories, health formalities are strongly applied. It is entirely likely that proof of recent cholera inoculation will be required. Otherwise there are the usual customs and immigration checks. These will be carried out on board off the airport. Anchor or circle in that area, and do not proceed to any other anchorage or yacht club berth until cleared. Visas are unnecessary.

ANCHORAGE

There are no bays where a private vessel might anchor and still offer her crew convenient facilities. Even Hebe Haven, where there is a separate yacht club, good facilities and a large shopping centre after a while feels isolated for those wanting to see Hong Kong proper during their visit.

Under the circumstances the visitor is advised to proceed to the Royal Hong Kong Yacht Club after clearing customs in the hope of finding a mooring at this excellent, if crowded, facility. If nothing is available then the latest information regarding a sensible alternative should be available.

Royal Hong Kong Yacht Club Situated on Hong Kong Island under the shadow of towering highrise blocks, this wonderful club offers a vast range of services from a travel-lift haul-out to a high class restaurant in superb surroundings. There are also squash courts, bowling alley and swimming pool as well as a selection of dining rooms. Very much a yachtsman's club, local races are sponsored as is the biannual Hong Kong to Manila race which is held every two years and cruising folk are welcome to participate.

HONG KONG
Slipways are available near the yacht club at Hong Kong as well as at other yachting centres in the area. The club has a travel lift.

Double decker trams, ferries and underground serve Hong Kong around the clock.

A deposit of around US$100 is required by the club against services not being paid for, and moorings, if available in the first place, must be vacated after two weeks.

WEATHER

The climate of Hong Kong is subtropical being very steamy in the summer (wet season) and delightful during winter. The best months from a tourist's point of view are November and December when temperatures are most stable and comfortable. The average winter temperature is about 15°C whilst in summer it is 28°C. The average rainfall is 85 inches per annum, 75 per cent of which falls between May and September.

May to October is the southwest wind monsoon period when temperatures are at their hottest and there is a likelihood of typhoons. These are most common in the latter half of the season. The southwest wind is reliable enough for fair passage from Singapore, but calms often dominate.

November to April brings the dry northeast monsoon when typhoons are rare except early in the season. The best months for sailing south from Hong Kong are January, February and March. These are also the safest months for the near neighbours, the Philippines.

Water taxis offer the best way of getting ashore in Hong Kong, their price being low and availability regular.

FACILITIES

The wonderful facilities of the Royal Hong Kong Yacht Club have been advertised. Here it need only be pointed out that Hong Kong is one of the best stocked cities in the world where everything can be found. Sail-making is possibly its greatest claim to cruising fame, there being a number of companies specialising in not only making and repairing sails and associated equipment but in keeping their promises regarding delivery. Previously the cheapest sailmaking centre in the world, the competitive gap has been narrowed considerably with improved wages, the high cost of material and now, the economic apprehension.

Other than sails, the visitor will enjoy having clothes tailor made at reasonable prices, eating out at some of the remarkable Chinese restaurants and visiting such sights as Peak Tram, the Kam Tin Walled Cities, Ocean Park and other ancient or commercial sights. The everyday sight of a fifty storey skyscraper being built using bamboo scaffolding will take a lot of beating.

The ubiquitous sampan of Hong Kong performs many tasks from cargo delivery to taxi. This is Aberdeen, the other side of Hong Kong Island from the main harbour.

A typical street scene, Hong Kong.

Indonesia

POSITION

Stretching between and including the island of Sumatra in the west to the western half of mainland New Guinea, known as Irian Jaya, in the east. Passing within 200 miles of Australia's north coast and extending north to Malaysian Borneo and the Philippines.

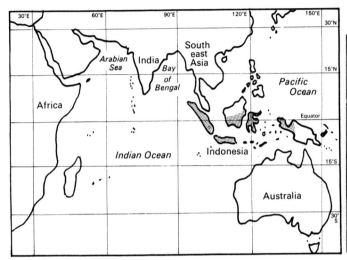

Indonesia is an island country stretching from Malaysia to Papua New Guinea.

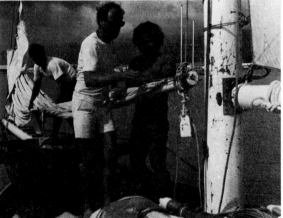

Frenchman Philippe Petiniaud had an Indonesian *prau* built in Bali in 1977 and has cruised the islands with two locals. Named *Sri Noa Noa,* her simplicity has attracted a lot of Western interest.

GENERAL DESCRIPTION

The islands of Indonesia number some 7900 of which 3000 are considered large islands and nearly all are tropical, scenic gems. Rain can be prolific being along the Equator, and as a result dense vegetation is common. Coral reefs and wonderful sandy beaches fringe most islands and there are enough bays and inlets to offer different anchorages virtually every night from one end of the country to the other.

Indonesia is the world's largest archipelago and is divided into three main groups. These are; Greater Sundas, Lesser Sundas and the Moluccas. From east to west the archipelago stretches some 3000 miles whilst from south to north it is about 1200 miles.

Except for the Hindu island of Bali and a few scattered Christian centres, the religion of Indonesia is Islam whilst the government is Republican. Despite free elections being required by the constitution every five years, only three have been held since independence from the Dutch in 1945. The army has been responsible for maintaining what amounts to a dictatorship in a country that, it might be fairly argued, demands such measures, for it must be recalled that its expanse over so many islands presents many problems of administration.

Fundamental diplomatic mistakes commonly made by the western visitor to Islamic countries are best avoided. See page 3 for a list of dos and don'ts which apply in lesser and greater degrees to all Islamic countries.

Most government officials are Javanese to ensure loyalty and to maintain a strong line of command. As a further measure of loyalty, department heads and often their underlings are posted to outer islands for a limited time only so that loyalties cannot fade or change. And whilst this practise may help keep the country in line, the fact is, an elitist leadership has emerged which keeps indigenous leaders down whilst making the Javanese the modern day colonisers of the country. It scarcely needs adding that the island of Java is by far the wealthiest place in the whole country, yet it is the tiny head of a huge body.

Regrettably, the head leans towards corruption. Nothing happens in Indonesia without someone's palm being greased. It is Egypt all over again with the outstanding difference that the country is physically so beautiful as to dampen one's outrage and is worth visiting despite itself.

The people of Indonesia number 153,000,000 and are scattered over a total landmass of 735,000 square miles. In some places population density is the greatest in the world whilst in others it is the least. Generally speaking they are friendly people tending towards being small with delicate features. Many of the women are nothing short of exquisite and all have strict codes of moral behaviour which are easily outraged by the western visitor who is sometimes looked upon as a crude barbarian. He is also looked upon as being rich and therefore fair game for theft; watch your belongings in a crowd and seek local knowledge as to where a boat might be subject to petty theft. Broadly speaking, the further away one sails from Java, the more friendly the population becomes until in

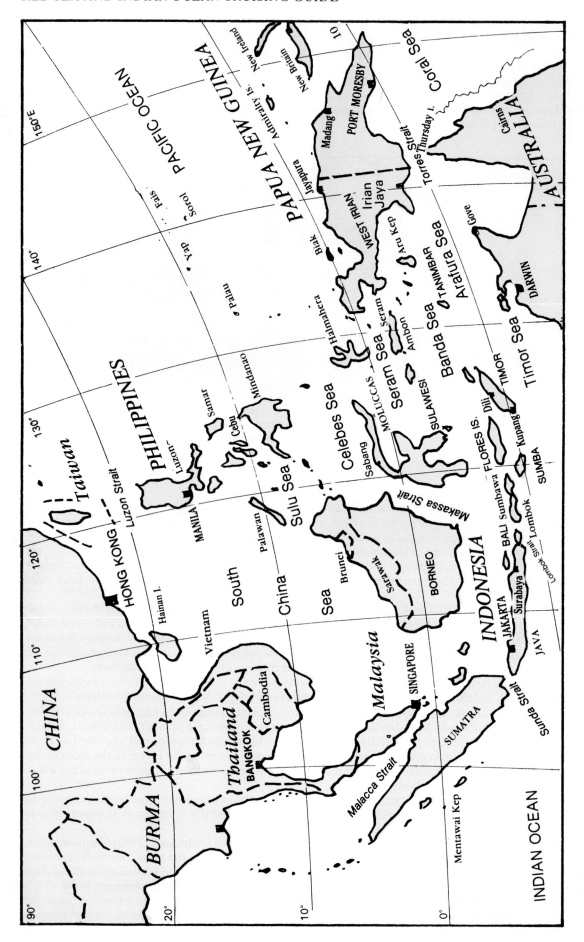

INDONESIA

Indonesia comprises the large islands of Sumatra, Java, most of Borneo, Sulawesi, Timor, Halmahera and half of New Guinea. Including her smaller islands and islets her territory embraces nearly 8000 islands. All private vessels must have a sailing permit before entering the country.

the eastern area one almost forgets about backsheesh and theft.

But not too far east. West New Guinea, which was handed over to the Indonesians from the Dutch in 1961 and is now called Irian Jaya, experiences border scuffles with Papua New Guinea. These are very much storms in a teacup in which New Guinean bow and arrows have proven no match to Indonesian jet fighters. The conflict involves but a handful of mountain people and rarely touches the visitor but he should not expect the hand of welcome in Irian Jaya.

The capital city of Indonesia is Jakarta on the northwestern end of the island of Java. The second largest centre is Surabaya, also on the island of Java, which is very much a maritime town with a large and bustling port. There is a yacht club here but it is a club very much in the sense of an Egyptian club.

Of great interest to the railway buff is the fact that Indonesia still employs a number of ancient and not so ancient steam locomotives on its limited railway (also on the island of Java).

FORMALITIES

Upon arriving in any Indonesian port, whether it is your first, last or any in between, the cruising sailor is obliged to clear customs, immigration, harbour master and police; and because there is often a pecking order in every port, different from the last, it can help to know who is the top man. Usually another yachtsman in port can advise who to see first.

In some ports the yacht cannot even go daysailing from a base port without clearing out and in all in the same day! Considerings the time this can take per office, and the time it takes to walk from one office to the other, there is never anything left of the day in which to go sailing. As a result, few go daysailing from, and back to, the same port and most cruising folk steer clear of any port of entry for as long as it is humanly possible. This, at least, is the good news: you may still actually sail past a port!

Before partaking in the above bureaucratic thrills and spills, the visitor must obtain a *Sailing Permit* prior to entering Indonesia.

SAILING PERMIT This gem of misguided wisdom is a way of keeping track of the private boat within Indonesian waters. Upon application, a basic route is stated in terms of ports to be visited and the anticipated E.T.A. at each. The application is processed by at least four government departments who, upon acceptance, send duplicates out to all ports on the list.

A permit is available for three months only and is best secured by writing in advance to:

P. T. Pedang Kayra Bhakti, Wismo Kosgoro, 4th Floor, Jakarta Pusat, Indonesia. Telex No. 46653 Wismak.

This company will forward an application form which should be filled in and returned accompanied by a payment of at least Australian $138.

Those anxious to obtain a permit at the last minute are advised that it is usually possible through the embassy in Singapore (for those approaching from the west) and Port Moresby (for those approaching from the east). Mostly, however, these embassies can only pursue an application already being processed.

APPROACH

Presuming an Indonesia Sailing Permit is in hand, the cruising boat may enter at any port as long as it is mentioned on the permit. Sometimes a blind eye is turned to the fact that a port is being entered not on the permit but no dependence should be based on this.

From Sri Lanka Those without permits and anxious to formalise Indonesian details whilst in Singapore should sail direct for Singapore, across the Bay of Bengal and down the Strait of Malacca. Where it is noted on a sailing permit already in hand, Sabang can be the landfall. This is a small island off the northern tip of Sumatra.

From Papua New Guinea Presuming it is the southeast trade wind season, the southern route through the Torres Strait is by far the best having a guaranteed wind flow right up until late November and possibly well into December. The first Indonesian port of entry on this route is just 80 miles beyond the Torres Strait at Merauke, Irian Jaya; otherwise, one of the eastern group such as Aru Kep or Tanimbar Kep can be recommended. From this region, the entire Indonesian chain can be cruised from east to west but an approach around July-August is suggested so as to use the trade wind as far as possible. By November, the wind often fails completely in the Indonesians.

Those cruising over the top of Papua New Guinea will experience largely windless conditions at any time of year and can enter Indonesia at Jayapura, a northern border town in Irian Jaya. Otherwise sail direct for Ambon in the Moluccas.

From Darwin The Darwin Sailing Club sponsors an annual ocean race from Darwin to Ambon and the cruising yachtsman is recommended this as an easy way into Indonesia on the basis that the way is paved, somewhat, bureaucratically. This is not always true, however, Australian organisers having been driven to distraction at times, so the visitor interested in this race should contact the Darwin Sailing Club ahead of time for race confirmation. The race is usually held in late July.

Otherwise, cruising people leaving Darwin en route to Africa or Europe may touch on Indonesia at Kupang (Timor) then cruise the fabulous Flores Islands, Sumbawa Island and Lombok before sightseeing, then clearing from, legendary Bali. Because Bali is the most popular and logical port en route into the south Indian Ocean, it enjoys greater detail later.

WARNING   Do not approach too close to the eastern half of the island of Timor nor attempt to enter its north port, Dili. This region was, until 1974, Portuguese territory but has been in dispute since their departure. Civil war continues in varying degrees and yachts close in to shore have come to be regarded as amusing targets.

WEATHER

Being mostly between the Equator and 10° south, Indonesia experiences the same fundamental weather influences as those described for the south Indian Ocean towards the end of this book. However because an Equatorial area tends to be a calm area in terms of dominant wind or noticeable differences between seasons, the following is an attempt to clarify the situation.

May to October inclusive This should be a dry season with southeast trade winds. In fact, over the windward sides of high, large islands there is considerable rainfall derived from the moisture collected over thousands of miles of ocean by the wind. The wind, meanwhile, often fails from 5° south to the Equator leaving stifling calms and variables in its wake. Thunderstorms are common at any time of year near the Equator, but are mostly very brief.

During this period, the best developed trade winds are between 5° and 10° south with landmasses commonly channelling the southeasterly into an easterly or even a northeasterly wind. The months of greatest activity are June, July and August.

November to April inclusive Whereas rain occurs in the dry season owing to localised precipitation, it occurs during this season because of the superior conditions for the formation of clouds with or without the assistance of uplifted wind against an island. In other words, it can rain anywhere at this time of year although the windward sides of large islands remain the most common areas.

A northwest wind flow passes over the Indonesian islands from about 5° south to beyond its southern limits, this sometimes commences later than November and finishes earlier than April and is an extension of the northern hemisphere's northeast monsoon which warps over the Equator to appear in the southern hemisphere as a northwesterly and often a true westerly.

In the areas where the wind changes from a northeast monsoon to a northwest wet season, the wind can be anything from a fair and reliable northeasterly to a totally unreliable northerly. Most commonly the whole country lies under a calm during much of the wet season although in certain areas where wind-channelling can occur, a steady and sometime rumbustious wind can blow for days on end.

Cyclones This subject enjoys its own description in the chapter 'Destructive Winds' where it was noted that cyclones rarely touch on the southwestern fringes of the Indonesian islands. Mostly, cyclones are unknown and the wet season is a safe one: albeit, annoying with its rain, calms and thunderstorms.

BEST CRUISING TIME

This is undoubtedly during the so called 'dry season' from May to November at which time the southeast trade wind does its best to dominate the area. As a result, the logical direction of progress is west.

Because this book emphasises the passage from Europe to Australia, which is eastabout, it is obvious that the Australian-bound yacht will be obliged to utilise the rather poorly defined and often drenchingly wet November to April wet season. This cannot be avoided unless one chooses to remain in Singapore until the dry season then start off through the Indonesian chain of islands. This is quite feasible but implies that headwinds will be battled periodically.

BEST PASSAGE TIME

Keeping in mind that the best time to *cruise* in Indonesia is between May and November and that the best resultant direction is east to west it can be appreciated that passage in the opposite direction must be undertaken during the wet season if favourable winds are to be expected.

In this context — and only in this context — the best time to leave Singapore for Australia's most logical northern port, Darwin, is late November through to late February.

The exact time between these parameters will be dictated by the length of time required in Singapore after the crossing from Sri Lanka. Weather has little to do with it because the wet season extends from November to April as stated earlier. However, there is a tendency for the northwesterlies to become more reliable during the months of January and February.

Whatever the personal preferences, the seasonal ones suggest that the navigator get his vessel down to Darwin before the beginning of the southeast trade wind. This means that Darwin should be reached no later than the end of March. It can be appreciated, therefore, that to leave Singapore early is to have more time to sail through the Indonesian islands.

The navigator should not try to spend too much time in the Indonesian Islands because the wet season is not a comfortable time to actually cruise the area, nor are all its anchorages safe with the wind in the northwest quarter. This should be seen as a semi-passage, not a cruise. Later, after revictualling in Darwin, the southeast trade season from May to November can be used for a return to the Indonesian chain so that it might be cruised properly and with less anxiety about anchorages.

In closing this section, it should not be presumed that anchorages are unavailable during the west season. Obviously, those bays suitable when the wind is southeast are unsuitable with the wind in the northwest (or calm and threatening from that direction, as is more often the case). But bays unsuitable during the trade wind become satisfactory in the wet season. Also, of course, all ports are secure and there are a few totally enclosed anchorages safe in all weather.

ANCHORAGES

I suspect it would be beyond the scope of a large, single volume to describe all the anchorages in the Indonesian chain and I therefore do not propose to attempt it. However, it can be confirmed here that anchorages are everywhere along the islands, some bad, some magnificently secure and some apparently perfect which prove too deep to be sensibly used.

The navigator will have a full set of detailed large-scale charts from which anchorage decisions will be made. The limiting factors are depth and protection in relation to the wind direction. In the Equatorial areas of calms and variables the combination of the two can be worrying indeed and where these are encountered, it is often safer to remain at sea even if it means drifting and standing watch all night.

Quite a few anchorages demand that the anchor be grappled into a steeply shelving coral reef leaving no room to swing should the wind change. This type should only be used where the sightseeing is irresistible and the wind is holding true and fair. Otherwise accept that occasional nights must be spent at sea and compensate with those anchorages offering total and absolute security.

BALI

This tiny Hindu island of 3 million people often attracts one third its population again in tourists every year being one of the world's legendary areas of classic beauty and amazing culture. Regrettably, the weight of tourism is at last making an impression so that now one witnesses a lot of 'instant culture' staged without subtlety for money wielding foreigners. It scarcely need be added that much of this social destruction is encouraged more by outside rather than local investment.

Despite it all, by going inland to some of the mountain villages which have changed little over the centuries, Bali as it was can still be seen. The waterfront scene, though culturally shattered, can prove amusing for a cruising person.

The only port of entry is Benoa, a reef-fringed inlet almost severing a small peninsula on the southern tip of Bali. The largest town is Denpasar, about 15 kilometres distant to the north.

Officials at Benoa are accustomed to heavy yacht traffic and in 1984 enjoyed a reputation for being friendly and helpful (the latter being a relative term in Indonesia). Yachts are occasionally afforded the facilities of the port for a limit of three days without a Sailing Permit but this depends on the official on duty and do not assume that this will happen. Listen to the grapevine.

Two young men in Benoa harbour run a small business called Bali Yacht Services and enjoy a reputation for good service and honesty. They will assist with any facet of the boating scene from fuelling to victualling and will watch a boat whilst the crew are ashore.

VISAS

The following countries no longer require visas when visiting Indonesia: Australia, Austria, Belgium, Canada, Denmark, Finland, France, Great Britain, Greece, Iceland, Italy, Japan, Luxembourg, Malaysia, Netherlands, New Zealand, Norway, Philippines, Singapore, South Korea, Spain, Sweden, Switzerland, Thailand, U.S.A., West Germany.

Papua New Guinea

POSITION

Papua New Guinea extends from the border with Indonesia on the New Guinea mainland in the west to the eastern tip of Bougainville Island in the east. It stretches from the most southerly islet of the Louisiade Archipelago to islets off the northern tip of New Ireland.

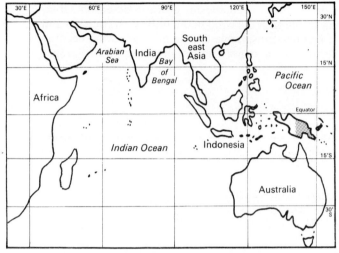

Sharing its major island with Indonesia, Papua New Guinea offers one of the most interesting cruising grounds in the world.

NEW GUINEA
Thatching is still used exclusively at the village level in Papua New Guinea. This is a church being built in the Louisiade Archipelago.

GENERAL DESCRIPTION

The mainland of Papua New Guinea is shared with Indonesia, has a total area of 312,000 square miles and it is the third largest island in the world after Australia and Greenland. Geologically, it is only recently separated from Australia, the two countries sharing the same continental shelf and being separated by a shallow maze of reefs and islets. This is the Torres Strait, which enjoys its own description later.

Almost wholly contained between the Equator and 10° south, it is very much a tropical country with a steamy climate, yet contrasting sharply are the below-freezing temperatures of the highlands. And there are many such contrasts in this fascinating country which is a melting pot of different cultures, attitudes and stages of development. It is in every sense, a wonderland for the cruising yachtsman. Papua New Guinea was discovered so recently by white men that to this day there are villages where the young people have yet to have their first sight of a European face, and life here covers the range from the Stone Age to the sophistication of modern life. The cruising boat can still visit areas only touched upon by occasional trading vessels, or it can anchor off a city as modern as anywhere else in the world. There are government officers whose ears or noses bear the slits originally made for bone or shell decoration and villagers who still wear such ornaments.

Although the first recorded European to touch on New Guinea was the Portuguese navigator Dom Jorge de Menesses who named it Ilhas dos Papuas, the country was divided up in the late 1800s by the Dutch, German and British, the latter reluctantly so until the Germans showed an interest. Since then the Dutch half has gone to Indonesia whilst the German northeast section was lost after the First World War. Eventually Australia found herself the caretaker of both the German and English parts, which included many scattered islands to the east and northeast. The country was granted independence in 1975 but continues to enjoy a gift economy from Australia.

FORMALITIES

Yachtsmen from most countries may enter without first acquiring a visa. Inquiries can be made ahead to your nearest Papua New Guinea embassy or consulate when in doubt.

Logical ports of entry from the various directions of approach are as follows; from the west, Port Moresby; from the northwest, Wewak or Madang; from the northeast, Kavieng; from the east; Kieta; from the southeast, Samarai.

Unless otherwise instructed, remain aboard until cleared.

WEATHER

The weather of Papua New Guinea is identical to that described for the south Indian Ocean on page 152. The southeast trade wind, from April to November or December, is extremely well developed along the south coast and north west Coral Sea, where winds commonly blow Force 5-6 for weeks on end, after which only a day or two respite is experienced before blowing at that strength and for that duration again.

The southeast trade wind commonly fails completely for many days and sometimes weeks at a time along the north coast of mainland New Guinea and on similar latitude in the islands to the east.

The wet season between December and April is often calm and variable although good northwesterlies do sometimes blow along both the south and north coast. In the islands a southwesterly is not uncommon at this time of year.

ANCHORAGES

I can do no better than to suggest the reader buy my cruising guide, *Cruising Papua New Guinea*, whilst in Port Moresby or a major town in Australia. Meanwhile it can be confirmed that some of the most beautiful anchorages will be found in many ports of the mainland and islands, and only on rare occasions will the skipper be defeated by excessive depth or boisterous conditions unfavourable to a particular area.

GETTING THERE

From the east, out of the Pacific Ocean, Papua New Guinea is easily approached using the wonderful winter (dry season) trade winds. From the west, from such areas as Indonesia, Singapore or north Australia, there is a problem in as much as the favourable northwest wet season is often too wet and too variable to be depended upon.

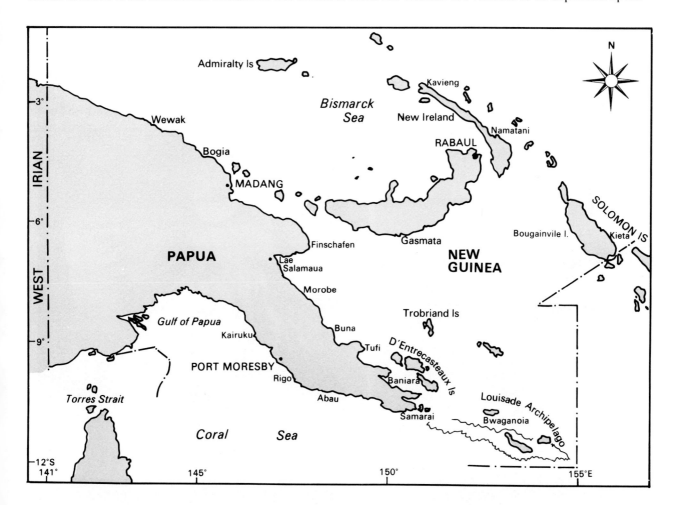

PAPUA NEW GUINEA
So complex is the culture of Papua New Guinea that in a country of about 2 million folk nothing less than 500 totally different languages are spoken. After 100 years under Australian guidance, English and pidgin English are the dominant languages. It borders the Solomon Islands in the east.

One of the many splendid anchorages to be found in Papua New Guinea, this is called English Harbour and is on the island of New Ireland.

Ceremonial dress is still worn occasionally in Papua New Guinea without a tourist promotional reason. The fellow on the left has recently been widowed whilst the *Duk Duk*, right, was once considered fatal if viewed by females. Here he entertains friends but it remains a sight essentially for men only.

However, by using the engine mercilessly, the calms and clear periods of the December to April wet season can be used to advantage and a passage can be forced either south or north of the mainland. The north is recommended for its gentler trade winds when they return so that easting can still be made should it return prematurely or the visitor choose to remain downwind too long. Madang, for example, is the type of place that will trap the romantic for months if he allows it.

BEING THERE

During its recent development Papua New Guinea like many developing nations, had an ambivalent attitude towards the expatriates working and living there and many returned to their home countries.

Then, as services declined, Europeans were welcomed again, but by then most Australian expatriates were well and truly re-established back in their own country. As a result, and because Papua New Guinea has advertised worldwide for technicians and advisers today there are all nationalities in the country but Australians still dominate, English and Canadians are common whilst a number of European countries are also represented in the advisory work force.

Economies and attitudes work in waves and on this basis it can be said that a visiting yachtsman might find employment in Papua New Guinea. Many do, some don't. It depends on the mood in both corners at the time. But one thing that can be said about Papua New Guinea is that its attitude towards outsiders is not volatile. There has never been a case of intimidation towards a visitor apart from the obvious one of the exploitation of tourists. But that is rare. Generally speaking Stone Age, late-to-be-discovered Papua New Guinea has made one of the most peaceful transitions into the twentieth century of all developing nations.

NEW GUINEA
Dugout canoes which have been planked up are used for inter-island work in Papua New Guinea. Note the bailer shell on the mat platform. This is literally used for bailing.

Australia

POSITION

Between the Pacific Ocean and the Indian Ocean in the southern hemisphere east to west and from about 10° south to nearly 44° south. Part of the southwest Pacific area known as Oceania.

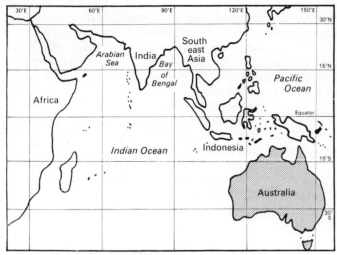

Settled by the English as a penal colony in 1788, Australia covers an area of nearly 3 million square miles.

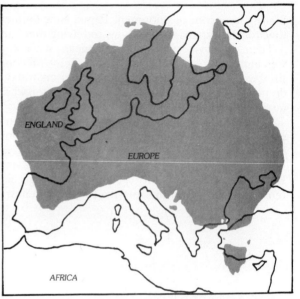

Australia is seen here superimposed over Europe. With only 15 million people she is underpopulated by comparison with most countries in the world.

GENERAL DESCRIPTION

The accompanying map shows Australia's size relative to the United Kingdom and Europe. It has an area of 2,968,000 square miles. But emphasising its size more than any other single factor is its population. This is an almost insignificant 15,276,000 (1984 figures). Most of her 12,446 miles of coastline is uninhabited and virtually impossible to control by an affordable navy, a fact which encouraged her alliance with the West generally and England and America in particular. In the past, threats to Australia's vulnerability have proved unfounded and the upheavals in the neighbouring areas since the Second World War — in Malaya, Indonesia, Vietnam and China, have not affected her although they may have given reason to the controversial and isolationist white Australian policy, a policy which has been abandoned for a liberal outlook on foreign affairs and particularly towards coloured immigration, Aborigines and neighbouring emerging nations.

Australia was claimed by Captain James Cook for the Crown in 1770 and eventually settled as a penal colony by England in 1788; she was proclaimed a commonwealth in 1900 after which her first commonwealth government was formed. Since then two major parties have competed for leadership, these being the socialist-leaning Labour Party and the capitalist-leaning Liberal Party.

Being founded by Mother England, many Australian habits and attitudes are English. This is especially true in both humour and drinking habits, the former being more Monty Python than Bob Newhart, the latter in evidence by the pub on every corner; like the English they encourage the erection of these monuments to frivolity then penalise everyone using them in taxes and fines. The random breath testing laws in Sydney and Melbourne may yet revolutionise the Australian drinking habit but certainly they are sending a lot of pubs to the wall.

Mixed up with the humour, grog and quarantine laws (described later) is a country with tremendous future potential for economic wealth and independence. There is little the country cannot produce, from a barrel of oil to the winner of the America's Cup. And those yachtsmen disinterested in racing will discover some of the most splendid cruising grounds to be found anywhere, from a fjord-like inlet in Tasmania to the world's longest coral necklace, the Great Barrier Reef.

FORMALITIES

The accompanying map shows all the ports of entry around the Australian coast. Any vessel entering the country is bound to clear customs, immigration and quarantine and under no circumstances may any member of a crew venture ashore until boarded. Visas are not necessary for most friendly nations but check with the Australian representative en route. There are representatives in Singapore, Port Moresby and Fiji.

PORTS OF ENTRY
All ports shown on this map are legal points of entry.
Visitors are not permitted ashore until boarded by
customs. Quarantine is strict.

AUSTRALIA

Thursday Island
Gove
Wyndham
DARWIN
Cockatoo Island
Derby
Broome
Port Hedland
Port Walcott
Dampier
Exmouth
Carnarvon
Geraldton
PERTH
Bunbury
Albany
Esperance
Cape Thevenard
Port Lincoln
ADELAIDE
Port Augusta
Whyalla
Port Pyrie
Wallaroo
Port Giles
Edithburg
Rapid Bay
Port Stanvac
Portland
Geelong
Crib Point
MELBOURNE
SYDNEY
Newcastle
Botany Bay
Port Kembla
Eden
Coffs Harbour
BRISBANE
Maryborough (Urangan)
Bundaberg
Glads.one
Rockhampton
Hay Point
Mackay
Bowen
Townsville
Lucinda
Mourilyan
Cairns

Beauty Point
Devonport
Bell Bay
Spring Bay
Burnie
Port Latta
Stanley
HOBART

Sternfast mooring is extremely rare
anywhere in Australia except at
certain marinas. This exception is
in the tiny breakwater harbour of
Kiama on the southeastern
coast of Australia.

117

AUSTRALIA
Thanks to her islands, reefs, headlands, rivers and ports, much of Australia's coastline can be day-hopped. Only the Great Australian Bight, in the Southern Ocean, lacks havens of any description.

The following details should be digested by the visitor so that ill feeling will not be generated upon arrival in an Australian port; her very strict quarantine laws are referred to here.

Regardless of which country you left prior to arriving in Australia, all foods are subject to inspection. Dairy products including milk, cream, butter and dried processed milk will be confiscated unless they are from New Zealand, Canada, United States or Ireland. Sprouting beans, lentils and so on must be destroyed unless from Australia and staple foods such as flour, sugar and cereals will be inspected for weevils. If 'alive' the food will probably be confiscated. Polished rice is unrestricted whilst brown or unhusked rice is prohibited. Cheese is acceptable as long as produced in foot-and-mouth disease-free countries and in its original sealed package. Eggs are banned. Honey is unrestricted whilst soups are restricted only if containing pieces of meat. Tinned tuna and other fish products are unrestricted but tinned meat, unless produced in Australia, must be dumped.

Those wanting to keep their artifacts from the South Pacific must have them sprayed by an officer who may confiscate any part consisting of animal skin.

Animals cannot be landed in Australia except in quarantine which is expensive, especially as the minimum period is nine months. Shipboard pets may be kept aboard but are subject to a bond and regular inspection by officers of the Department of Health. Any vessel with an animal aboard must remain in midstream and under no circumstance may it venture alongside for any reason.

The modern, bustling city of Sydney contrasts sharply with the flat, dusty inland of Australia. Of her nearly 12,000 miles of coastline, the east coast is by far the most popular thanks to the mountain chain which runs full length and the Great Barrier Reef which extends for 1200 miles. Sydney is on the east coast.

DANGERS

Realising that many folk using this book will visit Australia for the first time, I am honour-bound to flip the other side of the Australian coin which shows the natural dangers that are more or less unique to Australia. The person from Europe will have been spoilt by harmless spiders, snakes and a total absence of dangerous sharks. He or she must not take the attitude ashore or into the water here.

Sharks Australia has had its fair share of overseas divers whose specific purpose was to prove that her sharks were no more dangerous than elsewhere. They all failed. One, who theorised that underwater screams send a shark scurrying, was sent scurrying himself.

In fact, there have only been about 100 shark fatalities since Australia was first settled. That is about one every two years and many of those were immigrants who simply did not understand the dangers, or divers who spent most of their working lives in the water anyway.

However, the fact is, a hungry shark in Australian waters will be attracted by undue splashing. The visitor is therefore advised to avoid surface swimming open waters and to restrict aquatic activities to diving which is much safer.

Crocodiles After decades of decimation by hide hunters, the crocodile became a fully protected animal in the early 1960s. Now they are recovering in such numbers that many northern centres are concerned and there is now pressure to reintroduce limited hunting laws.

Darwin, Australia's northern capital city, has an ever-increasing problem as crocodiles are commonly sighted in her harbour. Indeed, there was a sign posted in the Darwin Sailing Club begging boating folk to report all crocodiles. One fellow who sighted one from his windsurfer claims the world speed record for running on water carrying a windsurfer!

Gove, about 500 miles east of Darwin, recently lost a tourist who swam near the mouth of a river and it is claimed that more Aborigines are taken by crocodiles than is generally realised.

Crocodiles may exist along the coast of Australia as far south as the Tropic of Capricorn (23⅓° south). They may venture out to islands along the north coast but not on the east. Mostly they restrict themselves to rivers and for this reason the visitor should never consider slipping into the water whilst anchored within any river in the crocodile zone. Beware also of picnicking on a low river bank, the crocodilian feeding habit is to take cattle and other animals as they come to drink or forage for crabs and roots.

Sea Wasp Also known as the box jelly fish, this horror drifts around the surface with a number of string-like tentacles hanging below. A swimmer entangled in these tentacles has about three minutes to live. Whilst deaths occur from sea wasp stings, many folk survive because they were touched by, as against entangled in, the tentacles.

Sea wasps only appear during the wet season in the southern hemisphere and are most commonly encountered on a lee shore during a northwesterly wind. It is folly indeed to swim from such a shore.

Snakes There are many deadly varieties in the bush of Australia including the rather sluggish death adder, which often lies in hot, loose dirt and sand to react when trodden on; and the taipan, one of the world's most fatal vipers. They are most prolific in April and will only bite when trodden on. The obvious advice then is to watch your step when bushwalking.

Considering that a snake, reacting to being trodden on, will most likely strike somewhere above the ankle, a form of leg protection is more important than boots. The enthusiast bushwalker should therefore wear high boots or a form of spats.

In truth one rarely sights a snake and there are very few fatalities. Nevertheless, the possibility is there and government bodies have seen fit to produce a line of antivenins which have saved many lives but are of little use to a person bitten in isolation and who cannot reach hospital within hours. It is advisable to buy a publication showing the types of snakes and their level of danger. As a very broad rule of thumb, brown snakes are deadly whilst green, yellow and some black snakes are relatively non-venomous. However, the largest species of all, which can appear quite brown in colour, is the carpet snake and he is quite harmless.

Stone Fish A tropical reef and rock dweller, this fat, incredibly ugly fish sits on the sea bottom where he disappears into the background, living up to his name and looking like a stone.

But a stone with a difference; when trodden on, thirteen spines are erected, these easily pierce the toughest bare foot, automatically releasing a deadly poison from sacks at the base of the spines. A full injection would almost certainly prove fatal.

The reader might take heart from the fact that in a quarter of a century of cruising, most of it in coral waters, I have personally found only five stone fish. I have, however, witnessed Torres Strait divers making a game of discovering them by the dozens in certain rocky areas.

The best defence is again protection and the best protection is a good quality sand shoe worn whenever reef or rocky shore walking. In fact, the spines of a large stone fish would still pierce the sole of a sand shoe but the penetration is limited to a non-fatal dose.

Coral Certain corals sting more than others whilst all are capable of giving distress in greater or lesser doses. This is dependent upon a person breaking the skin against a pierce of coral so care is the best advice that can be offered here. In fact, a pair of spats is again appreciated for the ankle area is mostly scraped when walking a coral reef.

The Coasts

So that visitors might understand the differences, and thus plan their destination more sensibly, the coast of Australia is described here in sections. The final section, the north coast, enjoys the greatest detail not because it is physically deserving but because anyone following the suggested routes in this book will make his landfall there.

EAST COAST

This runs from the Torres Strait at about 10° to nearly 38° south at Cape Howe. Embracing the northern state of Queensland and the southern state of New South Wales, it includes the capital cities of Brisbane and Sydney respectively, along with dozens of major towns and many more minor towns. There are abundant natural and manmade harbours as well as countless anchorages, although the latter favour Queensland thanks to its Great Barrier Reef extending along 1200 miles of its coast.

Without question, the Great Barrier Reef provides the best cruising in Australia and can be highly recommended. However, because it experiences a persistent southeast trade wind throughout the months May to November an approach from the north can prove tiresome. This subject is dealt with in greater detail later in this section.

Australia boasts many interesting rivers for the yachtsman to explore. This is the Myall River, New South Wales.

Many east coast rivers are trained near and around their entrances with rock walls making them safer for small boats crossing their bars.

SOUTH COAST

Included here is the island state of Tasmania which with its anchorages and scenery provides excellent cruising but is rather too cold during winter, being in the path of the Roaring Forties westerlies. However, during the summer months of November to March and especially towards the end of the season, it can be most pleasant on all counts.

The south coast of mainland Australia stretches from Cape Howe on the southeast corner to Cape Leeuwin on the southwest corner. Spanning some 35° longitude, it includes some rather inhospitable coastline, hundreds of miles of which is quite without anchorages or even an identation worthy of note.

Embracing the coasts of Victoria, South Australia and Western Australia, the prettiest scenery and greatest collection of anchorages is found in the east between Cape Howe and Cape Adieu on the western side of the Eyre peninsula.

The land behind much of the south coast of Western Australia is backed by the well-known Nullarbor Plain which is the southern edge of the huge Great Victoria Desert. It is this coastline that forms the Great Australian Bight which is so completely without anchorages and that commits yachtsmen to remain at sea whilst passing through the area.

Anchorages become available again in the Albany area, and Albany itself is a port of clearance making it very handy to those sailing to Australia via the Southern Ocean.

Capital cities encountered along the south coast of Australia are Melbourne, the capital of Victoria, and Adelaide, the capital of South Australia, but neither city can boast a harbour which has attractions worthy of a special visit.

WEST COAST

The entire west coast belongs to the state of Western Australia and towards its southern extreme is sited the state's capital, Perth. In fact, Perth's main port is Fremantle and it is here that in 1987 the Americans will try to wrest back their cup lost to Australia in 1983.

For all intents and purposes, the west coast is not a cruising ground on a day-to-day basis. There are, however, enough ports and anchorages to offer some respite after a few days at sea.

The coast is uninspiring scenically but cannot be denied its very special wild quality which is most appealing to the adventurous. The weather can be unexciting being commonly from the south although southbound boats have been known to reach Perth on a fair breeze, but the norm is hard sheets and expectation of a dusting.

Without doubt, the best cruising ground along the west coast is in the Shark Bay area. Here there are many snug and fascinating anchorages as well as good fishing and a fleet of crayfish boats.

The classic view of Sydney harbour.

A typical Australian east coast river anchorage.

NORTHWEST COAST

This is an area of big tides and often fast currents with enough islands and coastal indentations to make daysailing a possibility for much of the way, but the navigator must remain on his toes for it is a coast about which little is known. Despite good coverage in large scale charts there remains opportunity for misadventure.

Between North West Cape and Darwin are a number of mining as well as old established towns such as Broome, Derby and Wyndham where victuals and fuel can be purchased.

NORTH COAST

DARWIN TO TORRES STRAIT is dealt with here in greater detail than its natural claim to fame would normally justify because this is the logical area of landfall for the yachtsman from Europe via Singapore and Indonesia. However, it is a wild and rugged part of Australia with a unique attraction which cannot be denied, appealing more and more to folk anxious to really 'get away from it all'. Also, it is a popular coastal route for those about to make passage overseas. Being 'under the lee' of Australia, so to speak, much of this part of the coast experiences a common, year-round onshore-offshore wind flow despite it being in the southeast trade wind belt. This is looked at in greater depth later, but for now it can be appreciated that anchorages enjoying protection only from the south and east are not necessarily secure. The wind can, in the afternoon, swing right around to onshore.

Considering this problem, the navigator should only anchor behind headlands or open islands whilst the trade wind is obviously well established and then try to find totally enclosed anchorages when the wind is light. The alternative is to remain at sea as the situation dictates.

There are parts of the coast which oblige the stranger to exercise caution. Although shown in excellent detail on large scale charts in most areas. The most critical area is in Castlereagh Bay between Cape Stewart and Elcho Island.

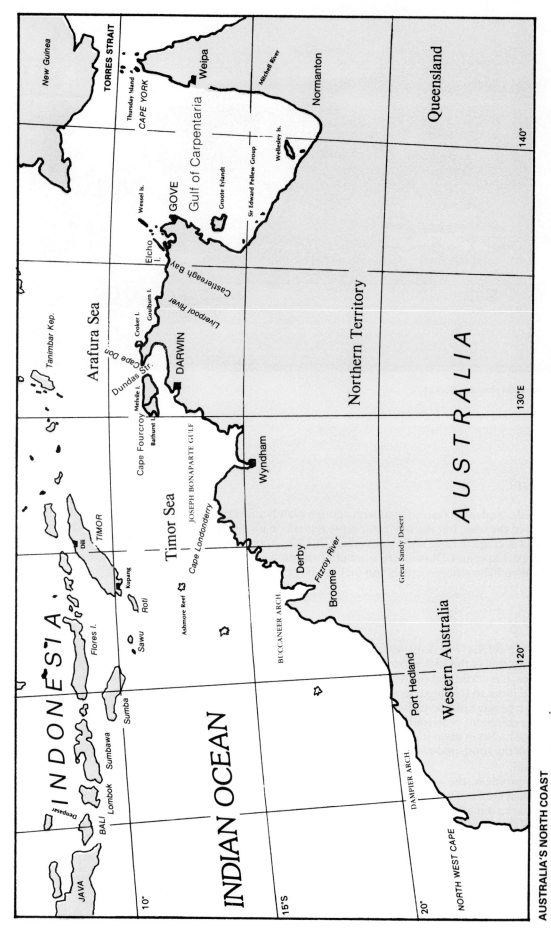

AUSTRALIA'S NORTH COAST

The northwest and north coasts of Australia comprise mostly uninspiring scenery except for those gorges and rivers west of Darwin. But the whole coast offers anchorages and adventure for those who enjoy isolation, hunting and fishing.

Elcho Island is the root, so to speak, of a long chain of islands, the Wessel Islands, projecting from the coast in a northeast direction and offering wonderful cruising in themselves. In the description of the Wessel Islands will be found the twin chain of islands in the same area known as The English Company's Islands.

Gove harbour is also fully covered later and this is the only other major settlement outside of Darwin on this, the Northern Territory coast.

Gove lies on the northwest corner of the enormous Gulf of Carpentaria which is best crossed direct by the small boat unless her crew are determined to coast-hop. This cannot be recommended in the gulf owing to the headwinds down the west coast during the trade season and the fact that much of its scenery is uninspiring. There are, however, a few groups of islands as listed here.

Groote Eylandt Leaving no doubt as to which nation found this group first, Groote Island lies 110 miles south from Gove and is a major prawn fishing centre with trawler facilities. There is also an Aborigine settlement.

Sir Edward Pellew Group is a scattering of islands nearly 100 miles south of Groote and in the southwest corner of the gulf.

Wellesley Islands More commonly referred to by the name of the major island, Mornington, there is another Aborigine settlement here as well as it being a prawning centre. The group is at the head of the gulf.

CAP DON TO TORRES STRAIT Anchorages between Cape Don and the Torres Strait are many and varied. Starting from Cape Don, they will be discussed briefly here. (For much of the information following I am indebted to Jackie Curran and Joe of the Waterwitch ketch *Banda Naira*.)

Cobourg peninsula This jagged scrap of land terminating at Cape Don has many bays slashed into its side some of which offer haven during a well-developed south or easterly trade wind. All-weather anchorage will be enjoyed in Port Essington and Port Bremer whilst Bowen Strait, between the peninsula and the Aborigine settlement island of Croker is troubled only by windward-tide. The most easterly anchorage on this peninsula. Cape Cockburn in Malay Bay experiences swell regardless of exact wind direction.

Cape Cockburn to the Wessel Islands This part of the coast is very much catch-as-catch-can, the bays often facing the wrong way and the headlands proving insubstantial. However, dependent on the exact nature of the wind at the time, it is possible to daysail and total security will be enjoyed in the Liverpool River off the Aborigine settlement of Maningrida.

Wessel Islands and Gove offer excellent anchorages and harbourage respectively and are described in full later.

Gulf of Carpentaria Its islands which all offer good anchorage have been noted but the fair passages between each make visits difficult to justify except on the basis of pure adventure. It is best to sail the 330 miles across its mouth in one hop, choosing the right time of year as noted under the heading 'Weather'.

Torres Stait This passage between Australia and Papua New Guinea is fully described later. Here it can be confirmed that anchorages exist and the main port and township of Thursday Island offer facilities as well as being an entry port.

ABORIGINE LAND Much of the coast so far described as the Northern Territory is called Arnhem Land over which Aborigines enjoy absolute land rights. It is therefore a matter of courtesy to always request permission to land at any Aborigine settlement. These are listed here in order from west to east: Garden Point Mission, on Melville Island to the north of Darwin; Snake Bay Mission also on Melville Island; Croker Island; Goulburn Island; Maningrida on the Liverpool River; Milingimbi Mission on the west side of Castlereagh Bay; Elcho Island in the Wessel Group; Yirrkala at Gove; Groote Eylandt in the Gulf of Carpentaria; Mornington Island also in the gulf; Mitchell River Mission on the east coast of the gulf and finally, Weipa Mission on the same coast.

APPROACH to the coast should be made so as to avoid a last minute windward beat to the destination. Those sailing from Indonesia to Darwin are best advised to depart Kupang in the November to March northwest season (wet season) to landfall on the north Australian coast at Cape Fourcroy on Bathurst Island (next to Melville Island immediately north of Darwin).

Darwin is best approached via the Dundas Strait under Cape Don from all points east and northeast during the southeast trade wind season. Otherwise, the Wessel Islands present a good landfall as discussed under their own heading later and Gove Harbour is a port of entry.

Beware of blundering onto the coast anywhere other than the above points as the low-lying land can prove difficult to identify. There are also many offshore hazards.

WEATHER The southeast trade wind is well developed across this area its strength being related to the temperature of the Australian mainland. It can be appreciated that from Gove right across to North West Cape, the two seas between north Australia and the Indonesian chain are under the lee of Australia. This alone is enough to interfere with the steady trade flow but rising heat from inland deserts exaggerates the situation.

As a result, whenever the trade wind eases over the Pacific Ocean or Indian Ocean, it tends to lift and disappear altogether to the north of Australia, especially in the western Arafura and eastern Timor Seas. Having lifted, it can sometimes be replaced by a wind that is attracted shorewards and thus we have the phenomenon of a north-westerly blowing during the southeast trade wind season.

The navigator can work on the following basic information:

When the trade wind in the Pacific Ocean (north west Coral Sea specifically) is at full strength, the same wind will blow with considerable strength and reliability right across the top of Australia. It may be as much as 20 per cent weaker but it will not fail.

When the wind drops below 15 knots to the east, it will probably carry across Australia as far as the longitude of Darwin beyond which it will fail altogether in the eastern Timor Sea and perhaps as far west as Bali. Close in to the land, it will blow southeast (offshore) during the night then ease and eventually calm towards midday after which a light onshore (northwesterly to northeasterly) will blow until dusk.

When the trade wind is exceptionally light to the east it will be non-existent across the top of Australia from the approximate longitude of Gove as far west as Bali. Close inshore, there will be the same calms as experienced in the Arafura and Timor Sea with little opportunity for a wind to develop either onshore or offshore.

During the November to April northwest (wet) season, conditions tend to be mostly calm with the greatest opportunity for actual northwesterly winds being during January and February. Before and after these months the winds tend light and variable or non-existent. Rain can be heavy but is not continuous in a daily sense.

The best time for crossing the Gulf of Carpentaria from west to east is immediately after the trade wind season. This might be as early as late October or as late as mid-December.

TIDES In the extreme south portion of the Gulf of Carpentaria, tides commonly occur only once each extreme per day. Otherwise, all other part of the north coast of Australia behave normally with two highs and two lows every 24 hours.

The range varies from around 7 metres in Darwin to 3.5 metres at Gove and Torres Strait.

HISTORY The earliest voyage of exploration to Australia which can be substantiated in history was that of the Dutch vessel *Duyfken* in 1606; fully 164 years before Captain James Cook, and whilst there is little doubt whatsoever that the north coast was visited by Malays, and also possibly by Chinese and Arabs there is no hard evidence to support this. *Duyfken* first touched on the coast near the present mining town of Weipa, on the eastern side of the Gulf of Carpentaria anchoring in Albatross Bay, the headland to which bears the vessel's name.

From Albatross Bay the vessel continued south into the gulf but turned north again probably due to the return of the southeast trade wind. En route up the coast a crewman was lost in a skirmish with Aborigines and in crossing the Torres Strait there was probably a temptation to press east but the trade wind would have prevented such endeavour.

Despite hundreds of natural harbours, breakwater harbours are found here and there along the Australian coast. This is Wollongong harbour, southeast coast.

Upon returning to the Dutch-held East Indies (now Indonesia), the commander of *Duyfken* reported that the new land was not encouraging. He found that there was 'no good to be done there'.

Later, in 1623 another voyage of discovery was launched using two Dutch vessels, the *Pera* and *Arnhem* which broadened navigational horizons west to the Northern Territory and confirmed that the country appeared dismal. More skirmishes with Aborigines did little to raise enthusiasm.

I cannot help but speculate as to whether or not Australians would now be of Dutch or Portuguese descent had explorers from those once powerful nations ventured beyond the north and down the east coast. There they would have found reef waters stretching for 1200 miles and containing a wealth of beche-de-mer, pearl shell and fish, whilst ashore the mountain ridge parallel to the coast for the entire length of the eastern seaboard would certainly have impressed them. They might have even waxed lyrical over the rain forests, the mountain streams and safe harbours, and had they reached down as far as fabulous Sydney harbour they could only have stopped to settle as the English did nearly 200 years later. It took Captain James Cook to discover the east coast of Australia and explore its length before claiming it for England and in so doing he secured a fine piece of real estate that would be squandered on convicts and their guards for many years after.

Except for a visit by Abel Tasman in 1644, the area was not looked at seriously again until Captain Matthew Flinders charted part of the coast in 1803 for the British Government who had occupied Sydney, thousands of miles to the south.

Soon after Flinder's hydrographic voyage, pressure was brought to bear on the Colonial Department to create a northern port somewhere in Australia. It was argued that trade might open up with the Dutch in Indonesia and the Portuguese in Timor whilst offering distressed sailors a place of refuge. Also, by having their own port in the north, British ships might find refuge without paying taxes to the Dutch for in that period most vessels went by way of Timor or Java.

In this way one of Australia's shortest lived ports was created at Port Essington in 1838; the child of earlier and futile attempts to start a settlement in the area, Port Essington also was doomed to failure. It proved too remote and survived only eleven years and remains of the settlement can be still seen in the southwest corner where the town of Victoria was built.

During the Port Essington period, buffaloes were brought over from Timor starting what was to become a major tourist industry in the north, that of safari hunting. Otherwise little happened along the north coast of Australia until uranium and bauxite, two minerals that established the area as a most valuable asset to the country as a whole, were discovered. Today, uranium is shipped through Darwin whilst the town of Weipa on the eastern side of the Gulf of Carpentaria, where the Dutch ship *Duyfken* first discovered Australia, lies on the world's largest bauxite deposit. There is also a twin bauxite deposit of enormous wealth where the *Arnhem* discovered the Northern Territory. Those early Dutch reports that there was 'no good to be done there' were slightly off base and not without irony it would seem!

DARWIN

POSITION Northern Territory coast 12°27'S 130°50'E.

GENERAL DESCRIPTION Darwin is Australia's most isolated capital city lying at the top of the Northern Territory, a state of Australia which is, in itself, considered a remote and desolate area.

Darwin's isolation is its very attraction; it is a modern, sprawling oasis at the end of a seemingly endless road. The very fact of being able to survive there is an achievement which sets Darwinites apart from other city dwellers. Despite the constant high temperatures, excessively high cost of living and somewhat unexciting surroundings, the people are most independent and more friendly to visitors than those in east coast cities and towns. The visiting yachtsman is made very welcome here, but considering the problems and more attractive alternatives, he needs a very special reason for visiting the city as will be realised by the end of this description.

With a population of around 50,000 in the 1980s, Darwin has doubled its numbers since the fateful cyclone on Christmas Day 1974. Cyclone *Tracy* toppled so many buildings and dwellings and killed so many inhabitants that Darwin was obliged to completely rebuild. Many people attracted by the high wages and ample employment during this period remained, swelling the ranks and helping to consolidate the local economy. Some people say Darwin has never been the same since, having lost her very special frontier personality and much of her friendliness. I have visited the area a number of times, both before and since *Tracy* and am tempted to agree.

The fact is, in the mid 1980s, Darwin has become an almost impossibly expensive place in which to live unless locally employed and thus enjoying inflated wages. The cost of transporting freight across the desert from Adelaide, from where it mostly emanates, is enormous and is further inflated by the local suppliers' propensity for adding large profit margins. Suffice it to say that I have seen items sold at trade price in Darwin costing much less at retail on the east coast. Such high costs, the lack of decent anchorages and the distance lost by diverting into Darwin explain why a yachtsman needs a special reason for visiting the place.

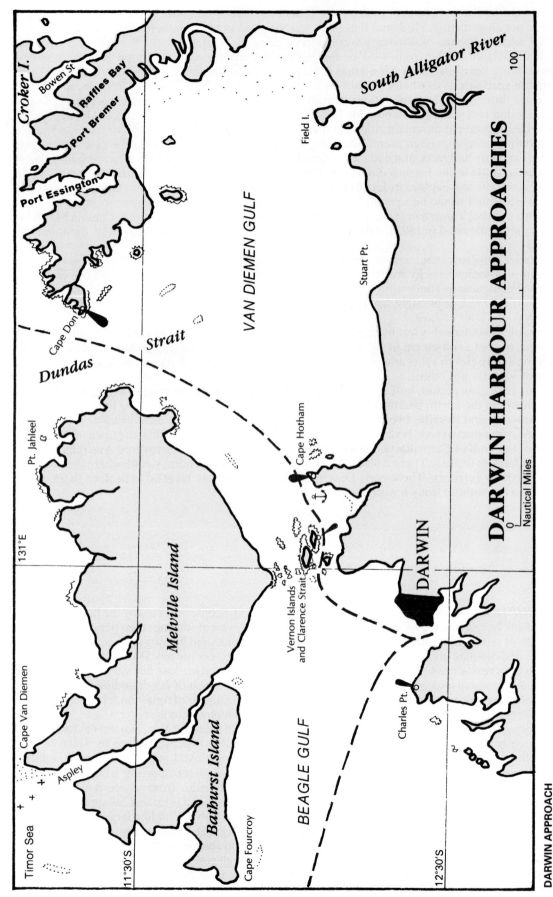

DARWIN HARBOUR APPROACHES

0   Nautical Miles   100

DARWIN APPROACH

Vessels approaching from the west or northwest may enter Darwin via Beagle Gulf whilst those coming from the east or north are best taken through the Dundas Strait into Van Diemen Gulf. The Clarence Strait is a reef and islet-restricted channel where strong tides are experienced.

General view of the Darwin Sailing Club yard and clubhouses. Visiting boats may be hauled out and stored here but living aboard once on the hard is not permitted.

Although I cannot recommend Darwin without qualification to the passing sailor I do, of course, recommend it to the person intent on coastal hopping. His experience would not be complete without a few weeks spent in this very special part of Australia.

APPROACH   The entire Northern Territory coast is predominantly low lying and landmarks are few and far between until the coast is close aboard. Persons making a landfall in the area after a few days at sea and out of sight of land should pay attention to their celestial findings so that a minimum of confusion arises when identifying landmarks. This is especially so when approaching from the west and northwest.

The most common approach is from the east by vessels coming from the Torres Strait or Gove or perhaps along the coast. From this direction Cape Don is the most important mark being the rounding point out of the Arafura Sea and into Van Diemen Gulf. The distance is 100 miles from Cape Don to Darwin harbour and the first potential anchorage en route is under the lee of Cape Hotham, 70 miles south-southwest from Cape Don. Dependent on weather and crew stamina, the visitor might consider anchoring in the region of Cape Don to freshen up before the haul down to Darwin. Fair anchorage is available under Cape Don or, better still, in Port Essington, 20 miles to its east.

Once in Van Diemen Gulf, the vessel must pass west into Beagle Gulf through the constricting channels amongst the Vernon Islands between Gunn Point on the mainland and Cape Gambier on Melville Island. This passage is called *Clarence Strait* and experiences strong currents and it is sometimes profitable to wait under the lee of Cape Hotham for a fair current.

Leaving Clarence Strait astern and steering again towards the southwest, Darwin appears at about 12 miles off as a cluster of medium height high-rise buildings 'in the sea' with Cox peninsula showing as a low line of trees to its west. Casuarina Hospital is conspicuous on low land with buildings spreading from its right.

The final approach into Darwin harbour is made passing red buoys to port and green or black to starboard. All buoys are lit.

NAVIGATION AIDS   All important headlands from Cape Don and right into Darwin harbour support powerful, flashing lights. Cape Don is manned.

All harbour buoys and beacons are lit with flashing red to port and flashing green to starboard (entering).

ANCHORAGE   Soon aftering entering harbour, Fannie Bay will be seen to port and will be conspicuous during winter by the forest of masts within. On closer scrutiny, both the Trailer Boat Club and the Darwin Sailing Club will be seen on the foreshore behind the beach. The latter club's haul-out yard will be seen to its right.

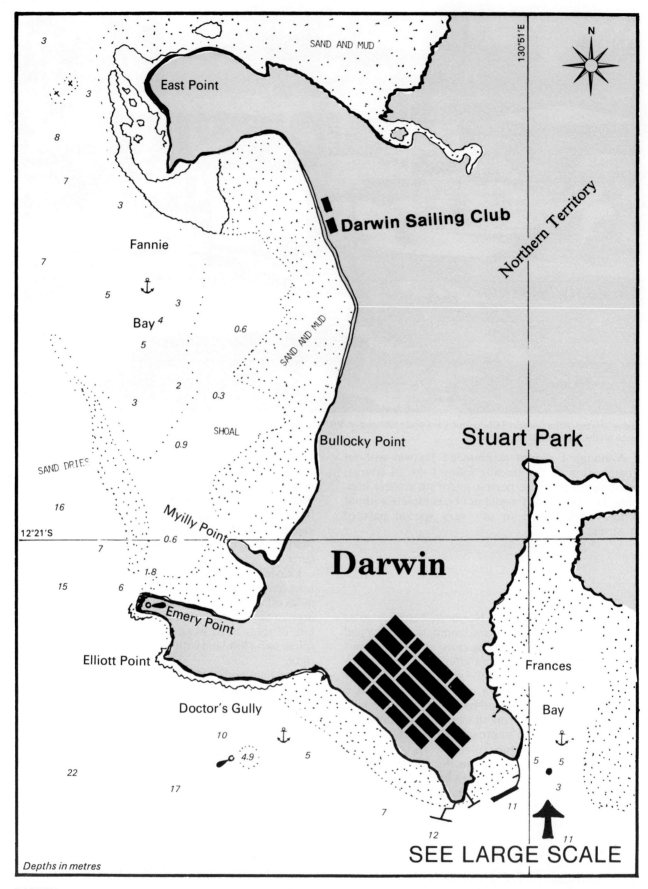

Depths in metres

DARWIN

The city and suburbs of Darwin are contained mostly on a west seeking peninsula which offers anchorage in Frances and Fannie Bay. Frances Bay is the less animated of the two.

Fannie Bay is entered more or less mid-channel between a rocky headland and the end of a long tongue of sand, and anchorage is taken wherever space
permits, but beware of interpreting the empty
space between moored vessels and beach, at high
tide, as being available for anchorage. This area
largely dries out at low water. Remember, tides in
Darwin harbour range up to around seven metres!

During trade winds of a persistency that allows
them to blow twenty-four hours a day, Fannie Bay
can be quite comfortable with only a modicum of
swell working into the bay. However, once the
wind dies, or is replaced by an onshore wind, the
area becomes very uncomfortable for living
aboard. Despite the wonderful facilities at the Sailing Club, it is often an investment in comfort to
move around to Francis Bay.

Those obliged to formalise their entry into
Australia in Darwin must proceed to Francis Bay
direct whilst those unwilling to row the long distances and suffer the rolling of Fannie Bay will prefer it despite a few difficulties of a different kind.

Francis Bay is immediately upstream of the main
shipping wharf which hooks out into the harbour
and encloses a small commercial area of ferries,
tugs and general workboats. The visitor will continue past this wharf and anchor where possible
amongst the moored craft in the vicinity. Beware
of cluttering up the lane used by coastal and ocean-
going barges which berth upstream from this
anchorage. Also, beware of anchoring too close to
other boats as windward-tide performances here
can be quite hectic when a spring tide ebbs against
the south-east trade wind. Use only a mud anchor;
the holding is good but the opportunity for fouling
one's own anchor is high if the wrong choice is
made.

Except when the trade wind is very strong and
the ebb tide stacks up waves against it, Francis Bay
is comfortable. Certainly there is no swell. The
greatest single problem here is in getting ashore
and then finding a safe place to leave the dinghy.
This problem increases in direct proportion to the
state of the tide.

The only place to put ashore in the dinghy is at
the ferry jetty inside the main wharf. But once
ashore, the dinghy must be moved. Very light dinghies can be carried up to the main wharf's deck
but heavier ones must be somehow tied so that
they neither obstruct commercial traffic, hang up
when the tide is low, or fetch under when the tide
is high. If you return to your dinghy three metres
underwater and flying from its painter like a kite,
you will certainly not be the first! Conversely, the
maddening business of finding the dinghy caught
up on the wharf's steel braces, many feet above low
water is not uncommon.

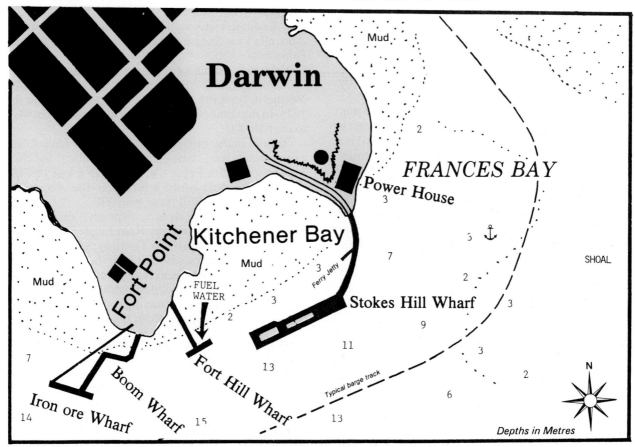

FRANCES BAY
Despite windward-tide conditions during a southerly wind, Frances Bay is essentially comfortable and offers the most
convenient access to the city of Darwin. When anchoring, allow for the passage of very large barges working
upstream.

I find the best solution to this problem is to use a long painter the end of which is taken up to the main wharf's deck. There it is taken in along the main wharf between ferry jetty and embankment and is belayed to a water pipe or handrail. There is still a chance of it drifting back under the main wharf and causing untold trouble but it most often carries clear with the current. If in doubt, a stern anchor can be dropped to hold it clear at all times.

Having solved, or learned to live with, the shore access problem in Francis Bay, the city of Darwin will be found an easy walk away. This is one of the greatest single advantages of this anchorage.

TIDES   Two highs and two lows occur every twenty-four hours with a spring high of around seven metres and a range of six. Neap tides tend to have a range of two to three metres. Resultant currents can run at up to three knots.

WEATHER   This subject is well covered in the south Indian Ocean description but details marginally more pertinent to Darwin are noted here.

Temperatures in Darwin tend to remain the same all year round. In the wet season (November to March inclusive) night temperatures rarely drop below 28° Celsius with day temperatures 33° and above. Extremely high temperatures, such as those experienced in southern parts of Australia during heat waves, are rare.

During the dry season (April to October inclusive), night and early morning temperatures can get down to 15° during a cold snap but mostly hold above 20°. Day temperatures range around 31°. Rain virtually never occurs in the dry season whilst it is brought by thunderstorms during the wet season.

As a matter of interest, whilst fitting out *Tientos* in Darwin in 1981, we had three consecutive dry season days of total overcast, periodic drizzle and a constant day temperature of 22°C. It was the most unusual weather for thirty years and felt like a freeze compared to the norm.

During the dry season the dominant wind is the southeast trade wind which, when strong, can hit Darwin with a slight southerly slant to it and when weak can be lifted into the stratosphere and be replaced by calms or even onshore northeasterlies or northwesterlies. For this reason, anchorages 'under the land', such as Fannie Bay, can be actually less comfortable in calm weather than when the trade wind is at full strength.

STAYING DURING THE WET SEASON
Because of the various problems confronting the live-aboard yachtsman in Darwin, it often pays to have the vessel lifted out into the Darwin Sailing Club Yard for the duration of the wet season. But this, unfortunately, presumes you will rent an apartment or find employment with accommodation, for living aboard 'on the hard' is not permitted.

Those wanting to remain afloat will find Frannie Bay, near the Sailing Club, untenable for most of the duration and Francis Bay becomes out of bounds

from the beginning of November unless the vessel moves to an approved mooring. This little bit of bureaucratic meddling is a hangover from the hysteria created by cyclone *Tracy* as the wet season is now looked upon as disaster time.

The yachtsman living aboard wishing to remain afloat in Darwin harbour has no option but to move up into one of a number of tidal creeks all of which place him so far away from the city and general facilities that they seldom meet his needs. It is almost obligatory, therefore, to take a tidal berth on Dinah Beach where comradeship aplenty will be found and the distance from town not too overwhelming.

MARINA   There is a strong possibility of a marina being built in Darwin, either in Francis Bay, upstream from the anchorage, or in Fannie Bay. If in the latter, it will almost certainly take the form of a basin excavated from dry land behind the beach and united to the harbour by a dredged channel. In all probability it will be contained by a lock gate and be open to traffic only at high tide. Those determined to seek employment in Darwin and to live aboard their vessel during the wet season might phone ahead regarding this potential facility. The Darwin Sailing Club should be able to advise.

HISTORY   The town site of Darwin was surveyed in 1869 and a year later the first pole for the overland telegraph from Adelaide to Darwin was installed. Port Essington was rather too remote as a base in Australia's far flung north being out on the Cobourg Peninsula.

Previously administered by South Australia, the Commonwealth Government took over in 1911, the Northern Territory became an independent state in 1978. In that time, Darwin's population rose from 944 to over 50,000.

Darwin is the only Australian city to have fully experienced war, being heavily bombed by the Japanese on 19th February, 1942 with a loss of 243 people. The post office which was the worst hit enshrines the names of those who fell.

Darwin's future prosperity depended on the discovery of uranium at nearby Rum Jungle and later in other areas of the Northern Territory; cattle farming and other industries also formed the basis of the town's economy. Tourism, interestingly enough, has boomed; the area's crocodiles, buffalo, wild pig, dingoes and good fishing attracting overseas sportsmen to the many safaris available in the area.

FACILITIES   Marine engineers, aluminium and steel fabricators, ship chandlers and all boat-orientated industries are very well represented in Darwin. There are also slipways, cranes, shipwrights, timber, resins and so on available as well as the wonderfully relaxing facilities of the Trailer Boat Club and the Darwin Sailing Club in Fannie Bay.

The shops of Darwin and the enormous supermarket complex out at Casuarina provide everything the yachtsman could ask for and there are public buses and taxis for those without wheels.

Such is the range of the tide in Darwin harbour that careening is no problem. This grid is owned and rented out by the Darwin Sailing Club. Darwin offers all boat support services.

Water and fuel can be piped directly aboard under the 'T' head of Stokes Hill Wharf as shown on the map, and the ferry wharf may be used for limited berthing whilst bulk loading and being boarded by customs on exit. An incoming vessel must wait at anchor.

THE ALTERNATIVE TO DARWIN Presuming the reader is not anxious to visit Darwin for employment or sightseeing purposes, he is well advised to consider other venues for his needs. Gove will be found to be superior on every point except availability of goods and services. Otherwise, Christmas Island has a very well-stocked small supermarket where prices are much lower than anywhere in Australia. This is discussed under its own section immediately after the south Indian Ocean description.

FORMALITIES Customs, immigration and quarantine authorities are all represented in Darwin and the main office is shown on the map. The officers are patient and courteous but are obliged to uphold Australia's stringent laws on the importation of animals or animal products. There is also a drug problem with the close proximity of Indonesia and Thailand. An incoming vessel from another country must not come alongside nor may any of its crew come ashore until the vessel has been boarded and cleared. Fly the quarantine flag and call on VHF Channel 16 if unnoticed.

When clearing out of Australia from Darwin, the skipper need only visit the office. If duty-free goods are required he must have them delivered to the waterfront by the agent under the eye of a customs officer.

Those sailing for Indonesia will find the Indonesian consulate off the highway at the suburb of Stuart Park.

THE WESSEL ISLANDS (Australia)

POSITION The Wessel Islands lie along a north-east-southwest line projecting from the northeast corner of the Northern Territory in the Aborigine reserve area known as Arnhem Land. Approximately 100 miles in length, the chain of islands have their approximate centre at 11°40′S and 136°E.

GENERAL DESCRIPTION The Wessel Islands can scarcely be called lofty with a maximum elevation of only 120 metres (Raragala Island). However, their windward sides are dominated by rather impressive, sheer cliffs giving them an appearance of height. Under their lee is 100 miles of fabulous calm-water sailing regardless of the strength of the trade wind. There remains, however, an element of doubt owing to the incomplete surveys of the southern area. Nevertheless, with eyeball navigation southwest from Raragala Island, the average navigator will not experience difficulty and the area does, in fact, appear free of isolated dangers.

The English Company's Islands parallel and to the south of the Wessels are included in the general description here as they are similar in every respect and also offer anchorages to a vessel passing through the area. These also have been incompletely surveyed but appear to be free of uncharted hazards.

All islands in the area under scrutiny here give promise of anchorage and all except Elcho Island are uninhabited. Elcho has a large and well-established Aborigine settlement on its southwestern tip. The whole group being Aborigine land, however, means that Aborigines might be found camping out, or in semi-permanent residence, on any island at any time.

The character of the land in the entire area tends to be rather uninspiring but unique for some of the strange rock formations, caves and cliffs to be found. There are no coconut palms leaving only a poor collection of stunted indigenous scrub to struggle against the elements.

In the uncharted areas, the seabed tends to be very undulating and one might occasionally panic whilst watching the echo sounder, but usually shoals do not threaten the average small boat. It is wise, however, to be always alert.

Inhibiting eyeball navigation to a certain extent is the lack of clarity in the water which can be deceiving as it gives the impression of clear water, but in fact is quite difficult to penetrate. For example, a coral head easily sighted two metres down at low tide can be impossible to sight at high tide with five metres over it. Fishing can be very disappointing considering the area's isolation, but absolutely outstanding if you come across a good patch. Lure trailing is recommended.

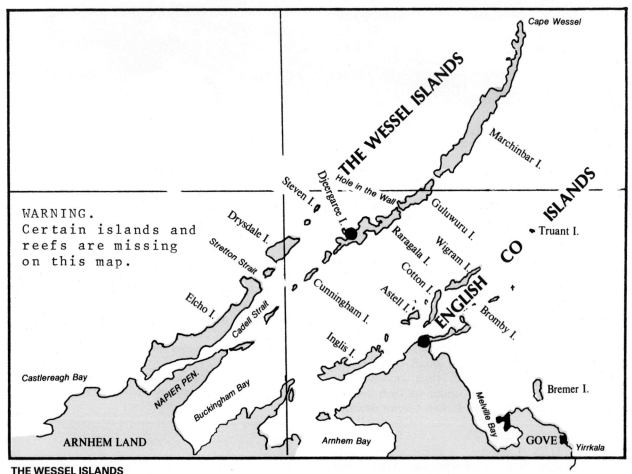

THE WESSEL ISLANDS
Projecting from the northeast extreme of Arnhem Land, the Wessel Islands offer a variety of anchorages.

A typical rock formation amongst the ancient, weather-worn islands of the Wessel group off the northeast corner of Arnhem Land, Australia.

Beaches are mostly of white to light yellow sand and are pleasant enough without being remarkable. It is always difficult finding a beach from which to swim since many have rock ledges at the neap low tide mark.

As a rule the coral in the area is of a very low grade and more often it tends to be a parasite on rocks rather than an entity of its own. Soft corals are common.

APPROACH Vessels sailing west direct from the Torres Strait, with no intention of stopping at Gove, should steer to raise the north tip of Marchinbar Island (Cape Wessel) fine on the port bow. The island's cliffline is visible in fair weather from about fifteen miles and there is a major unmanned light on the point. Beware of cutting in too close in rough weather as a considerable disturbance can occur off the point and extend to sea fully half a mile.

Those planning to rest at the Wessels can round up under the lee of Marchinbar Island and choose an anchorage from one of the many bays.

From Gove harbour, the approach to the islands is by logical elimination. It is the approach from the west that can cause some concern and doubt.

Any vessel making a passage from points west to points east should landfall onto Cape Wessel and pass it wide. Those planning to anchor within the group and/or bound for Gove from the west are advised to landfall on Stevens Island, half-way down the Wessel chain, so that immediate orientation is possible and anchorage can be sought before night makes it impossible.

Stevens Island rises as a low scattering of trees but quickly comes together as a low mound with no distinctive features. Closer in, however, a sand dune appears in the centre of the island after which a small cliff can be seen to its right.

Closer in, the sand dune takes shape as an irregular grass line above a beach that circles the island and later a rock ledge at the low neap tide level will be seen around much of the beach.

It is safe to hold Stevens Island close to starboard (entering), the water there carrying a minimum nine metres. Disturbed water in this area stretches north from the island and can appear from a distance like a breaking reef. Take care and steer outside this disturbance if in doubt.

Once inside Stevens Island, a remarkable ledge of red rock will be noted on its southern tip and its east coast should be favoured to clear a detached shoal to its east.

Having safely entered into the Wessel chain, anchorage can now be sought. Otherwise, those pushing on towards the English Company's Islands and Gove are advised to pass out of the Wessels through the passage between the second and third of the Cunningham Islets opposite Drysdale Island where a reef extends southwest from the larger islet and has three smaller islets atop its extreme edge. This will be found on a course south from Stevens Island. Reefs are shown on the chart in this passage but were not sighted by the author. Nevertheless 'eyeball' your way out or, if in doubt, other passages further south might be preferred.

Having cleared the Wessels, and now en route for the English Company's Islands, the best entrance in the latter group is to the south of Astell Island.

The islands of Astell, Cotton and Wigram are not visible from the above described Wessel exit, but those to their southwest are obvious although not necessarily definable. Soon after leaving the Wessels, however, all major islands of the English Company's pop above the horizon allowing course adjustment as you proceed.

From the English Company's Islands, the Wessels are below the horizon except for the cliffs on Raragala Island.

ANCHORAGES Charts show excellent large-scale detail of the Wessel's most northerly area (Marchinbar Island) where a number of anchorages are available in the various bays. To the south, under the lee of such islands as Guluwuru, Raragala, Cunningham, Drysdale, etc., anchorages may be chosen at random depending on mood and weather. It was my experience, however, that many of the bays shown as blank areas on small-scale charts are full of coral or rock patches amongst which anchorage cannot be recommended. Some are shoal overall.

The bottom in most potential anchorages is predominantly sand with scattered weed patches. These can appear from above as reef which they occasionally are, so a good lookout is vital when coming up to any anchorage.

Depending on individual choice, anchorages around the Wessel and the English Company's Islands will be found to be free of serious swell, but not necessarily of movement. Currents can bring a semblance of swell into certain areas. But, well chosen, most are secure and comfortable enough.

Two anchorages not shown on large-scale charts are illustrated. These are a mainland anchorage opposite Pobassoo Island in the English Company's Islands and Djeergaree Island in the Wessels. Anchorage, it has been stated, can be found in many other areas, and those yachts leaving or approaching Gove will find fair shelter under Cape Wilberforce.

135

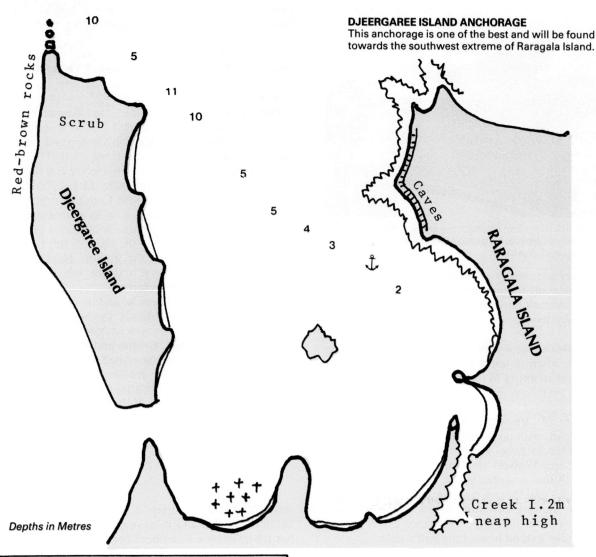

10

5

11

10

5

5

4

3

2

Red-brown rocks

Scrub

Djeergaree Island

Depths in Metres

DJEERGAREE ISLAND ANCHORAGE
This anchorage is one of the best and will be found towards the southwest extreme of Raragala Island.

Caves

RARAGALA ISLAND

Creek I.2m neap high

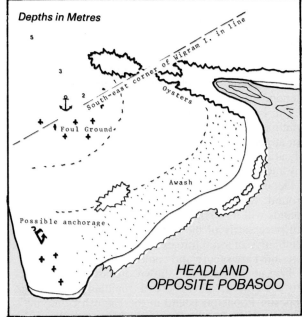

Depths in Metres

5

3

2

1

South-east corner of Wigram i. in line

Oysters

Foul Ground

Awash

Possible anchorage

HEADLAND OPPOSITE POBASOO

POBASOO ANCHORAGE
This unnamed bay is on the mainland opposite Astell Island.

CADELL STRAIT This is a shallow, calm-water passage between the mainland, at Napier Peninsula, and Elcho Island. Any navigator is advised to work a rising tide to around the halfway point from where the falling tide will assist rather than inhibit. If in doubt as to the whereabouts of the deepest water, work a making tide all the way through. There is not enough water in the channel for deep-keeled yachts at spring low tide.

The strait is beaconed but these are used more by radar-equipped vessels for distance-off measures. The visitor can only use his common sense and it is suggested that he speak to a Darwin-Gove barge skipper whilst either in Darwin or Gove prior to navigating the strait.

GUGAN RIP Also very aptly named 'The Hole in the Wall', this narrow passage separates Raragala Island from Guluwuru Island. Considering the choice of alternative passages through the Wessels it is not recommended to the visitor owing to its excessive current which can create rather spectacular overfalls at its eastern end when running east against a trade wind. During spring tides the current can cause loss of control forcing a vessel to back and fill to hold it off the rocks to each side whilst it is swept out into open waters.

This situation is not the norm, but despite adequate depth and freedom from detached reefs within, the passage is narrow enough to give rise to speculation on entering. It is thus described here only for those who enjoy a little low-profile adventure. Certainly it can be a most remarkable way through the Wessels, but neap tides and fair weather should be worked by the newcomer.

STRETTIN STRAIT This passage lies between the top of Elcho Island and diminutive Graham Island to its northeast. It represents one of the most common passages out of the Wessels (westbound) and has been used by the author without difficulty. However, I have since met a yachtsman who struck bottom in the strait and suggested that a warning be included here. Under the circumstances I feel that the passage over the top of Stevens, as recommended under 'Approach', is the better way into and out of the Wessels.

WARNING Visitors from another country (logically Indonesia) who have not previously cleared into Australia must, under no circumstances, anchor anywhere within the Wessels or along any other part of the coast. Formalities can be completed at Darwin or, closer to the Wessel Islands, Gove.

GOVE (Australia)

POSITION 12°12'S 136°38'E Northwestern corner of the Gulf of Carpentaria and northeast corner of Arnhem Land in Melville Bay.

GENERAL DESCRIPTION Gove harbour comprises Inverell and Wanaka Bays and tends to be from two to seven metres deep. It provides secure haven for small craft being fully enclosed and having good holding. To its northwest is Nabalco's aluminium plant and to the west is the aluminium loading conveyor wharf which accommodates bulk ships one at a time. Approximately ten kilometres from the harbour is the company town of Nhulunbuy and further along the road is the bauxite strip mine. Branching off this artery is the road to Yirrkala, an Aboriginal settlement from which mining rights were gained.

Typical of northern Australia, mountains are non-existent and hills commonly rise to only seventy metres. Naturally occurring palm trees are unknown, despite the climate, allowing common Australian trees to dominate. Many species are stunted owing to the harsh conditions of weather and soil.

Beaches tend to be of a reasonably fine yellow sand and the coastal water is clear, but seldom as sharp as that around well-developed reefs along Australia's northeast coast. Coral exists in the Arnhem Land area but is rarely found in dense clusters and is mostly poor.

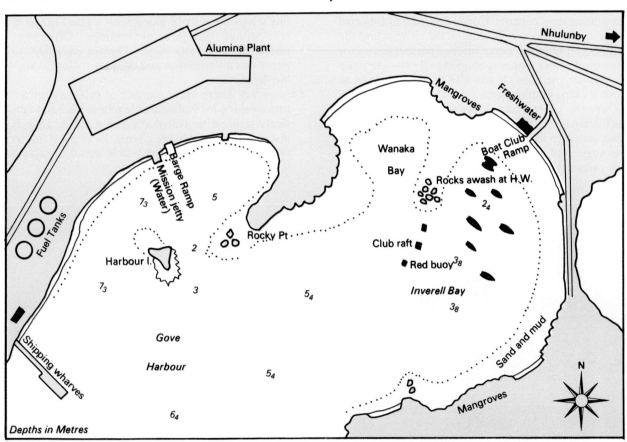

GOVE HARBOUR
Superior to Darwin in comfort and security, Gove is a bauxite mining town where most facilities will be found in severely restricted numbers.

APPROACH   Many yachtsmen using this book will approach from the east, their last port being Thursday Island in the Torres Strait. From this direction a proper landfall after the 330 mile crossing of the Gulf of Carpentaria will raise Gove Peninsula which will appear as a long flat-top 'island'. This 'island' is, in fact, Mount Saunders, on which will later be sighted the ABC's radio tower. Final approach, as marks become obvious, can safely be made between the mainland and Bremer Island; there being ample depth and minimal extensions from the coastal tidal fringe.

Those making a night landfall are advised that a new light was established on Veronica Island in 1983. There is also the older light on Truant Island. Both are to the north of Gove harbour and both oblige a yacht to haul hard on the wind for the final beat into the harbour. A daylight landfall is recommended.

Those approaching from the west or north will pass through the two island chains; the Wessels and the English Company's. As a result, a series of anchorages may well precede arrival in Gove and landmarks will be identified easily. The description of these two island chains precedes this section.

ANCHORAGE   All private vessels, as well as the Police and Fisheries vessel *Salloo*, moor or anchor in Inverell Bay. The holding is outstanding here over good sticky mud and only a severe westerly wind can cause any semblance of discomfort. Even then, most discomfort is found in trying to land the dinghy without wetting its occupants. Considering the isolation of the area, the enforced honesty of the citizens and the exceptional holding, Gove offers a perfect haven for any vessel whose owner is obliged to fly elsewhere on business or pleasure. It can also prove attractive to those seeking employment.

Over the years I have known Gove, Inverell Bay has filled with visiting and local boats to a point where close access to the Boat Club area is impossible. It is thus suggested that a person planning on an extended visit carry a dinghy outboard motor.

Wanaka Bay remains empty of boats and can provide excellent anchorage to those willing to travel the extra distance to the Club. At an extreme low tide this can oblige one to skirt around the rocks which start to dry at half tide and which are connected to the land by a rocky bank which remains awash. Beware of these rocks when moving around the harbour at high tide.

TIDES occur in Gove harbour twice a day and tend to be half the range of Darwin. This suggests a realistic maximum of 3.7 metres spring high down to a low of zero. They occur approximately three hours after Darwin.

FACILITIES   Considering it has a population of only 4,500 Gove offers a remarkable cross section of facilities for the visitor. These are listed here:

Gove Boat Club is situated on the beach front in Inverell Bay and offers honorary membership to all visitors. Launching ramp, showers, toilets, washing machine, boat stowage, under-cover odd-job area, a fully stocked bar and recreation area are available.

Slipping Nabalco's heavy equipment is available to anyone whose need to crane out is urgent. Otherwise, normal underwater work is carried out at the Boat Club's tidal grid.

A 3 metre tide easily places a vessel of 1.9 draught into the cradle. Maximum beam is 4.8 metres. A charge is levied.

Yacht Hardware A limited range is carried in Nhulunbuy's hardware store along with a good range of antifoulings and general coatings. Otherwise, phone direct to any of the Darwin chandlers to enjoy instant attention and delivery by first available flight.

Engineering There are a number of private contractors working for Nabalco able to machine and fabricate steel parts. Nabalco's own machine shop is also available to private clients. Because stainless steel 316 is the only permissible metal in certain

The alumina bulk loading facility at Gove harbour, northern Australia.

Approaching Gove harbour from the northeast, the alumina refinery dominates. The town of Nhulunbuy is ten kilometres south.

aspects of alumium refining, the local dump is a rich source of very useable pieces of this precious metal.

Timber Not much available but enough to make basic repairs if necessary. Certainly no dress timbers. Go to Industrial Park near Nhulunbuy or check dump for furniture, packing cases etc.

Upholstery can be made and repaired at Industrial Park. Basic sail repairs possible.

Spare Parts for most engines, pumps and so on can be ordered by phone from Darwin.

Fuel is available from the Mission Jetty. The best time is during light weather since most of the fleet is out, otherwise trawlers tend to cluster here, leaving no berth open. Phone BP first.

Water Although from an underground water table, the local water is excellent and there is no shortage. Demijohn it off from the Boat Club or hose it in from the Mission Jetty when possible.

Transport Nabalco run a regular free bus service between the town of Nhulunbuy and the refinery, or 'plant' as it is known. Walk from Boat Club up dirt road to sealed road and wait under conveyor belt.

Otherwise, walk towards town along sealed road to bus stop 32 at Wallaby Beach. There is a taxi service based in town.

Regular 727, DC9 and Fokker Friendship flights west to Darwin and east to Cairns. The latter much more expensive for some reason or another. Book with either Ansett or TAA in town.

Formalities No trouble clearing in and out of Australia here. Customs office is over near tug wharf.

Communications STD and ISD calls can be made from all public phones at the Nhulunbuy post office plus a few scattered around the area. The closest to the anchorage is near the Mission Jetty. Air mail is regular and reliable and, c/o Post Office, Nhulunbuy, NT 5797 is the best address for transients. Barges also serve Gove from Cairns and Darwin offering a useful service to a yachtsman wanting heavy items brought in. There is no road transport to Gove although a track from the Darwin-Tennants Creek Road is open to 4WD vehicles in the 'dry' (May to October, but often closed up until July. Local police will advise).

Accommodation is available at the Walkabout Hotel in town or at a motel at the airport. Both are expensive.

Money Just the one bank here, Westpac (ex Bank of NSW) capable of all transactions. No trouble with hard currency but Australian dollar is the best. The post office is a Commonwealth Bank agent but withdrawals of up to $50 per week only are permitted.

Shops include hardware, snack and coffee bar, newsagent (books, toys, tobacco etc), butcher, Woolworths supermarket, chemist, boutique, service station.

Gove Gazette is the name of the little local newspaper. It is available every Friday morning outside the newsagent free of charge and is valuable to the yachtsman for its general information and tide table.

Recreation There are many clubs in Nhulunbuy covering most sports as well as a modern air conditioned cinema, public swimming pool and regular sailing events. Darwin ABC and commercial TV here also.

WARNING Buffaloes are common in the Gove peninsula area and might be encountered on the main road when driving or walking. Approach with caution and proceed only when a beast decisively 'takes to the bush'. Crocodiles are also prevalent and swimming should be restricted to known areas. Up until the early 1970s they were often sighted on the beach around Inverell Bay but human activity in this area seems to have driven them away. There is also the possibility of the deadly sea wasp being encountered in the area during the wet season months of November to March inclusive. Beware of swimming during onshore winds or else wear protective clothing, such as skivvy and panty-hose.

SIGHTSEEING Being a small community in an isolated area, much pleasure is derived from social contact despite the stultifying effect of television. However, the visitor is recommended the weekly tour of the bauxite refinery and/or the strip-mining operation out of town. He will also find a most delightful freshwater swimming hole inland from the south corner of the anchorage. This crystal pool is the result of earth being taken to form the causeway between the mainland and the island in Inverell Bay.

COASTAL SURVEILLANCE Planes operate under contract to the Australian Government on a daily basis from the local airport. They range south to the Roper river and west towards Croker Island.

WEATHER The weather over the northwestern corner of the Gulf of Carpentaria is identical in basic character to that described for the south Indian Ocean. The centre of that area, Gove harbour, differs only in that the 'wet season' occasionally occurs slightly prematurely, fair westerly winds sometimes occurring as early as November. Cyclones are virtually unknown here but are possible.

HISTORY Gove shares the general history of the area as outlined in the section on Australia's 'North Coast'. Here it is of interest that Gove itself was named only recently after the American Lt Gove who was killed in action whilst based here during the Second World War. The present airstrip is an improvement of the American-built strip whilst certain meaningless sealed roads in the bush and the remains of two aircraft on display remind us of their endeavour.

Huge bauxite deposits were discovered in the 1960s attracting the Swiss-based multinational, Nabalco, who were obliged to pay handsome royalties to the local Yirrkala tribe for the right to mine an 80,000 acre lease. Production commenced in 1972 and the deposit is expected to be productive until the year 2060 at a mining rate of 28,000 tonnes per day!

Of interest; such are the power demands of this operation that Gove's power station produces more kilowatts than Darwin's and its mine-to-refinery conveyor belt is the longest in Australia at 27 kilometres.

Torres Strait

POSITION Between 9°00' and 11°00'S at 142°20'E.

GENERAL DESCRIPTION Within the rather loose boundaries noted above, this strait separates Australia from Papua New Guinea. Between the two closest points of land it is exactly 81 miles wide, however, a giant trying to step across would be assisted by the numerous stepping stones in the form of the large islands of Prince of Wales, Banks, Mulgrave and Saibai. If he trod carefully, he might use the smaller islands of Horn, Hammond, Mount Ernest, Jervis and Turnagain plus countless smaller islands, coral and sand cays.

Most of the islands mentioned above lie in a broad band the width of Cape York running across the strait north to New Guinea. There are, also, a variety of islands and cays to the east as the strait scatters through hundreds of coral reefs out into the Coral Sea. The whole area, in fact, can be described as a maze of islands and reefs between the two mainlands.

Ships with a maximum draught of 48 feet can, and regularly do, pass through the strait. They are assisted by the famous Torres Strait pilots and many lights, buoys and beacons provided by Australia's Department of Transport and maintained by its special division known as 'Nav Aids'.

All major channels are thoroughly charted leaving any properly equipped navigator in no doubt as to his whereabouts at any one time. There are, however, a few problems presented by weather, tides and anchorages as will be discovered under their own headings.

Thursday Island is the area's administration centre and largest town and enjoys its own description at the end of this section. It, and the Torres Strait, are also described fully in my book *Cruising the Coral Coast*. Here it is repeated in an updated, but slightly condensed form.

APPROACH There are four directions from which a yacht might approach the Torres Strait. These are: from the southeast along the Great Barrier Reef coast (this area is fully covered in *Cruising the Coral Coast*); from the east across the Coral Sea from Port Moresby; from the west across the Gulf of Carpentaria; and from the south, out of the Gulf and, typically, from Weipa. They will be looked at independently here starting with the most common approach. The possession of proper charts is presumed.

From the Coral Coast Having passed the tip of Cape York at Eborac Island, steer direct for Flinders Passage; the most conspicuous landmark, when closing the island group consisting of Prince of Wales, Horn, Wednesday, etc., is the 'horn' on Horn Island consisting of two distinct hills together. When entering Thursday Island harbour (Port Kennedy) use Flinders Passage. Boat Passage is safe but its western end can be difficult owing to sandbanks and fast flowing water.

Those bypassing Thursday Island to pass directly into the Gulf of Carpentaria can use either Endeavour Strait or Prince of Wales Channel.

From the Coral Sea The Torres Strait is entered from this direction by rounding Bramble Cay (light) and steering to the southwest down the Great North East Channel. The distance from Bramble Cay to Thursday Island is approximately 140 miles. It can be travelled safely overnight thanks to the many excellent lights but caution should be exercised regarding currents (see 'Tides'). Otherwise, overnight anchorages can be used.

The greatest problem with the approach to Bramble Cay from the Coral Sea is one of weariness after the short, 200 mile passage from Port Moresby. You need to be mentally bright and physically active but in fact can be shattered which makes it difficult to seek out the low cay and its trellis light structure from a sea that is more often rough than not, being as it is in one of the world's most persistent trade wind areas.

The navigator should beware of landfalling too far south where the northern end of Australia's Great Barrier Reef fragments or too far north where the shoals of New Guinea's Fly River might be found.

Sighting Bramble Cay is one of navigation's necessities and can be its greatest trial. Those without a satellite navigator should consider timing their arrival off the light at dusk so that the midday latitude sight can give an accurate position line along which the course might be steered or from which it might be adjusted.

Bramble Light is visible for seven to nine miles and sits atop a 21 metre high steel lattice tower. In daylight it is visible at around 11 miles. It gives a full one second flash.

From the west Inevitably a vessel approaching from the west must cross the Gulf of Carpentaria. This is discussed under Australia's 'North Coast', but pertinent to approaching the safest landfall is the Car-

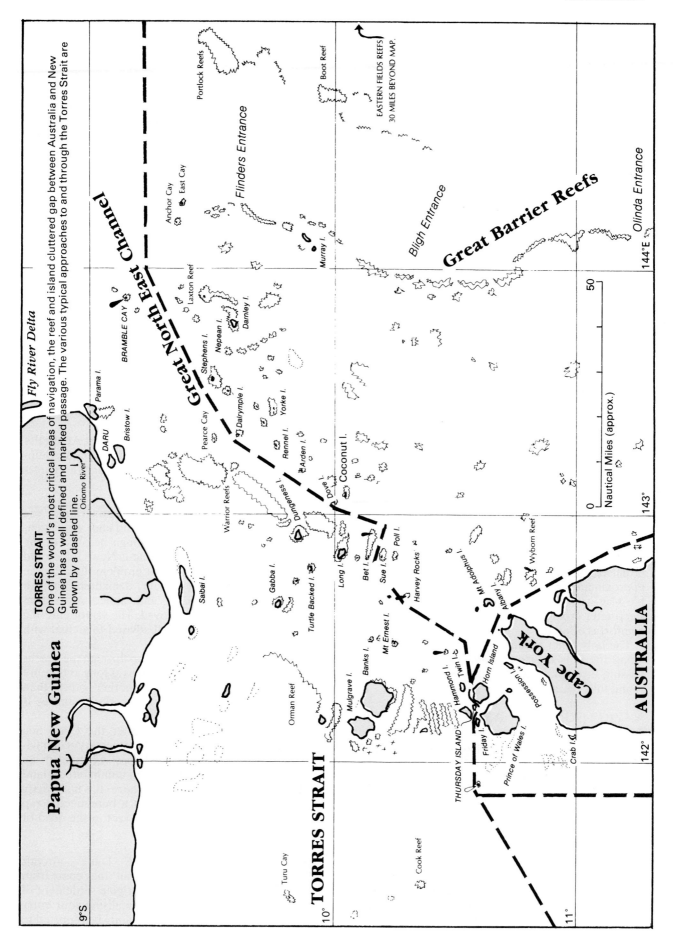

Papua New Guinea

Fly River Delta

TORRES STRAIT
One of the world's most critical areas of navigation, the reef and island cluttered gap between Australia and New Guinea has a well defined and marked passage. The various typical approaches to and through the Torres Strait are shown by a dashed line.

Great North East Channel

TORRES STRAIT

Great Barrier Reefs

AUSTRALIA

Cape York

pentaria lightship situated on the 7 fathom bank known as Carpentaria Shoal southwest from Booby Island.

The Carpentaria lightship is a red steel vessel with a single light structure standing amidships on its well deck. Its light carries for many miles. After this light is the major, manned light on Booby Island from where Thursday Island harbour is best entered between Friday and Goodes Islands. Beware, during a night approach, of over running marks when the current is favourable. This passage can produce rates of up to seven knots, but three to four is more common.

From the south Vessels approaching the Torres Strait from the south invariably come from Weipa, a bauxite town on the west coast of the Cape York Peninsula and approximately 125 miles from its tip. The mainland coast along this stretch is featureless having a continuous sandy beach broached by a few rivers. There are few good marks enroute, however, when the trade wind is well developed on the east coast, the west coast provides perfect calm-water sailing.

Endeavour Strait, between the mainland and Prince of Wales Island, can be entered from this direction outside Crab Island. But beware of the numerous sandbanks in the area and utilise a rising tide whenever possible.

ANCHORAGES It is difficult to find a truly peaceful place to rest within the Torres Strait, owing to the swift currents, strong trade winds and reefs and islands of a shape not consistent to good anchorage.

Those anxious to seek comfort at anchor will find the Oriomo River, opposite Daru and on the New Guinea mainland, very peaceful whilst certain parts of the enormous Warrior Reefs eliminate swell. But the only reasonable anchorage to be found along the Great North East Channel is behind Rennel Island approximately 50 miles in from Bramble Cay. Bramble Cay itself is often used by those desperate for sleep after crossing the Coral Sea but absolutely no comfort is offered.

The only other anchorage within the Torres Strait along the only course recommended to yachtsmen passing through, is at Thursday Island. This will be found fully described later.

NAVIGATION AIDS Australian navigation aids are taken very seriously and are installed and maintained by a division of the Department of Transport. Rarely will they be found extinguished or faulty thanks to the constant vigil of those on the service ships and workshops.

In the Torres Strait there are 26 light structures and 8 buoys which are maintained by such vessels as the *Cape Moreton* and *Lumen* on the advice of the chief mechanic stationed at Thursday Island.

TIDES AND CURRENTS I suspect there are more tidal stations within a given area of the Torres Strait than anywhere else in the world. These give a clear picture of height and flow to the many deep-draught ships moving through the Strait — especially Prince of Wales Channel — every day and night. A clear picture is demanded on two accounts; firstly because maximum draught, minimum depth is being worked and, secondly, because the tides are remarkable for their behaviour, often flouting man's finest prediction based on his years of experience and sophisticated tools.

Remembering that we have the Arafura Sea to its west and the Coral Sea to its east, it can be appreciated that the bit between, the Torres Strait, is under attack from two opposing directions. Added to this is the fact that the tidal range to the east is lower than that to the west. Thus there is a constant seesaw effect through the shallow Strait waters which are further restricted by reefs and islands. It is entirely possible to have a spring 'run' with little to no vertical movement or, conversely, a neap 'run' with considerable vertical movement. It very much depends on which sea is overwhelming the other at the time in question.

The visiting navigator will find a fairly well-behaved tide in the Great North East Channel but it becomes increasingly wayward the closer to the centre one gets. And the tidal centre, like the administrative centre, is Thursday Island. There the most remarkable performances will be witnessed; tides turning for no apparent reason, currents weaker or stronger than expected and so on.

The *Queensland Tide Tables* or relevant Admiralty publication, should be considered as essential equipment aboard any vessel venturing through the Torres Strait.

FORMALITIES Customs and immigration are well represented at Thursday Island and, whilst generally fair, they can be quite tough because of the close proximity of the area to Papua New Guinea and the resultant illegal immigrant problem. Quarantine authorities are no less lenient, demanding that all fresh food, especially eggs, and canned meats from any other country be destroyed. The visitor entering from another country is well advised to victual with this in mind.

Those intending to sail nonstop through thg Torres Strait are free of formal obligations as long as they are going from one country to another other than Australia. Anchoring under these circumstances is forbidden.

Those yachtsmen dog-tired after the Coral Sea crossing and unwilling to risk the necessary reef navigation down the Great North East Channel in an exhausted state may anchor at an uninhabited island as long as they do not venture ashore. It is not strictly legal but certainly better to get a bureaucratic rap over the knuckles than hitting a reef in the dead of night.

COASTAL SURVEILLANCE Daily aircraft flights watch the entire Torres Strait; they come from the airstrip at the mainland Aborigine settlement of Bamaga. If anchored before formalising your entry into Australia, you will most certainly be reported to the relevant authorities for sneaking ashore.

WEATHER It is a fact that the Torres Strait experiences one of the world's most persistent trade winds. Its consistency is often difficult to describe to a person who hails from another trade wind area, let alone those from areas of fickle winds. Facts would be difficult to exaggerate and are as follows.

During the months April to November, inclusive, the southeast trade wind blows through the Strait at a regular fifteen to twenty knots for twenty-four hours a day, seven days a week. It more commonly rises to twenty-five with gusts nudging thirty-five knots then eases, although calmer winds are not unknown with two or three days every four or five weeks of very light breezes, always from the southeast. Complete calms are rare but these, too, can actually occur for a day or two.

It is an essential part of their character that the trade wind seasons never change, but there is no doubt that some years are better, or worse, than others. For example, one year it blew for two months without any respite and only eased for three days before rising again and blowing hard for another six weeks continuously. During that particular year the trade wind actually dominated right through the summer northwest season! Another year might see the trade wind a little friendlier with less power to its gusts, with more frequent and longer periods of light-to-calm conditions but the difference will be more apparent to the local than the visitor unaccustomed to trade wind conditions; even a light season seems like endless weeks of strong winds to the stranger.

The southeast wind is the winter trade wind right around the southern hemisphere between, approximately, 5° and 25° south. It is most persistent between 10° and 15° south and always occupies the months April to November although in some less dominated areas the wind can start later and retire earlier.

Being between the two most critical latitudes, Torres Strait lies in the thick of the wind belt, but the greater persistence and higher speeds are due to a number of accelerating effects in the area. There is the effect of slightly warmer air rising off the shallow Strait waters causing wind to rush in to replace it and there are the lofty mountains of western New Guinea (now called Irian Jaya and part of Indonesia) lifting the inrushing air to cold and dizzy heights exceeding three thousand metres to further encourage air to rush in and replace it and lastly, and most profound of all, there is the funnelling effect. Wherever landmasses come together to restrict a large ocean, stronger winds are inevitable. It happens at the entrance to the Red Sea, between India and Sri Lanka, between Tasmania and Victoria and in the Torres Strait.

Having emphasised my point I will not soften the truth. The fact is the Torres Strait can be thoroughly unpleasant to anything but a sailboat going in the right direction. It makes anchorages already poor even worse; it makes walking unpleasant and it makes southeasterly passages utterly miserable and often impossible. But there is one thing we can say for it: it is reliable as well as being a known factor which one need not fear.

The southeast trade wind is a safe wind in as much as it never backs or veers and when anchored on the north-west side of a reef or island during the season one need never fear a lee shore. However, it tends to follow a physical characteristic; for example, along the Queensland coast especially from Cairns north to Torres Strait, it is very much a southeasterly because that is the direction of the land but in the Torres Strait itself, it can warp towards east-southeast as it tries to curve into, and through, the Strait. Rarely, it will reach a true easterly slant but it never attains northing except during the summer season.

In summer, known as the 'wet' season, the southeast trade wind progressively fades towards Christmas offering many total calms as it does so. Around Christmas there tends to be a period of unsettled, fickle winds before the north-west wind, carrying tons of rain, comes in from Indonesia and blows for around six weeks. Thunderstorms are common during this period and there is no guarantee that an open anchorage will not suddenly become a lee shore and for this reason navigation can be worrying making the wet season a good time to be settled in a secure harbour. Otherwise, those trying to work their way south and east should grab the transitional calms between seasons. Late December and early to mid-March tend to be the best times, but movement will depend almost entirely on engine power. 'He who waits for the wind, waits for the wrong wind' at these times of year.

The wet season is also called the 'cyclone season' for the simple reason that cyclones are likely between November and April but tend to be most common during January and February. In fact, the Torres Strait rarely experiences a destructive wind; most such winds travel south before becoming a threat to man, and gusts of over seventy knots are most unusual in the area and mostly emanate from thunderstorms.

To generalise, the wet season is a dominantly calm period but can be disturbed enough to make navigation hazardous.

INHABITANTS The Torres Strait islander is a race apart. He is certainly not related in any way to Australia's mainland Aborigine (at one stage it was beneath his dignity to intermarry with them) and looks more Papuan without the colour and feature extremes of that race. Because of their similarity, the immigration department have a difficult time preventing Papuans moving into the area undetected.

The islanders are very much a maritime race and lived on most of the major islands, especially Darnley and Murray out on the edge of the Coral Sea as well as Mulgrave and Banks above the Cape York peninsula. Most historians depict them as fierce and bloodthirsty warriors setting traps for European vessels then eating the hapless crew, and much of this might be true but 'hapless' Europeans asked for much of it by their total disregard for the locals' culture and human rights. The islander was little more than a cheap diver for the white man's pearl ships. What was once known as the Department of Native Affairs

(DNA), later to be called the Department of Aboriginal and Island Affairs and latterly the Department of Aborigine and Islander Advancement, is a Queensland Government section that caters to the needs of the Australian native whether he lives onshore or offshore. Needless to say, the department does nothing right according to most Aborigines and islanders but it does manage to hand out welfare cheques in apparent gay abandon and this has, in my opinion, been the greatest single blow to indigenous culture. Today there is no obligation to work and, I fear, the once proud and incredibly industrious Torres Strait native is but a shadow of his former self. In the main, he runs his affairs and his islands rather well, but nowhere will the visitor see a scrap of the past. Whether from white man's cruelty in the past or his overindulgence now, Australia's native races have taken giant steps backwards in terms of their culture.

HISTORY In 1605 Pedro Fernandez de Quiros set out from the Spanish colony of Peru with a fleet of three ships in search of the 'Great South Land'. He landed at, and named, St Phillips and St James Bay on Espiritu Santo Island in the New Hebrides, (now Vanuatu) and attempted settlement. Calling the settlement *La Nueva Jerusalem* and holding the first Christian service in that part of the Pacific Ocean, he placed responsibility for handling any conflict with local natives in the hands of one of his commanders, Luis Vaez di Torres.

Owing to illness amongst the crew, the settlement in St Phillip and St James Bay lasted only twenty-five days after which the fleet apparently split up, leaving Torres sailing west alone. Thus, in May 1607 Torres and his crew arrived in Manila in the Philippines by way of the Moluccas, after passing through the gap between Australia and New Guinea late in 1606. His name was given to the area by the noted British Hydrographer, Alexander Dalrymple, in 1767 and Torres Strait was annexed to Queensland in 1872.

Along with its remarkable tides and its persistent trade winds, the Torres Strait can also claim a most remarkable history being the venue for some of the most adventurous characters imaginable. The temptation to dive into this veritable sea of fascinating stories will be resisted here to be replaced by a recommendation that the reader endeavour to obtain relevant works for himself; discussions on Captain Cook's third voyage, Captain Bligh's mutiny, the wreck of the *Pandora*, convicts escaping by boat, or the pearling industry will include the Torres Strait.

THURSDAY ISLAND (Australia) (no large-scale plan)

POSITION 10°35'S 142°13'E. In the Torres Strait 20 miles west-northwest of Eborac Island on the tip of Cape York.

GENERAL DESCRIPTION Thursday Island, one of the smallest islands of its group at less than two square miles, is the administrative centre for the Torres Strait area and the only town of note being also called the town of Port Kennedy. It is contained by Hammond Island to its north, Horn Island to its east, Prince of Wales Island to its south and Friday Island to its west. Other islands, such as Goodes, Wednesday and Tuesday Islets, contribute to the creation of its harbour (Port Kennedy but more often called Thursday Island harbour). Regrettably it is a rather poor anchorage as noted under the specific heading later.

It is surrounded by a fringing coral reef of a moderately low continental type, varying in width and quality its top mostly dries at low water springs. The currents around it are often strong and occasionally unpredictable as described under the heading 'Tides' in the Torres Strait description previous to this.

APPROACH The safest approach for the newcomer from the east is via Flinders Passage between Horn Island and Wednesday island. It is well buoyed with lights showing red to port and green to starboard on entering the actual harbour.

Alternatively, Boat Passage, between Horn Island and Prince of Wales Island may be used when approaching from the east, but a long sandbank running like a spine down its centre often confuses and traps the unwary.

Jardine Rock, at the eastern mouth of Boat Passage, should be passed to port. It is marked by a red beacon and light.

Vessels approaching from the west are best taken through the passage between Goodes and Friday Island after landfalling on Booby Island. Beware of over-running navigational marks when working in with a strong east-setting tide.

ANCHORAGE Thursday Island was chosen more for its exposed anchorage rather than its protected anchorage to give the (then) engineless vessels a promise of fair wind which, if used wisely in conjunction with a current, would not necessarily carry the vessel back onto a lee shore. But a lee shore Thursday Island very definitely is and, as such, is most uncomfortable.

THURSDAY ISLAND
The township of Thursday Island is a typical country town with more than typical country prices. The visitor is advised to avoid victualling in bulk here.

Those determined to remain close to Thursday Island itself should anchor amongst, or outside, other vessels between Main Wharf and the Fuel Wharf (still referred to by some as the 'Naval Jetty'), or west of the Engineer's Jetty. In this area a strong trade wind makes conditions most uncomfortable when blowing against a current and also the holding is not reliable. The Admiralty Pattern (Fisherman's) anchor is best here but beware of windward-tide antics fouling the flukes.

Horn Island opposite Thursday Island, offers vastly superior anchorage in terms of both security and comfort. It lacks only convenient access to the latter's shopping centre and this can be offset by travelling across to Thursday Island by ferry or by using the dinghy. If the latter, make sure the dinghy is capable of thumping back against some formidable wind and currents. The reefs en route can be passed over by outboard at one metre tides and over.

Anchorage can be taken anywhere along the northwest face of Horn Island. The bottom is good-holding sandy mud with a minimum of weed inviting the use of the Danforth or plough. With enough scope, any vessel will hold here during the worst trade wind gusts. During very strong trade winds a swell of about half a metre at some six metres apart invades the anchorage when the current runs north but otherwise movement is minimal, created by wind.

When entering this anchorage beware of numerous cultured-pearl rafts.

FACILITIES The shopping centre at Thursday Island offers all essentials but all prices are inflated beyond a fair and reasonable freight-included level making it one of the most expensive places to victual so the yachtsman is thus advised to keep his purchases to a minimum. If en route to Gove he will find prices easier there and if sailing direct for the Indian Ocean, he will find Christmas Island, only 2500 miles away, one of the best places for victualling.

Fuel, water, fresh baked bread, soft and alcoholic beverages, etc., can be purchased at Thursday Island and Burns Philp and Island Industries Board's store nearby tend to be the cheapest for all galley lines.

Communication is good from Thursday Island with a post office, telegraphic facilities and operator-connected trunk calls to anywhere in the world. There are taxis on the island and Ansett runs almost daily flights from the Horn Island airfield to Cairns via Weipa, Iron Range and, sometimes, Cooktown. This service is outrageously expensive.

FORMALITIES Details have been noted under the same heading for Torres Strait. Here it should be noted that customs, immigration and quarantine authorities are based at Thursday Island with the customs house being near the Main Jetty. Yachtsmen entering Australia for the first time are obliged to fly the yellow flag and remain on board until boarded although it is permissible to anchor at Horn Island to await formalities if the Thursday Island anchorage is untenable.

WEATHER This subject has been covered under the Torres Strait section but will be recapped here.

The April to November southeast trade wind sometimes strikes Thursday Island slanted to the east-southeast. This makes little difference to the anchorage beyond creating slightly more windward-tide movement when the current is running north.

Being a child of high pressure systems passing over southern Australia and the Tasman Sea, the higher the pressure, the stronger the trade wind. A typical example is given here:

With a high pressure system centred over the Tasman Sea with a ridge up the Queensland coast and whose central pressure is 1035 millibars, there will be winds of about 15 to 20 with gusts to 25 knots between Cooktown and Thursday Island. The barometric reading at Thursday Island will be around 1013 millibars. Skies can be fully overcast or crystal clear depending on the amount of moisture collected by the wind but rarely does it rain during the trade wind season. Precipitation mainly occurs at this time of year close to steep mountains.

Thursday Island can be a charming place in the December-March wet season at which time its harbour is dominantly calm and its baked foliage turns lush and green. At this time of year Thursday Island itself is a better anchorage than Horn Island.

HISTORY Possibly named by Captain James Cook in 1770, but more likely named by Lt Phillip Parker King surveying in 1819 aboard the *Mermaid*, Thursday Island was formally acknowledged in 1877. At that time the coaling station at Somerset in Albany Passage (on the mainland) was transferred to Port Kennedy (Thursday Island).

Thursday Island, a base for government control and private exploitation, became the administration centre for the Torres Strait as well as the base for many large pearl-diving companies.

It was not until the mid 1900s that the pearling industry collapsed as plastics replaced shell in the manufacture of buttons and trinkets. The cheaper Trochus shell was tried and then, when it seemed the diving industry would die on its feet, cultured-pearl farming was commenced, bases being established at Horn Island, Friday Island and in other areas of the Torres Strait. Soon afterwards came the discovery of prawns in the Gulf of Carpentaria and Thursday Island became a major repair and maintenance base for the hundreds of trawlers that flocked to the grounds.

Today, pearl shell, crayfish diving and the prawn industry are Thursday Island's main backstays. Welfare cheques, however, are a major source of income as is reflected in the local shopkeepers' 'easy-come-easy-go' price structure.

The Great Barrier Reef

POSITION

Stretching almost full length along the northeast coast of Australia off the state of Queensland from the Torres Strait down to Lady Elliott Islet off the city of Gladstone. Approximately 1200 miles long.

GENERAL DESCRIPTION

That part of Queensland paralleled by the Great Barrier Reef is often referred to as the 'Coral Coast' for the obvious reason that the world's longest chain of living coral lies off the coast along the general line of the continental shelf.

The water between the coast and the first line of reefs, although often thought of as an impossible area to navigate, is, in fact, travelled annually by thousands of ships of all sizes. The greatest restriction to commercial vessels passing along the entire length of the coast is not the number of reefs along the way but the limited depth when breaking out of the Torres Strait. Thus vessels over 48 feet cannot enter or exit at the extreme north but they can, however, come and go from the south or via a great number of passages through the reef between the two extremes.

It can be appreciated that the inner route, as that part between the coast and reefs is known, is very definitely navigable and is therefore very well charted at both small and large scales and taking advantage of this is a large fleet of visiting boats who trek north from southern Australian ports annually or who arrive from overseas countries to spend a season 'on the reef'.

As well as visitors, the Queensland sailor himself is well represented; his yachts, motor cruisers and runabouts cramming every port along this fascinating coast. Tourists discovered the area long ago so facilities at the local ports are nothing less than international in standard. Quite apart from coastal resorts, there are twenty island resorts, two of which are on coral cays.

As yet, the tourist has not destroyed the option of isolation, for just as surely as he or she can fly from a capital city down south and be in tropical paradise within hours, so too can the yachtsman find an anchorage so remote as to be cut off from civilisation for as long as desired. It is this remarkable contrast that remains one of the greatest single attractions of the Coral Coast.

PORTS AND ANCHORAGES

As author of Australia's first cruising guide, which happens to be a guide to this coast, I cannot resist pointing out that my book, *Cruising the Coral Coast*, is now in its fifth edition and is available from all major and some minor bookstores along the coast.

Until confirmation can be extracted from its pages, the navigator can rest assured that the Coral Coast can very definitely be sailed by day. At no point along the coast is it obligatory to sail overnight but it is possible thanks to the excellence of navigational aids.

Anchorages range from isolated and rather exposed reefs to snug bays, inlets and passages and there is a major port every 200-odd miles except in the far north where a stretch of 450 miles must be covered between ports. Because nearly all anchorages, regardless of their type or nature, are mud or sand bottomed, the standard mud anchor is more than suitable. It pays, however, to have an Admiralty Pattern as the second bower ready for those times when there is a little more coral on the bottom than normal. This will only occur, of course, behind coral structures.

FACILITIES

Every major port along the Coral Coast has no less than one, and as many as four, yacht chandlers. Also, most towns have haul-out facilities or slipways as well as congenial yacht clubs, public and marina moorings. There are sailmakers, specialist electronic sales and service centres, stainless steel and aluminium fabrication shops and so on. In brief, it can be said that any repair can be effected along the coast at any one of the dozens of boat-building yards.

FORMALITIES

All major ports are ports of entry. Do not anchor (unless dangerously tired and willing to argue the point) anywhere until legally cleared.

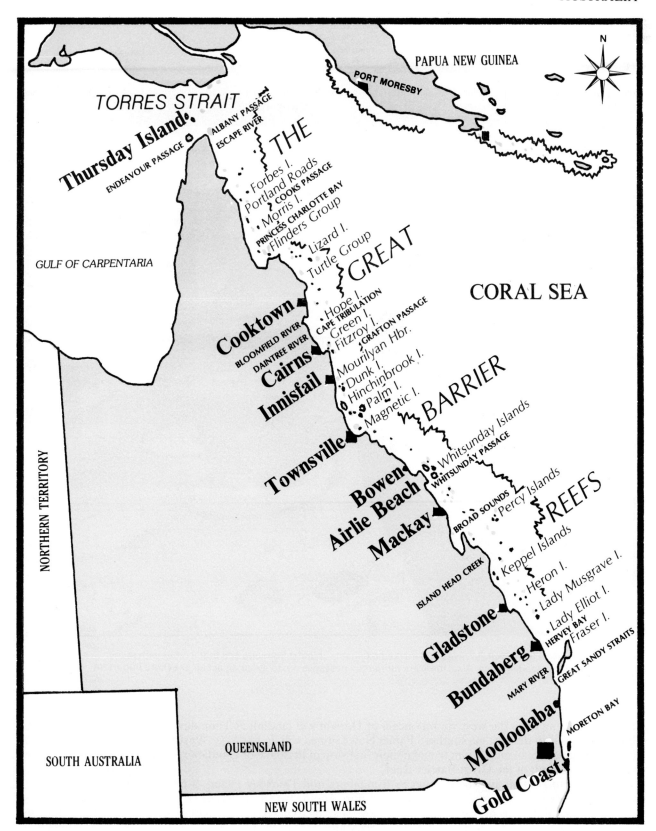

GREAT BARRIER REEF
A favourite cruising ground of national and international vessels, Australia's Great Barrier Reef stretches 1200 miles along the state of Queensland's coast.

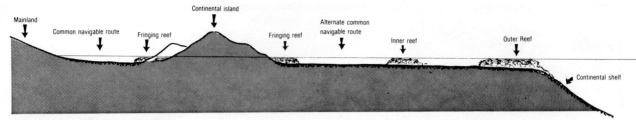

BARRIER REEF CROSS SECTION
In concentrated and simplified form, the Great Barrier Reef area looks like this in cross section. The outer barrier reefs tend to lie along the continental shelf whilst inner reefs are scattered between it and the mainland. Many inner reefs support cays whilst continental islands all have fringing reef.

BARRIER REEF
The Great Barrier Reef has a well surveyed and marked navigable channel from one end to the other with many alternative channels along the way. Also, there are numerous passages out to the open ocean, the more important ones being beaconed.

LANDFALLS

The sailor coming from the west via Indonesia or Darwin will landfall at Thursday Island in the Torres Strait. Those coming from the east via southern Papua New Guinea will do likewise. Westbound sailors coming out of the south Pacific Ocean mostly aim to make their first stop in Brisbane or Bundaberg. Both these ports are south of the southern limit of the Great Barrier Reef.

To attempt to landfall anywhere between Bundaberg and Thursday Island, a distance of some 1200 miles, means that the barrier reefs will be encountered before finding land and this can be dangerous if the navigator is in any way doubtful of his prowess. However, those wishing to make such a landfall are recommended Grafton Passage outside the port of Cairns, as not only is the outer edge of the passage well marked but a major light will be found on an isolated reef further offshore. This is Bougainville Reef which provides an ideal preliminary reference.

BEST TIME TO CRUISE

The best time is undoubtedly the winter season. This occurs between May and October during which time there is an absolute minimum of rain, if any, and the wind remains true from the southeast subject to variations as noted next.

WEATHER

This is the same as in the Torres Strait, south Indian Ocean, and so on, but deserves mention here because of a few special conditions that can occur to the sailor's advantage.

North part Between Thursday Island and Cairns there is a very boisterous and reliable southeast trade wind. This blows almost without let up from April to November. Commonly Force 5 it reaches Force 7 for 3 days every couple of weeks.

Between December and April the trade wind is largely replaced by the northwest wet season but in most years this fails to affect the coast any further south than halfway between Thursday Island and Cairns. The southeasterly prevails although with less gusto and between many lengthy periods of calms. This is the cyclone season and the area from halfway down to Cairns is cyclone-prone.

Cairns to Bundaberg This includes the remainder of the actual Coral Coast. The Queensland coast in fact extends down to its capital, Brisbane, another 300 miles south.

Basically, similar conditions prevail, the southeast trade wind dominating the winter April to November season. However, the transition periods, April to May and then October to November, can bring promise of more calms and variable winds and the spring transition (October-November) can bring very useful and often strong northerlies. These can be used to great advantage when planning a cruise north from which a return south is anticipated.

During the December to April wet season, the southeasterly returns and prevails but again with greater periods of calms and chance of variables. When a cyclone occurs, however, the wind is invariably southeast and can reach destructive strength.

The inner route, between the Great Barrier Reef and the Queensland coast is used constantly by commercial ships of all sizes such is its well defined and surveyed deep water. Only at certain bottle necks is the private boat obliged to pass close to larger ships.

GREAT BARRIER REEF
Contrary to popular belief, most anchorages along the Great Barrier Reef are behind mainland headlands or continental islands. Rarely is one actually obliged to anchor behind coral alone. This is under the lee of Cape Grenville and the island in the background (Sunday Island) is where Captain Bligh's authority was challenged during his epic open boat voyage.

South Indian Ocean

The reader should refer to the current and wind charts on page 22.
The following describes the south Indian Ocean for those intending to cross it from east to west whether their passage takes them back to the Red Sea or to South Africa. In the interest of clarity, the description stops at the Equator, those seas and countries above the Equator having been described earlier. This section is followed by specific anchorage guides to Ashmore Reef, Christmas Island, Cocos (Keeling) Islands and the Chagos Archipelago.

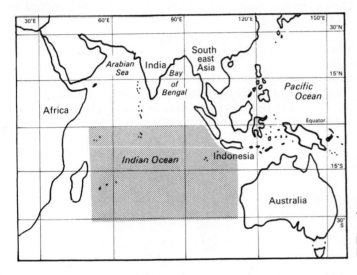

The second largest ocean in the world, the Indian Ocean bridges Australia and Africa. Here it stops at the Equator for simplicity's sake. Detailed maps will be found in the chapter, 'The Best Route'.

GENERAL DESCRIPTION

The south Indian Ocean represents to the cruising boat the second longest passage in terms of crossing oceans. Very broadly speaking, such a passage in the Atlantic Ocean is around 4000 miles whilst in the Pacific Ocean it is 8000 miles. In the south Indian Ocean it is 5500 miles.

Only those yachtsmen on endurance runs need to produce this high nonstop mileage as all oceans offer anchorages en route and the Indian Ocean is no exception, her longest obligatory stretch being the 2500 miles between the Cocos Islands and Rodriguez.

For reasons to be explained, the south Indian Ocean is recognised as one of the least comfortable for small vessels on account of its very well-developed trade wind regime and areas of cross-swell. But discomfort should not be read as dangerous for a great variety of very small yachts make this passage annually in absolute safety.

DEPTHS

In the centre of the West Australian Basin between North West Cape and the Cocos Islands, depths exceed 6000 metres. The deepest point is in the Sunda Trench below Java at 7450 metres. Most other basins tend to be around 5000 metres deep and the majority of the ocean has depths down to 2000 metres.

CURRENTS

A broad band of west-flowing current assists the westbound vessel all the way from Australia to Africa. This is known as the Equatorial Current. Its counter current, sometimes known as the Indian Counter Current but more often referred to as the Equatorial Counter Current, runs eastward in a band roughly 5° north and south of the Equator. This is commonly very weak or missing altogether although it is capable of rates up to 3 knots.

THE SEA

There is nothing extraordinary about the basic behaviour of wind-driven waves. Indeed, in certain areas they are exceptionally orderly and predictable and, as a result, comfortable. However, a persistent beam swell upsets this order in other areas and can make life aboard rather trying most noticeably in the northeast corner of the ocean between the Timor Sea and the Cocos Islands. It sometimes extends south to the southern limit of the trade winds and west beyond Cocos Keeling.

The above mentioned swell is dominantly from the southwest suggesting that it is a child of the Indian Ocean high pressure system which creates the trade winds over its northern part and westerlies along its southern part. To its east a swell pattern moves north to attack the area noted at right angles to the south-east trade wind.

Basic observations made by the author during a total absence of wind suggests this swell runs at heights of up to 3 metres with crests approximately 100 metres apart.

WEATHER

From April to November inclusive the southeast trade wind blows with monotonous continuity between latitudes 5° and 25° south with the best developed and most persistent band being between 10° and 15°. This period is free from cyclones although unseasonal blows have been recorded. As with any other destructive wind area, the Equatorial belt is entirely free of cyclones all year round.

By rule of thumb, the navigator can expect absolute freedom from cyclones during April through November with December mostly safe towards the Equator. In the southern area, especially around the island of Mauritius, cyclones commonly develop as early as November.

From December to March inclusive, the high pressure system moves south maintaining a southeast wind flow over the southern area but admitting a northwest flow from the northern hemisphere. This is a warping of the northeast monsoon and is mostly very poorly developed in terms of reliable wind. It does, however, bring rain and can blow persistently during the months of January and February.

In the 'collision' area between the southeasterlies and the northwesterlies, tropical revolving storms develop from where they track west and south to cause most damage in a belt between 10° and 25° south although cyclones outside these boundaries can occur.

It is because cyclones are produced in the vicinity of 5° or 10° of latitude that they rarely become dangerous until moving south beyond the area of their birth and whilst their exact track can never be predicted with absolute accuracy it can be said that they never venture north. It is this fact that makes the Equator quite safe.

The December to March cyclone season is often called the 'wet season' or the 'northwest season', the last description being the most misleading to a yachtsman because the northwesterly cannot be viewed as useful passage making wind.

POLITICAL

Because of the oil flowing out of The Gulf from Iran, Iraq and other producing nations, the Indian Ocean as a whole experiences a lot of attention from the superpowers. Russia may have occupied Afghanistan for an eventual 'window to the sea' and in the meantime Russia has dozens of peepholes scattered around in the form of sympathetic nations and it is rumoured she has a base in India's Laccadive Island whilst Aden is virtually hers to do with as she wants. In the south, recently independent nations have swung hard left and can probably be counted on as base sites in the future. To counter this trend, America leased the Chagos Archipelago from Great Britain, displaced all its inhabitants and set up a major air and naval base right in the centre of the ocean. It would appear that stalemate has been reached although neither side really admits to playing a game.

Between the heavies are other countries who depend on the Indian Ocean for trade and commerce and their plea is, of course, for stability. India's intention is for the entire area to be a 'zone of peace' whilst supporting those who would have America thrown out of the Chagos archipelago in favour of the return of the inhabitants; an idealistic view not quite in accord with today's realities.

Regrettably, today's realities imply that world peace is only possible through constant threat of war and in this context the Indian Ocean enjoys peace. There are very few places out of bounds to the private boat and, interestingly enough, the only place totally out of bounds is owned by the United States! In fact, American-controlled Chagos can be cruised in part as noted in detail at the end of this book. Meanwhile, the following is a roundup of countries in or around the south Indian Ocean.

AUSTRALIA   This has been fully described earlier. Its west coast is the south Indian Ocean's eastern boundary.

CHRISTMAS ISLAND, COCOS (KEELING) ISLANDS, CHAGOS ARCHIPELAGO are all described after this section.

RODRIGUEZ ISLAND   The first land encountered after departing Cocos Islands for the classic run across to Durban in South Africa, Rodriguez was an important cable and wireless station whose history has been closely linked with Mauritius from where it is governed.

Visitors are welcome and permission to stop in the main port of Port Mathurin may be obtained by radio from the resident commissioner but those without radio should find the authorities friendly enough if entry is made without prior warning. According to English circumnavigators Mike and Di Garside, Rodriguez is a most enjoyable place to visit.

MAURITIUS Some 400 miles further west than Rodriguez and a standard stopover for nearly all cruising boats, Mauritius is a lofty island of spectacular beauty both inland and round its coast. Mauritius was discovered by the Portuguese in 1508 and named by the Dutch after Prince Maurice of Nassau in 1598; the French colonised the area for nearly a century up to 1810 at which time England won control. Independence was granted in 1968 and in 1982 its government became Marxist overnight after a landslide victory for the socialist party. The island is overpopulated with 720 square miles and a population of nearly one million and it is overdependent on sugar. Tourism is consequently something of a holy cow that not even a Marxist government dares upset and as a result visitors are welcome.

The port of entry is Port Louis where yachts are usually moored alongside the waterfront near the customs landing steps. Firearms must be declared to the boarding officer and a vaccination certificate against yellow fever is required of visitors from infected areas. Cruising Mauritius is permissible after proper entry at Port Louis with the most popular destination being Grande Port on the southeast side.

Mauritius seems to attract an unreasonable number of early cyclones suggesting that the small boat should be out of the area, or well entrenched, by mid-November.

REUNION Réunion is a craggy island some 3069 metres at its highest peak and still a French colony with a gift economy adequate enough to dull any thoughts of independence. Its active volcano and lava flows make for some splendid scenery whilst the main town and port of entry, St Denis, is a piece of Paris transplanted into the Indian Ocean and despite a high cost of living it is well recommended.

MADAGASCAR is easily the largest island in the Indian Ocean whose bulk obliges a vessel to pass to its south en route from the above noted islands to Durban. Late in the year the southeast trade wind readily rises to gale force for brief periods and thunderstorms with spectacular displays of lightning are not unusual.

A few yachts have stopped at Madagascar but reports suggest the situation is rather uninspiring; the strongly Marxist government not quite bending over backwards to welcome visitors. The general advice is that Madagascar is safe enough for those determined to stop but scarcely does the effort prove worthwhile.

EAST AFRICAN COAST This is dealt with in the chapter 'Safe and Unsafe Countries'. Most yachts following descriptions thus far will automatically continue to Durban in South Africa, which is a completely secure and safe country from every point of view and where there is still a good opportunity of gaining employment.

Persons contemplating a cruise down the East African coast will more logically approach from the Seychelles in which case they will sail down the Mozambique Channel. This passage is noted as Route A9 in the chapter, 'The Best Route.'

SEYCHELLES Returning to the passage from Cocos (Keeling) Islands to the Seychelles Islands the reader is reminded that both the Cocos Islands and the group en route to the Seychelles, the Chagos Archipelago, are fully described after this section.

Another Marxist governed country, the Seychelles seem to experience rather regular coups which somehow occur without upsetting its tourist economy too greatly. Indeed, talking to one yachtsman who was in port for the 1981 coup, tourists continued to sunbake on golden beaches whilst the bullets flew not far away and whilst yachtsmen were more intimidated because of their position in harbour; there was no feeling of aggression towards outsiders. It was annoying, however, that they could not legally leave the trouble area because they were not permitted ashore to clear customs!

For all that, the Seychelles are a beautiful area which once knew a continual stream of foreign boats and now sees only a dribble. But boats still go there and crews report enjoying the place immensely so the area cannot be placed on the dangerous list. It can, however, be pointed out that cruising the actual area has been severely limited, a fact that reduces its attraction as a destination in itself.

Unless en route for the African east coast, in which case the Seychelles are nicely on the track, they cannot be recommended because of the dogleg they introduce to a course for the Red Sea. By far the better way to return to Europe is to leave the Cocos Islands and steer direct for Sri Lanka from where the northern hemisphere route across the Arabian Sea is more direct. The best time of year to leave the Cocos Islands for this passage is late October and early November. This presumes the sailor wants to have as much time in the southern hemisphere as possible before the cyclone season yet still arrive in Sri Lanka in ample time to prepare for the passage across the Arabian Sea during its prime cruising season in January, February and March.

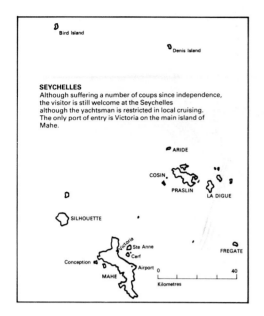

SEYCHELLES
Although suffering a number of coups since independence, the visitor is still welcome at the Seychelles although the yachtsman is restricted in local cruising. The only port of entry is Victoria on the main island of Mahe.

ASHMORE REEF (Australia)

POSITION Less than one hundred miles south of Roti Island, Indonesia (near Timor), and almost exactly on the border between the Timor Sea and the Indian Ocean.

GENERAL DESCRIPTION The islets of Ashmore and Cartier Reef belong to Australia and come under Northern Territory control although they are closer to Indonesia.

Ashmore Reef is a single coral structure supporting three islets, all of which are typical, low cays, the ground rising less than three metres with only stunted shrubs and stringy grass. Their host reef mostly covers at high tide with its uppermost portion exposing at low tide. Tides in the region appear to have a range of about three metres maximum.

The three islets of Ashmore are called East, Middle and West and can be seen from a distance of about six miles. In calm weather a green glow in the sky above the reef is often seen from a much greater distance.

The best anchorage is in ten metres, sand, off West Islet where fair holding will be found but seldom is the swell negated.

The area is a favourite — and strictly speaking, illegal — fishing area for visiting Indonesian *praus* who have a well on one of the islets.

For the above information I am indebted to Andy van Herk of the Canadian ketch *Eryngo*.

CHRISTMAS ISLAND (Indian Ocean)

POSITION 10°35'S 105°37'E 260 miles south of Sunda Strait and 650 miles south of west from Bali. Australian territory.

GENERAL DESCRIPTION Christmas Island is the coral encrusted tip of a long-extinct volcano that probably emerged some 50 million years ago. It rises more than 5000 metres from the ocean floor but exposes only about 300 metres above water and this exposed area is one of terraces and plateaus with an almost continuous cliff around the island between the two.

As it slowly emerged from the sea — probably as three distinct islands surrounding a lagoon — coral encrustation smothered the landmass to produce a limestone formation on and around the island. This was seeded by wind and bird-carried seed until it became cloaked in rich vegetation, much of which is rain forest. Bird droppings were also caught in the limestone base to become a rich source of phosphate for man to later mine and sell as fetilizer.

Today Christmas Island is a natural paradise, parts of which are being torn apart for the phosphate thereunder and all of which tends to be inhospitable to seaborne man for there is a distinct lack of secure anchorage. But the effort of getting and being there is worthwile for not only is it a unique area to see, but it also offers the best victualling in the Indian Ocean.

APPROACH As there is no anchorage during the northwest (wet) season it is presumed that yachts will approach Christmas Island only during the April to November southeast trade season. In this case the approach will be from the west.

In fair weather and by climbing the mast, the island is visible from a distance of about 35 miles, then from the deck at a distance of about 30 miles. From these distances it appears as two low, flat-topped islets, the northern one being larger than the other. The two join rapidly to become one long, low island with a moderate saddle between the two hills.

From about 20 miles off, mining activity on the south end is evidenced by a white scar along the hill top and in this area there might be experienced a slight south-setting current.

When loading phosphate at Christmas Island, ships moor to a pattern of buoys whch hold them in position under the bulk loading gantry. During the northwest wet season, this gantry is often smothered in spray from onshore wind and sea.

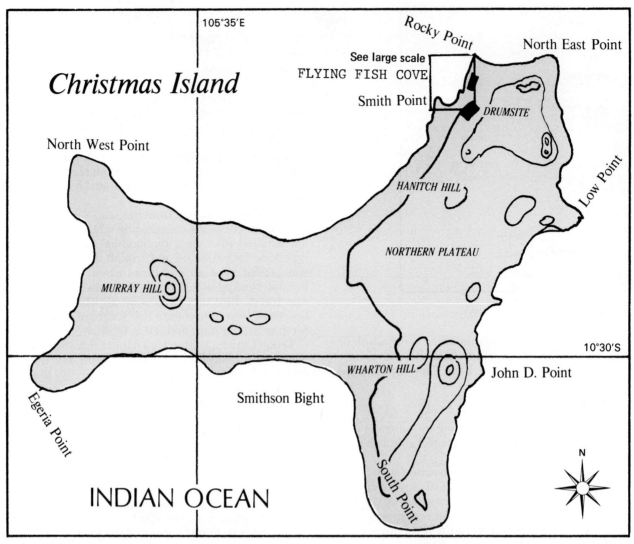

CHRISTMAS ISLAND
Lying along the favourite route from Australia to countries in the west, Christmas Island is Australian owned and is famous for its guano deposits.

Final approach into the only anchorage on the island (Flying Fish Cove) is made by rounding North East Point then following the coast around to the anchorage which will be more than obvious by the phosphate-loading gantries and other yachts at anchor.

The coast is quite free of offlying dangers the greatest problem being excessive depth rather than shoaling.

ANCHORAGE Flying Fish Cove, which lies under the lee of the northernmost headland, is the only anchorage available owing to its extensive shoaling in the bay (relatively speaking) and minimal disturbance from swell. This shoaling is in the form of a coral ledge over which the small boat is obliged to anchor; there is no alternative as the bottom dives off into great depths immediately off the ledge.

In the vicinity of the barge jetty there will be found a few coral-free sand patches, otherwise the bottom is a thick coral carpet with a few isolated gonkers higher than their surroundings. None of these present a danger to an anchored vessel unless too close to the fringing reef which exposes at low water springs. The holding is good with any anchor as it is unlikely that one would not grapple into the coral; the chain rumbles and snags a lot but it is secure.

The fringing reef is piled limestone with many boulders which expose over one metre at low tide. Do not anchor too close to this fringe as the swell backsurge could carry a vessel on.

During true southeast winds the anchorage is surprisingly comfortable with only a minimum of roll and surge, but when the wind favours the east the swell becomes pronounced from the north as it follows the coastline into Flying Fish Cove. The anchorage remains secure but the vessel tends to ride the swell more on her beam; also, with the wind in the east, gusts rounding the headland tend to carry phosphate over the anchorage. If a ship is loading at such time the visiting vessel will be covered in fine dust.

The worst swell condition is during a lull when the swell loses direction and mindlessly lops into the cove. With no wind to hold the vessel offshore, be certain the scope of your anchor cable prevents the vessel backing onto the fringing reef. Considering the swell in this area, total loss of ship would almost certainly follow a grounding.

Christmas Island appears from seaward as a long, low island comprising two distinct raised plateaus. This is the northern tip where, on closer approach, will be seen a two storied building. This is the golf club.

TIDES at Christmas Island occur twice daily and have a range of about 1.7 metres.

WEATHER Being in the south Indian Ocean trade wind belt, the weather here is identical to that described already. Pertinent to Christmas Island, however, is the fact that the moist trade wind air readily precipitates over the island and can thus bring rain at any time of the year. However, the most dominant wet period is the northwest 'wet' season between November and April with the wettest month tending to be March.

FORMALITIES Provided there is no suspicion of disease aboard the visitor may venture ashore to clear. If not met by police at the dinghy landing, call them on the phone which will be found at the barge jetty. If you have VHF, advise ahead on Channel 16 to Christmas Island Marine.

Visas are not necessary here but both customs and immigration procedures must be cleared, and are carried out at the local police station. Prior to clearing from Christmas Island it is necessary to settle any bills; especially the boat club's bar bill.

FACILITIES Christmas Island offers excellent facilities for the visiting boat. These are listed here.

Fuel Petrol must be demijohned down from the settlement but diesel can be piped aboard from the barge jetty. Arrange with the transport pool at the top of the hill for a tanker truck to come down to the jetty. Choose a day of least swell and berth anchor-out and sternfast to the jetty.

Gas and paraffin are also available from the transport pool behind the hardware division. Methylated spirits can be purchased at the supermarket.

Water comes from a waterfall not far from North East Point and is treated before use. It is slightly hard but one quickly acclimatises to it and it does not appear to effect the tanks in any way. It can be demijohned from a tap near the barge jetty or a collection of long hoses might reach the end of the jetty. Make sure there is no shortage before using the water.

Supermarket lines are well represented at the settlement's trade store opposite the service station. All freight is subsidised and taxes are waived making some food items much cheaper than Australian mainland rates and all grog just a little over half price (with the exception of wine which is not taxed anyway in Australia).

Fresh meat is available along with frozen chickens, fish and so on with many food lines imported from Singapore. As a result, the supermarket often displays a wide variety of items.

Toys, plastic goods, paint and basic hardware items are also available at the store many of which are half mainland prices.

Other shops North from the supermarket, on the other side of the road, will be found a line of Chinese trade stores which open in the evenings. Here will be found pirate music tapes for as little as one dollar each, photographic gear, clothes, Chinese food lines, souvenirs and so on. Also in this complex will be found a bar and the philatelic department of the post office.

The delightful self-serve boating club at Christmas Island where many facilities are available as just discovered by the author's wife, Patricia.

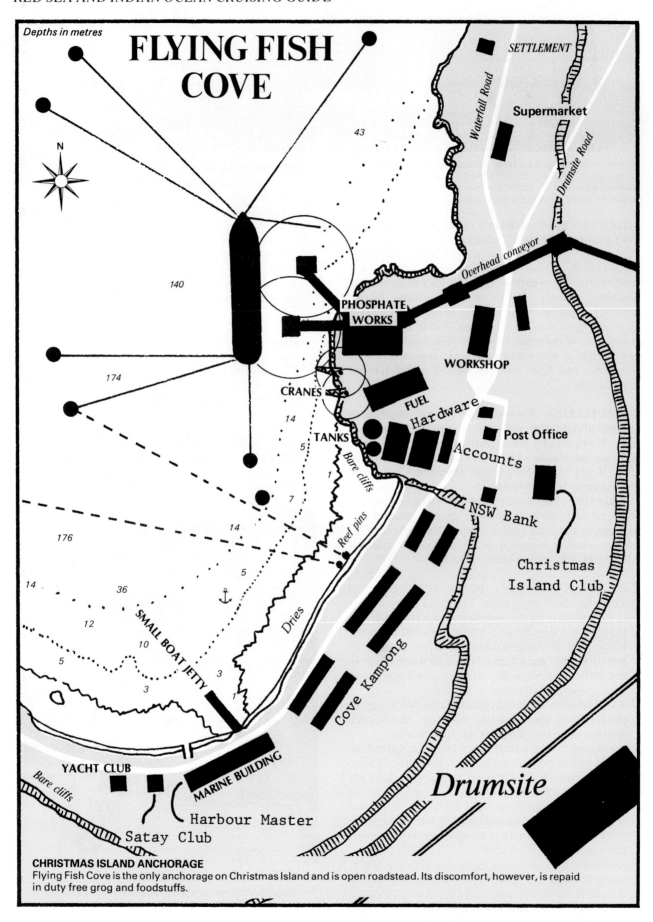

Depths in metres

FLYING FISH COVE

N

43

140

174

CRANES

14

5

TANKS

176

1

7

14

14 · 36

12

10

5

5

3

3

1

SMALL BOAT JETTY

Dries

Bare cliffs

Reef pins

⚓

SETTLEMENT

Waterfall Road

Supermarket

Drumsite Road

Overhead conveyor

**PHOSPHATE
WORKS**

WORKSHOP

FUEL

Hardware

Post Office

Accounts

NSW Bank

Christmas
Island Club

Cove Kampong

Drumsite

YACHT CLUB

Bare cliffs

MARINE BUILDING

Harbour Master

Satay Club

CHRISTMAS ISLAND ANCHORAGE
Flying Fish Cove is the only anchorage on Christmas Island and is open roadstead. Its discomfort, however, is repaid in duty free grog and foodstuffs.

Boat Club This delightful little club is situated to the south of the obvious dinghy landing and launching ramp. All grog and fast food is consumed on an honour basis, the purchases being entered in a ledger supplied and usually kept in the bar. Microwave ovens are used to heat fast food purchases and tables and chairs are provided for relaxing. There is also a barbeque, shower and toilet.

Payment for bar purchases must be made prior to obtaining customs clearance. This will include the temporary membership fee of $5.

Showers at the Boat Club are cold but tend to be warm generally. Clean up after use please!

Toilets are in the shower rooms and their use is encouraged on the usual antipollution basis.

Health There is an excellent hospital with full medical staff.

Restaurants will be found scattered around the settlement with fair prices dominating. The Chinese cafés at Drumsite usually offer the best value although the Satay Club, next door to the Boat Club, offers wonderful Malay food on Thursday evenings and Sunday mornings.

Transport The Christmas Island Phosphate Company (P.M.C.I.) provides free transport throughout the island.

Buses are either rather crude semi-trailers or small minibuses and they leave the anchorage (Cove Kampong area) every half hour. The hourly bus climbs the hill to Drumsite (Poon Saan) whilst the half hourly goes to the lower settlement.

A crew member leaving the boat at Christmas Island has a choice of a fortnightly flight to Perth or a fortnightly flight to Singapore, each flight alternating every Wednesday. Incoming crew will have to prove accommodation, as visitors not associated with the mining operation are not admitted.

Television There is a video transmitter here showing terrible programmes from late afternoon to early evening.

Radio Apart from the usual short wave transmitters, VHF and long wave radio telephone, there is a small broadcasting station working every day with music, news and Radio Australia.

Electronics are always available from a few Chinese Trade Stores (Settlement Shops and Drumsite) as well as a repair shop at Drumsite.

Entertainment There are two cinemas, two swimming pools and many sports regularly played from tennis to football. There are also social clubs apart from the Boat Club.

Wild Life The national parks of the island are represented by an officer of Australia's National Parks and Wildlife whose office is up at Drumsite. He can arrange occasional 4WD visits to the rain forest where one might see nesting boobies and possibly eight other distinct species of the nine major types of birds found at Christmas Island.

Communications are good with a radio telephone scrambler direct to Perth, Western Australia. To book a call either go to the radio shack direct or to the post office. Otherwise it might be arranged to take the call at a private phone if paid for in advance at the post office.

The anchorage at Flying Fish Cove, Christmas Island, is very exposed and subject to constant attack by swell. Only on days of minimal swell should small vessels go sternfast here to take on fuel and water.

Motorised barges are used exclusively at Christmas Island for handling ship's warps and ferrying ashore supplies. They are lifted and stored every evening via the gantry on the jetty in the background.

Mail comes in from Singapore and Australia, the latter arriving every second Wednesday on the fortnightly plane (Ansett and TAA alternately). The Singapore flight lands every other Wednesday.

Best address is Poste Restante, Post Office, Christmas Island, Indian Ocean. Add 'via Singapore' or 'Australia' if from another country as confusion might arise from the other Christmas Island situated in the Pacific Ocean.

Schools There is a primary and a secondary school near Flying Fish Cove with Australian teachers who do a two year stint from the mainland. It is sometimes possible to admit a transient child to the primary school.

Launderette There is a modern laundromat up the hill at Poon Saan along with a variety of other shops.

Hairdresser for both ladies and gents will be found in a shop at Cove Kampong (close to the anchorage).

Currency is the Australian dollar. Foreign exchange facilities are available at the Westpac Bank near the post office close to the anchorage.

Opening times Post Office 0800-1200 and 1300-1500 hours weekdays. Bank 1000-1500 hours weekdays. Launderette 24 hours. Telephone calls 0700-1700 hours weekdays, limited periods weekends. Supermarket (Trade Store) 0830-1700 hours weekdays and Saturday mornings. Other shops 1800-2100 hours. Boat Club any time as long as a permanent member can be found with a key.

Engineering Considering the number of vehicles, railway carriages and locomotives and general services to be maintained, it is not surprising to find Christmas Island well endowed with engineering facilities. Many items are available through the transport pool which are paid for on the spot at the relevant office. Such items as pipes and hoses, filters, oil, freezer parts and so on will prove no trouble to find but the difficulty might be in having work done. Employees of the mine are not available for freelance work but they may help in an emergency. Certainly, do not depend on finding services.

Haul out There is no haul-out facility at Christmas Island but it is possible to be craned out near the phosphate loading gantries in an emergency or if trying to escape the wet season swells and wind during a period of employment. Do not, under any circumstances, however, arrive at the island depending on this service.

TIME Christmas Island is seven hours ahead of Greenwich. Examples are; when it is 0800 hours at Christmas Island it is 0100 GMT, 0900 Perth and 1100 Australian east coast.

HISTORY The sighting of an island south from the Sunda Strait was recorded some twenty-eight years earlier but it was not until the 25th December, 1643 that Christmas Island was named by Captain William Mynors of the *Royal Mary* for conspicuous chronological reasons. Confusion caused by inaccurate plotting created the impression that there were a number of islands during the seventeenth century, this error being perpetuated on a number of maps of the period.

In 1688 William Dampier of the British buccaneer vessel, *Cygnet*, recorded the first landing on Christmas Island when two boats were sent ashore. Many landings followed over the next century but it was not until the 1820s that actual use was made of the island. This came about when John Clunies-Ross used it as a regular stopover for his supply vessels returning from Batavia to his holding on the Cocos Islands. Frigate birds, water and crabs, were collected for food; timber for building materials and the phosphate laden soil for soil enrichment were also gathered.

In 1872-6 the *Challenger* oceanographic expedition discovered phosphatic minerals and their naturalist, John Murray, urged the British Admiralty to examine the island in detail. This was eventually done and the island was annexed by the British Crown on 6th June 1888; later in the same year, a part of the Clunies-Ross family moved across from Cocos to become the first settlers at Flying Fish Cove, their intention being to cut timber.

At the same time that Clunies-Ross sought timber rights, so too did John Murray seek commercial rights. Some friction resulted but the two negotiated a seven year lease for the whole of the island in 1891 with a view to exporting timber, phosphate and other minerals that might come to light. Their first phosphate export occurred in 1895, after which they formed the Christmas Island Phosphate Company.

By the turn of the century Chinese labour had been imported, natural history had been studied and further phosphate deposits had been found. During the First World War the island enjoyed peace and the railway linking the strip mine to the anchorage was commenced, but the Second World War totally disrupted mining operations and most European and some Asian workers were evacuated to Australia. In 1942 a Japanese naval force bombarded the island but did not land. However, Indian troops garrisoned on the island mutinied and murdered or imprisoned their British officers surrendering the island to the Japanese a few weeks later.

By 1948 the mining company was struggling and its assets were bought out by the New Zealand and Australian governments who changed the name to the Christmas Island Phosphate Commission, with the British Phosphate Commission (of Nauru Island in the Pacific) the managing agents.

The island today has a population of around 3000 comprising Malay, Chinese, Indian and European people whose wages and working conditions are outstanding and whose future is as poorly defined as the future of the company. The combination of union demands, world economic recession and the increasing scarcity of the top quality A Grade phosphate has most experts predicting the end of the golden goose sometime in the late 1980s. Only increasing demand and the mining of B Grade ore at an economic price will save it and this may yet happen.

Meanwhile, and basing predictions on today's known facts, the 1990s may see Christmas Island become a tourist resort or a self-supporting community whose economy will be based on a variety of consumer needs and products. Australia will almost certainly pay the shortfalls and will possibly maintain control for the purpose of meteorological observation and defence.

MISCELLANEOUS Geologists tell us that Christmas Island is sliding northwards at a rate of about six centimentres per year. At the moment it is climbing the bulge along the edge of the Sunda (Java) Trench after which it will topple over, into the trench and disappear under the Indonesian Islands. This should occur, give or take a year or two, in about four million years.

The Red Crabs of the island live in a short tunnel from where they venture to bring in leaves for consumption and as a building material for the hatch of their burrow. Probably numbering in the millions, they cover the island from the shoreline to the highest hill throughout the dry season.

Early in the 'wet' season, around November-December, the adult crabs begin an amazing migration to the sea where they stand quietly as the waves wash over them. After a period that might last only a few minutes or a few days, the males move back to the shore and burrow where they await the females. There, copulation takes place. The males return to their inland homes leaving the female to lay her eggs in rock pools along the water's edge before also retreating inland. The babies, after a month's gestation and a month remaining around the marine environemnt, also head for the hills.

Very few cruising people will have the opportunity of witnessing the initial migration owing to the time of year. But according to all accounts the crabs move in a vast, red carpet, passing through private yards, across the golf course, down cliffs and across roads where the terrible massacre by vehicle traffic seems to have no effect on their determination to reach the coast.

During the 'dry' season, red crabs will appear around the Boat Club should rain occur; this is to quench their thirst and is not the beginning of a migration. However, they are seen in numbers enough to at least indicate the spectacle of the migration.

The dominant religion on the island is Islam and the visiting yachtsman is well reminded of that by being obliged to listen to the amplified tape recording bellowing from the small mosque at the anchorage. This starts before dawn and is repeated at least five times during the day.

Politically Australia is represented at Christmas Island by an administrator who lives in the Residence which will be seen to the south of the Boat Club set on a broad ledge above a low cliff.

Phosphate mining is concentrated mostly near the island's southern tip where ore is obtained by removing overburden and then picking up the exposed ore. The overburden is mostly rain forest which is inevitably destroyed after which C Grade ore is also stripped off, exposing B and then A Grade ores. The latter is the most economical in terms of demand, minimal treatment and price on the world market. It is this A Grade ore that is expected to expire by 1988, or therabouts, leaving only extensive deposits of B Grade. This is uneconomical to treat at the moment and is unlikely to prove worthwhile. As a result the whole mining operation may well close down.

In the meantime, the mined ore is carried by standard gauge railway to a treatment plant at Drumsite (above Flying Fish Cove) after which it is loaded into ships in bulk or bags. For this operation a ship is obliged to lay amidst a pattern of buoys as the swell creates too much surge to allow berthing alongside.

Ship mooring buoys are held in place by conventional methods but owing to the steep drop-off from the island's shelf, a chain is brought ashore where it is held by a steel peg or pin. These are noted on the chart as being 'Reef-Pins' and the chain running between a reef-pin and a buoy should be avoided when dropping anchor.

COCOS (KEELING) ISLANDS (Indian Ocean)

POSITION 12°10'S 96°52'E. Approximately 530 miles south of west from Christmas Island and 1720 miles northwest of Perth, the capital of Western Australia.

GENERAL DESCRIPTION The Cocos Islands comprise two atolls consisting of 27 coral islands nearly all of which are dotted around the southernmost atoll.

Known as North and South Keeling, the northern atoll is available only to dinghies in calm weather whilst the southern atoll provides anchorages for vessels of deep draught.

Referred to by the name 'Cocos' or 'Keeling', or by a combination of the two, the group is an Australian territory with a present day population of about 300 permanently settled Malays and 250 Australian expatriates. The Malays live on Home Island whilst all Australians live on West Island. All other islands are uninhabited.

Being a coral atoll, the water in the lagoon is spectacularly clear in most places and the beaches are of the finest white sand. All islands are planted in coconut trees, the tops of which being the highest part of any island.

Cocos Keeling as seen from three miles offshore. Like all coral cays, the islands here are low and featureless. Prison Island is under the arrow with Home Island left and Direction Island right.

APPROACH The navigator should plan his landfall so that the northern tip of South Keeling is found with a minimum of fuss; the entrance to the lagoon being there between Horsburgh Island and Direction Island but favouring the latter.

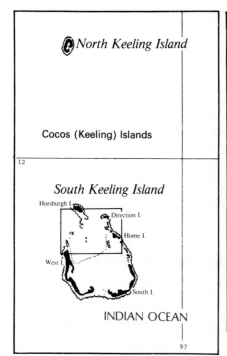

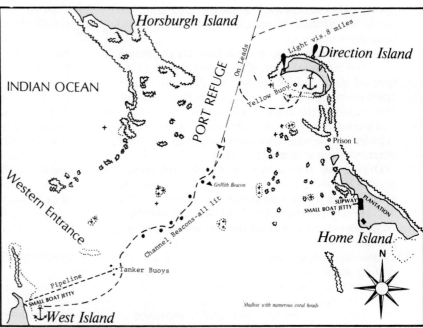

COCOS (KEELING) ANCHORAGE
The best anchorage in the Cocos (Keeling) group is under the lee of Direction Island in its own lagoon.

COCOS (KEELING) ISLANDS
Described by many circumnavigators as the world's most splendid anchorage, Cocos Keeling is isolated yet well serviced by a fortnightly plane from Australia.

Regardless of the direction of approach, the tops of the palm trees are visible at around ten miles off whilst the airport light, when illuminated, can be seen some 35 miles offshore at night by its distinct loom.

There are no offlying dangers anywhere around the group, the bottom rising immediately outside the lagoon entrance where the water changes colour from deep blue to light green as the sand bottom becomes visible. There may be some alarm felt by the many dark patches sighted on the bottom but these are mostly weed patches or low coral that does not threaten navigation.

On the western tip of Direction Island will be seen a light structure of open frame steel and immediately offshore from this light should be found a topless beacon. This indicates the extreme edge of the reef but should not be relied upon. Eyeball navigation is hard to beat here when in doubt.

Night entry is possible thanks to leading lights situated on beacons which also act as channel indicators when crossing the lagoon to West Island jetty. This jetty displays a very bright light which is not shown on the chart and might be a cause of confusion. All things considered, the navigator is warned against attempting a night entry unless equipped with the latest charts.

Once inside the lagoon the best anchorage is under the lee of Direction Island within its own separate lagoon as shown on the map. Those preferring to cross to West Island for any purpose, such as urgent communication, should be guided by the channel beacons, passing red to port and green or black to starboard. All these beacons are lit.

NAVIGATION There is a major flashing white light on the northeast face of Direction Island as well as a smaller light on its western tip.

Within the lagoon, there are entrance leading lights and port and starboard lights indicating the best water across to West Island. A powerful illumination light on the jetty at West Island might cause confusion.

When an aircraft is due to land the powerful airport light is switched on and the loom of its flash can be seen 35 miles to sea.

ANCHORAGE All visiting yachts are encouraged to anchor behind Direction Island, upon entering, although it is possible to anchor off West Island jetty. Direction Island is by far the better venue being good holding and very secure in the worst trade winds whilst the West Island anchorage is exposed to the full reach of the lagoon.

Direction Island lies on the northeast tip of the southern atoll and enjoys its own small lagoon within a lagoon. The bottom is clean white sand with a scattering of coral patches none of which reach to within two metres of the surface unless hard against the beach. One patch is, in fact, the wreck of a burnt out yacht.

To enter the Direction Island anchorage follow the dotted line on the plan but proceed with care over the tongue of coral that one would swear is only a foot or two below the surface. In fact, as far as I could determine, it is at least 3.6 metres under the surface, but cannot offer a guarantee with that information. Pass a topless beacon to port. Do not be tempted to enter via an apparently reef-free passage further towards the island; it is a sand shoal and carries less depth than the reef.

If an animal is aboard anchor outside the quarantine buoy. This necessitates a long row ashore but is quite comfortable. Otherwise, move in as close to the beach as you dare for greater comfort and convenience to the beach.

West Island The only purpose in using West Island as an anchorage is to avail oneself of the facilities at the settlement. The anchorage is wide open to the full reach across the lagoon and is not good holding unless one remains outside the weed line and then takes care not to drop into a weed patch. Lay out all the chain you can here for the vessel must be left to its own devices for a long time, the settlement being four miles from the jetty.

Having approached West Island via the already mentioned beaconed channel, steer from the last beacon direct for the now obvious jetty passing to either side of a group of tanker buoys. Anchor as close as depth and nature of bottom allow to the jetty and do not be tempted to go alongside; it is too shallow and is used regularly by local vessels.

FORMALITIES Advance visas are not necessary to visit the Cocos Islands, permission to land being granted on the spot. Customs, immigration (health where suspect) and quarantine regulations are represented on West Island and officers will board at either the West Island jetty anchorage or at Direction Island. They prefer Direction Island and visit it aboard the steel *Sir Zelman Cowan* every day. Rarely is a visitor kept waiting for long, but regardless, he must remain aboard until cleared.

In 1981 a High Security Animal Quarantine Station became operational on West Island. Its prime purpose is to provide a staging point for cattle being imported into Australia to improve her breeding stock. This, coupled with Australia's normal determination to keep animal diseases at bay, makes Cocos a highly critical quarantine station. Under no circumstances are animals to be taken ashore and all animal waste or food scrap is to be taken ashore at Direction Island for proper disposal. There are pits into which all waste must be thrown to be periodically burned using waste engine oil which is provided by the administration.

FACILITIES Too many yachtsmen rant and rave when they find that fresh food to outsiders is priced some 150 per cent above local price. Most make the point that Christmas Island administration does not penalise visitors in such a way, but it must be remembered that the population on the Cocos is small by comparison and as a result its own fortnightly victualling is often in delicate balance. All fresh food is flown in by plane from Perth and freight is subsidised. The simple truth is, the administration would prefer *not* to sell to outsiders and the heavy price loading is *intended* to discourage.

Other food lines, grog and cigarettes are available at local price. Alcoholic drink is cheaper than at mainland Australian prices by a considerable margin, there being no duty.

Fuel is available through the local agent, Shell petrol being twice the price of diesel and both being around fifty per cent more than mainland prices.

Water is caught in a tank on Direction Island but such is its popularity that rarely does its outlet do more than drip. Taps in town can be used but this presumes you find a way of demijohning water from the settlement on the jetty at West Island. There are definitely no available outlets close to the waterfront anywhere.

Communication is via radio telephone, telegram or mail. The telephone links with Perth from where it can be relayed to anywhere in the world. Reception is subject to atmospheric conditions. Mail is reliable and comes in once a fortnight aboard the Perth plane operated alternately by Ansett and TAA. Occasionally surprise deliveries are made by air-force planes en route to Malaysia.

The best address is Poste Restante, Post Office, Cocos (Keeling) Islands, Indian Ocean 6799. It might be worthwhile adding 'Via Australia' on mail from countries other than Australia.

Transport There are no taxis or buses on the islands and any visitor going from the jetty to the settlement on West Island is obliged to walk or hitch a ride; the sealed road of some four miles long is driven often enough. Otherwise, the dinghy might be taken down to the settlement and landed near the northern end of the airstrip.

Persons leaving a visiting vessel here may catch a once-fortnightly flight to Perth but should not presume space aboard will be available. Check as far ahead as possible.

A small tanker as well as a small freighter supply bulk needs to the island once every two months. Delivery of excessively heavy objects may be arranged with the administration but the time involved may stretch into many months.

Medical There is a small modern hospital at the West Island settlement that is manned by a full-time doctor and nursing staff.

The old fuel or water tank at the defunct cable station on Direction Island.

Shopping for food has been discussed and is executed at the island's only permanent store near the airport control tower. However, on Cocos, it seems that everyone has a franchise for something or other. It is thus possible to buy a variety of boutique items, toys, kitchen utensils and so on. Inquiries might start with the customs officer when he boards.

Cocos Club Visitors are welcome here by invitation. It has a fine bar and recreation facilities.

Barbeques can be held on Direction Island using one of the administration fixtures, but please leave it clean and tidy and obey quarantine rules regarding animals and food scraps (see 'Formalities').

Swimming is an absolute delight off the Direction Island beach where will be found a greasy pole and raft.

Slipping and repairs These services are offered by the Malay community on Home Island but there is a distinct lack of enthusiasm to stand by a firm arrangement and only vessels of a draught less than about four feet can reach the cradle.

Village industry The Malay community do some excellent wood carving and with better organisation ought to have no trouble selling it. As it was, during our visit, three attempts to inspect, and possibly buy, local carvings failed despite the best efforts of the administration to rouse the Malay council leaders. Having formalised our entry to Home Island three separate times it was disappointing to find that on each occasion we were completely ignored. I suspect they are only paying lip service to wanting to be self supporting and independent.

Radio For entertainment, local residents have a lot of fun running a small transmitter giving out news and music. There is also a short-wave radio watch.

Fishing I add this heading here to advise that spear fishing is not permitted on the southeast corner of Direction Island where a gutter offers a colourful spectacle for those prepared to snorkel only. There can be a strong current here.

Line fishing is rather poor in the area and the keen fisherman should utilise a calm day to trail a line down the outside weather-edge of the atoll.

Prison Island is a delightful little speck between Direction and Home Islands. It offers a superb venue for swimmers, snorkellers and picnickers. Please take your rubbish back to Direction Island for burial.

Chickens Periodically the administration allows Home Islanders to run their poultry on Direction Island. These birds are owned and are *not* wild game.

Coconuts are everywhere and can be taken from Direction Island. There is a husking post provided and all husks should be neatly piled and used as barbeque fuel when dry.

Booby birds are, unfortunately, hunted mercilessly by the Malays who will be seen with shotguns. One bird, however, has become tame and has been tagged with a piece of red rag. Do not remove this rag lest he be shot.

HOME ISLAND Known as such because it was the island chosen by Captain John Clunies-Ross for his home site, this island is now the settlement area for all Malays in the group. With a population of about 300, the community is self-determining in preparation for eventual independence. It is financed by the Australian government but decisions are encouraged at native council level and as a result, visitors are not permitted without permission. This can usually be arranged through the customs officer on West Island, the two islands being in telephone contact.

WEATHER Being in the thick of the south Indian Ocean trade wind belt the information given earlier is relevant to the Cocos Islands. Specific details are given here.

There seems to be reasonable proof that a southeast trade wind blowing across the Cocos lagoon increases in speed by about ten per cent. The islands being low coral cays have no gust-producing qualities of their own suggesting that the warmer air over the shallow lagoon creates a faster inrush speed. This is relevant to the cruising yachtsman only inasmuch as he can expect slightly easier conditions at sea when deciding on his departure time from Direction Island anchorage.

During the northwest season the group do not offer security being rather too open to that direction. Vessels of shallow draught would find fair haven hard in against West Island to the south of the jetty.

Temperatures are typical of any tropical area although the constant trade wind can maintain a very comfortable average both night and day. Only during calms does it become oppressive.

HISTORY It is believed that North Keeling Island was first sighted by Captain William Keeling of the East India Company in 1609 with the remainder of the area being charted within the next few decades. In 1826, Englishman John Hare settled the southern atoll and was followed in the following year by Captain John Clunies-Ross. Despite being business associates, disagreement followed and it is said that Clunies-Ross actually restricted Hare to the small islet between Home Island and Direction Island known as Prison Island.

Whatever the truth of the matter, John Hare left in 1831 leaving Clunies-Ross in sole control. The latter imported labour from Malaya and set about building a copra plantation empire, undisturbed apparently by his domain being declared a part of the British dominions by Captain Fremantle aboard H.M.S. *Juno* in 1857.

In 1878 responsibility for the Cocos was transferred from the Colonial Office to the government in Ceylon and later to the government of the Straits Settlement (Singapore). At this time, 1886, Queen Victoria granted all the land of the islands to George Clunies-Ross in perpetuity reserving just a few rights for the Crown.

Direction Island was used as a cable station and as such became a prime target during the First World War. On the 9th November, 1914 the German cruiser

Emden landed a raiding party to destroy the radio and cable installations. H.M.A.S. *Sydney* responded to an SOS sent from Direction Island and engaged the enemy. The *Emden* was set ablaze after which her skipper ran her aground on North Keeling Island to prevent her sinking. Her rusty stempost was a monument to this battle until fairly recently. It was Australia's first sea victory.

During and immediately after the Second World War, administration was bounced back and forth between the governor of Ceylon, the military, and the colony of Singapore until on the 23rd November 1955 the islands were accepted by Australia as a dependent territory.

Before the introduction of long-range jet aircraft, the Cocos were an important staging point for flights between Australia and Africa. When this was abandoned in 1967, they remained a useful meteorological outpost and communications link.

Since the War, control of labour and the welfare of the Malayan population has been handed across to the Australian government; the Clunies-Ross family being pushed into retirement. They now own a ten acre homestead block on Home Island.

The population of Cocos-Malayans was depleted over the years from 2000 to 300, most being returned to Malaysia soon after the Second World War and others later going to Christmas Island.

In 1981 a High Security Animal Quarantine Station was opened on West Island specifically for the importing into Australia of cattle breeding stock. For this reason, quarantine regulations in the group are very strict and the visitor must obey them to the letter of the law.

CHAGOS ARCHIPELAGO

Lying a little over halfway along the logical route from the Cocos to the Seychelles in the south Indian Ocean, the Chagos Archipelago is a scattered collection reefs, banks and coral cays. There are a number of excellent anchorages available despite the rumour that cruising boats are not permitted in the area. This is only partly true.

Owned by the British, but leased to the Americans who use Diego Garcia as a military base, all local inhabitants were resettled on Mauritius to the southwest leaving all islands, apart from Diego Garcia, uninhabited but with remnants of buildings and domestic gardens.

It is absolutely forbidden to land anywhere on Diego Garcia whilst anchorage and landing is acceptable at other islands.

DIEGO GARCIA is the southernmost group consisting of one snake-like island atop a reef and forming a long and distorted U-shaped lagoon in which excellent shelter is enjoyed. Across the open end of the 'U', to the north, is a large isolated reef supporting two small cays and forming two distinct channels into the lagoon. These channels are called Main Pass and Barton Pass.

The airstrip and main settlement is on the western side of the lagoon but, as stated, it is comprised entirely of the United States base and landing is strictly forbidden. It is unwise even to enter the lagoon, the chances of being chased out immediately being very strong. I know of one yachtsman who had organised anchorage and a possible landing weeks ahead by ham radio only to be given short shrift on his arrival. He was allowed twelve hours only and was denied shore access despite information to the contrary.

The visiting yacht is recommended one of the following anchorages where molestation is unlikely, the base having no patrol boats. Aircraft may fly over you at anchor but that is all.

EGMONT ISLANDS (Six Islands) lie 70 miles northwest from Diego Garcia and offer anchorage only to those willing to negotiate, and then anchor amongst, a lagoon full of coral heads. Entrance is to the west of north over a one to two fathom bank and the best anchorage during the normal southeast trade wind is in the southeast corner under the lee of Sudest Islet. Make sure conditions for visual navigation are ideal, the coral heads being difficult to see during overcast weather. Much better to go to the next anchorage.

PEROS BANHOS is a large, scattered group of islets and reefs in the northwest corner of the Chagos Archipelago. Very few of its islets provide good haven, their shapes being uncomplimentary to the prevailing wind. However, the favoured anchorage is in the southwest corner against Ile du Coin where the usual coconut palms will be seen as well as the remains of a jetty and a few buildings. Lemons may be found growing here and drums of diesel fuel were left for an expedition that never returned; no doubt they have been taken by now.

SALOMON ISLANDS Lying between Victory and Speakers Bank and to the immediate southwest of Blenheim Reef, the Salomon Islands provide the best security in the whole group. The lagoon is relatively small with only one limited entrance to its north whilst the bottom is good holding. Within the lagoon there are a scattering of isolated coral heads but these are easily seen in sensible conditions of visibility and there is plenty of space between them.

The two favourite anchorages are in the southeast extreme under the immediate lee of Ile Fouquet or in the southwest corner against Ile Boddam. Both islands are the usual flat coral cay type supporting coconut trees of about 20 metres high. On Ile Boddam will be seen the remnants of a settlement and pier.

The lagoon entrance has a maximum depth of 6 metres which will be found by holding the reef projecting west from Ile de la Passe (Passage Island) close aboard. A boulder on the end of this reef assists. It dries nearly one metre at low water springs.

TIDES in the Chagos Archipelago vary from a mean spring height of 1.6 metres at Egmont Islands down to 1.4 at the Salomon Islands.

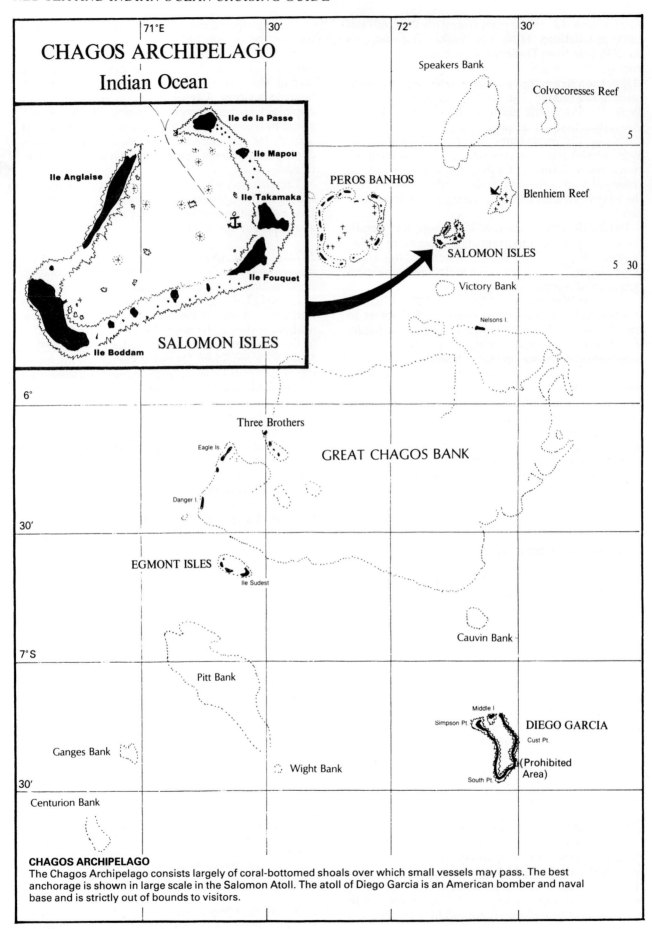

CHAGOS ARCHIPELAGO
The Chagos Archipelago consists largely of coral-bottomed shoals over which small vessels may pass. The best anchorage is shown in large scale in the Salomon Atoll. The atoll of Diego Garcia is an American bomber and naval base and is strictly out of bounds to visitors.

APPENDIX

I. ADDRESSES OF TOURIST OFFICES
IN LONDON

Australian Tourist Commission
Heathcoat House
20 Savile Row
London W1
Tel. 01-434 4371

Djibouti Embassy
26 Rue Emile Menier
75116 Paris
Tel. 727 49 22

Egyptian Embassy
Tourist Information Centre
168 Piccadilly
London W1V 9HL
Tel. 01-493 5282

Ethiopian Embassy
17 Prince's Gate
London SW7 1PZ
Tel. 01-580 3711/0174

Hong Kong Tourist Association
125 Pall Mall
London SW1
Tel. 01-930 4775

India Government Tourist Office
7 Cork Street
London W1X 2AB
Tel. 01-437 3677-78

*Indonesian Transport, Communications and Tourist
Attache's Office*
96A Mount Street
London W1
Tel. 01-409 3588

Kenya Tourist Office
13 New Burlington Street
London W1
Tel. 01-839 4477

Madagascar Consulate
15 America Square
London EC3
Tel. 01-481 3899

Malaysia Tourist Development Corporation
17 Curzon Street
London W1
Tel. 01-499 7388

Mauritius Government Tourist Office
23 Ramillies Place
London W1
Tel. 01-439 4461

Mozambique Information Office
34 Percy Street
London W1
Tel. 01-636 7108

Pakistan Tourism Development Corporation
52 High Holborn
London WC1
Tel. 01-242 3131

Papua-New Guinea High Commission
3rd Floor
14 Waterloo Place
London SW1R 4AR
Tel. 01-930 0922/7

Saudia Arabian Royal Embassy
30 Belgrave Square
London SW1X 8QB
Tel. 01-235 0831

Seychelles Tourist Board
50 Conduit Street
London W1A 4PE
Tel. 01-439 9699

Singapore Tourist Promotion Board
33 Heddon Street
London W1
Tel. 01-437 0033
Telex 893491

Somali Embassy
60 Portland Place
London W1N 3DG
Tel. 01-580 7140/7148

South African Embassy
South Africa House
Trafalgar Square
London WC2N 5DP
Tel. 01-930 4488

Southern Yemen Embassy
57 Cromwell Road
London SW7 2ED
Tel. 01-584 6607/9

Sri Lanka (Ceylon) Tourist Board
52 High Holborn
London WC1V 6RL
Tel. 01-405 1194/5

Sudanese Embassy
3 Cleveland Row
St James's
London SW1A 1DD
Tel. 01-839 8080

Tanzanian Tourist Office
Suite 2A
77 South Audley Street
London W1
Tel. 01-499 7727

Thailand Tourist Organisation
41 Albemarle Street
London W1X 3FE
Tel. 01-499 7679

II. BRITISH ADMIRALTY CHARTS AND PUBLICATIONS

The full list of Admiralty Charts for the area covered by this guide is available in the *Catalogue of Admiralty Charts and other Hydrographic Publications NP 131* which is published annually.

The World Catalogue, all Admiralty Publications and advice regarding Chart Agents overseas can be supplied by:

Imray, Laurie, Norie & Wilson Ltd.
Wych House, The Broadway,
St. Ives, Huntingdon, Cambridgeshire PE17 4BT. England
Tel. (0480) 62114 Telex 32496 KELOUK G

ADMIRALTY LIST OF LIGHTS

Vol. E	*Mediterranean, Black and Red Seas. NP78*
Vol. F	*Arabian Sea, Bay of Bengal and Pacific Ocean, North of the Equator. NP79*
Vol. K	*Indian and Pacific Oceans, South of the Equator. NP83*

RADIO PUBLICATIONS.
ADMIRALTY LIST OF RADIO SIGNALS

Vol. 1 (1)	*Coast Radio Stations. Europe, Africa and Asia (not Indonesia). NP281 (1)*
Vol. 1 (2)	*Coast Radio Stations. Americas, Australasia (including Indonesia) NP281 (2)*
Vol. 2	*Radiobeacons. NP282. Radiobeacon diagrams. NP282a*
Vol. 3	*Radio Weather Services. NP283. Map of forecast areas. NP283a*
Vol. 5	*Radio Navigational Warnings. NP285.*

ADMIRALTY SAILING DIRECTIONS

3	*Africa Pilot Vol. III*
13	*Australia Pilot Vol. I*
14	*Australia Pilot Vol. II*
15	*Australia Pilot Vol. III*
17	*Australia Pilot Vol. V*
21	*Bay of Bengal Pilot*
30	*China Sea Pilot Vol. I*
31	*China Sea Pilot. Vol. II*
33	*Phillipine Islands Pilot*
34	*Indonesia Pilot Vol. II*
35	*Indonesia Pilot Vol. III*
36	*Indonesia Pilot Vol. I*
38	*West Coast of India Pilot*
39	*South Indian Ocean Pilot*
44	*Malacca Strait Pilot*
49	*Mediterranean Pilot Vol. V*
60	*Pacific Islands Pilot Vol. I*
63	*Persian Gulf Pilot*
64	*Red Sea and Gulf of Aden Pilot (inc. Suez Canal)*

Ocean Passages for the World NP136.

III. APPROXIMATE DISTANCES (IN NAUTICAL MILES) BETWEEN MAJOR POINTS

Port Said to Suez	82
Suez to Port Sudan	705
Port Sudan to Aden	635
Aden to Salalah (Oman)	620
Aden to Cochin	2100
Cochin to Galle	440
Galle to Cocos (Keeling) Islands	1670
Galle to Singapore	1600
Singapore to Hong Kong	1520
Singapore to Darwin	1850
Darwin to Christmas Island	1520
Christmas Island to Cocos (Keeling) Islands	520
Cocos (Keeling) Islands to Chagos Archipelago	1700
Chagos Archipelago to the Seychelles	1100
Cocos (Keeling) Islands to Mauritius	2600
Mauritius to Durban	1750
Darwin to Gove	450
Gove to Thursday Island	330
Gove to Thursday Island to Brisbane	1400
Brisbane to Sydney	450
Thursday Island to Port Moresby	330

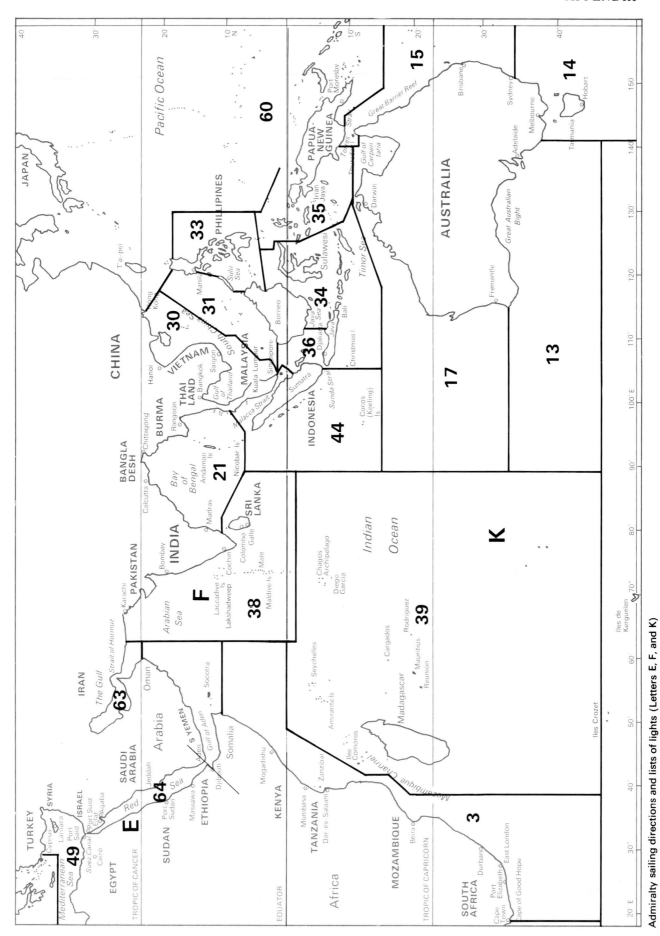

Admiralty sailing directions and lists of lights (Letters E, F, and K)

IV. CONVERSION TABLES

METRES TO ENGLISH FEET (100 metres = 328.09 feet)

Metres	0	10	20	30	40	50	60	70	80	90
0	Feet	32.8	65.6	98.4	131.2	164.0	196.8	229.7	262.5	295.3
1	3.3	36.1	68.9	101.7	134.5	167.3	200.1	232.9	265.7	298.6
2	6.6	39.4	72.2	105.0	137.8	170.6	203.4	236.2	269.0	301.8
3	9.8	42.6	75.5	108.3	141.1	173.9	206.7	239.5	272.3	305.1
4	13.1	45.9	78.7	111.5	144.4	177.2	210.0	242.8	275.6	308.4
5	16.4	49.2	82.0	114.8	147.6	180.4	213.3	246.1	278.9	311.7
6	19.7	52.5	85.3	118.1	150.9	183.7	216.5	249.3	282.2	315.0
7	23.0	55.8	88.6	121.4	154.2	187.0	219.8	252.6	285.4	318.2
8	26.2	59.0	91.9	124.7	157.5	190.3	223.1	255.9	288.7	321.5
9	29.5	62.3	95.1	128.0	160.8	193.6	226.4	259.2	292.0	324.8

ENGLISH FEET TO METRES (100 feet = 30.479 metres)

Feet	0	10	20	30	40	50	60	70	80	90
0	Metres	3.05	6.03	9.14	12.19	15.24	18.29	21.33	24.38	27.43
1	0.30	3.35	6.40	9.44	12.50	15.54	18.59	21.64	24.69	27.74
2	0.61	3.66	6.70	9.75	12.80	15.85	18.90	21.94	24.99	28.04
3	0.91	3.96	7.01	10.06	13.11	16.15	19.20	22.25	25.30	28.35
4	1.22	4.28	7.31	10.36	13.41	16.46	19.51	22.55	25.60	28.65
5	1.52	4.57	7.62	10.67	13.72	16.76	19.81	22.86	25.91	28.95
6	1.83	4.88	7.92	10.97	14.02	17.07	20.12	23.16	26.21	29.26
7	2.13	5.18	8.23	11.28	14.32	17.37	20.42	23.47	26.52	29.56
8	2.44	5.49	8.53	11.58	14.63	17.68	20.73	23.77	26.82	29.87
9	2.74	5.79	8.84	11.89	14.93	17.98	21.03	24.08	27.13	30.17

KILOMETRES TO ENGLISH MILES (100 kilometres = 62.137 miles)

Kiloms.	0	10	20	30	40	50	60	70	80	90
0	Miles	6.21	12.43	18.64	24.85	31.07	37.28	43.50	49.71	55.92
1	0.62	6.83	13.05	19.26	25.48	31.70	37.90	44.12	50.33	56.54
2	1.24	7.46	13.67	19.88	26.10	32.31	38.52	44.74	50.95	57.17
3	1.86	8.08	14.29	20.50	26.72	32.93	39.15	45.36	51.57	57.79
4	2.48	8.70	14.91	21.13	27.34	33.55	39.77	45.98	52.19	58.41
5	3.11	9.32	15.53	21.75	27.96	34.17	40.39	46.60	52.82	59.03
6	3.73	9.94	16.16	22.37	28.58	34.80	41.01	47.22	53.44	59.65
7	4.35	10.56	16.78	22.99	29.20	35.42	41.63	47.85	54.06	60.27
8	4.97	11.18	17.40	23.61	29.83	36.04	42.25	48.47	54.68	60.89
9	5.59	11.81	18.02	24.23	30.45	36.66	42.87	49.09	55.30	61.52

ENGLISH MILES TO KILOMETRES (100 miles = 160.93 kilometres)

Miles	0	10	20	30	40	50	60	70	80	90
0	Kilometres	16.09	32.19	48.28	64.37	80.47	96.56	112.65	128.75	144.84
1	1.61	17.70	33.80	49.89	65.98	82.08	98.17	114.26	130.36	146.45
2	3.22	19.31	35.41	51.50	67.59	83.69	99.78	115.87	131.97	148.06
3	4.83	20.92	37.01	53.11	69.20	85.29	101.39	117.48	133.58	149.67
4	6.44	22.53	38.62	54.72	70.81	86.90	103.00	119.09	135.18	151.28
5	8.05	24.14	40.23	56.33	72.42	88.51	104.61	120.70	136.79	152.89
6	9.66	25.75	41.84	57.94	74.03	90.12	106.22	122.31	138.40	154.50
7	11.26	27.36	43.45	59.55	75.64	91.73	107.83	123.92	140.01	156.11
8	12.87	28.97	45.06	61.15	77.25	93.34	109.44	125.53	141.62	157.72
9	13.48	30.58	46.67	62.76	78.86	94.95	111.04	127.14	143.23	159.32

CENTIMETRES TO ENGLISH INCHES (100 centimetres = 39.37 inches)

Cm	0	10	20	30	40	50	60	70	80	90
0	Ins	3.94	7.87	11.81	15.75	19.69	23.62	27.56	31.50	35.43
1	0.39	4.33	8.27	12.21	16.14	20.08	24.02	27.95	31.89	35.83
2	0.79	4.72	8.66	12.60	16.54	20.47	24.41	28.35	32.28	36.22
3	1.18	5.12	9.06	12.99	16.93	20.87	24.80	28.74	32.68	36.61
4	1.58	5.51	9.45	13.39	17.32	21.26	25.20	29.13	33.07	37.01
5	1.97	5.91	9.84	13.78	17.72	21.65	25.59	29.53	33.47	37.40
6	2.36	6.30	10.24	14.17	18.11	22.05	25.98	29.92	33.86	37.80
7	2.76	6.69	10.63	14.57	18.50	22.44	26.38	30.32	34.25	38.19
8	3.15	7.09	11.02	14.96	18.90	22.83	26.77	30.71	34.65	38.58
9	3.54	7.48	11.42	15.35	19.29	23.23	27.17	31.10	35.04	38.98

ENGLISH INCHES TO CENTIMETRES (100 inches = 254 centimetres)

Ins	0	10	20	30	40	50	60	70	80	90
0	Cm	25.40	50.80	76.20	101.6	127.0	152.4	177.8	203.2	228.6
1	2.54	27.94	53.34	78.74	104.1	129.5	154.9	180.3	205.7	231.1
2	5.08	30.48	55.88	81.28	106.7	132.1	157.5	182.9	208.3	233.7
3	7.62	33.02	58.42	83.82	109.2	134.6	160.0	185.4	210.8	236.2
4	10.16	35.56	60.96	86.36	111.8	137.2	162.6	188.0	213.4	238.8
5	12.70	38.10	63.50	88.90	114.3	139.7	165.1	190.5	215.9	241.3
6	15.24	40.64	66.04	91.44	116.8	142.2	167.6	193.0	218.4	243.8
7	17.78	43.18	68.58	93.98	119.4	144.8	170.2	195.6	221.0	246.4
8	20.32	45.72	71.12	96.52	121.9	147.3	172.7	198.1	223.5	248.9
9	22.86	48.26	73.66	99.06	124.5	149.9	175.3	200.7	226.1	251.5

ENGLISH GALLONS TO LITRES (100 gallons = 454.35 litres)

Galls.	0	10	20	30	40	50	60	70	80	90
0	Litres	45.4	90.9	136.3	181.7	227.2	272.6	318.0	363.5	408.9
1	4.5	50.0	95.4	140.8	186.3	231.7	277.1	322.6	368.0	413.4
2	9.1	54.5	99.9	145.4	190.8	236.3	281.7	327.1	372.6	418.0
3	13.6	59.1	104.5	149.9	185.4	240.8	286.2	331.7	377.1	422.5
4	18.2	60.6	109.0	154.4	199.9	245.3	290.8	336.2	381.6	427.1
5	22.7	68.1	113.6	159.0	204.4	249.9	295.3	340.7	386.2	431.6
6	27.3	72.7	118.1	163.6	209.0	254.4	299.9	345.3	390.7	436.2
7	31.8	77.2	122.7	168.1	213.5	259.0	304.4	349.8	395.3	440.7
8	36.3	81.8	127.2	172.6	218.1	263.5	308.9	354.4	399.8	445.2
9	40.9	86.3	131.8	177.2	222.6	268.1	313.5	358.9	404.4	449.8

LITRES TO ENGLISH GALLONS (100 litres = 22.01 gallons)

Litres	0	10	20	30	40	50	60	70	80	90
0	Gallons	2.20	4.40	6.60	8.80	11.00	13.20	15.41	17.61	19.81
1	0.22	2.42	4.62	6.82	9.02	11.22	13.42	15.63	17.83	20.03
2	0.44	2.64	4.84	7.04	9.24	11.44	13.65	15.85	18.05	20.25
3	0.66	2.86	5.06	7.26	9.46	11.66	13.87	16.07	18.27	20.47
4	0.88	3.08	5.28	7.48	9.68	11.88	14.09	16.29	18.49	20.69
5	1.10	3.30	5.50	7.70	9.90	12.10	14.31	16.51	18.71	20.91
6	1.32	3.52	5.72	7.92	10.12	12.32	14.53	16.73	18.93	21.13
7	1.54	3.74	5.94	8.14	10.34	12.54	14.75	16.95	19.15	21.35
8	1.76	3.96	6.16	8.36	10.56	12.76	14.97	17.17	19.37	21.57
9	1.98	4.18	6.38	8.58	10.78	12.98	15.19	17.39	19.59	21.79

INDEX